BUDDHIST LOGIC
AND
QUANTUM DILEMMA

General Editor

Dr. S N Bhavsar

Guest Editor

Dr Murli Manohar Joshi

15

BUDDHIST LOGIC AND QUANTUM DILEMMA

JAYANT BURDE

MOTILAL BANARSIDASS PUBLISHERS
PRIVATE LIMITED • DELHI

First Edition: Delhi, 2012

ISBN: 978-81-208-3552-8

MOTILAL BANARSIDASS

41 U.A. Bungalow Road, Jawahar Nagar, Delhi 110 007
8 Mahalaxmi Chamber, 22 Bhulabhai Desai Road, Mumbai 400 026
236, 9th Main III Block, Jayanagar, Bangaluru 560 011
203 Royapettah High Road, Mylapore, Chennai 600 004
Sanas Plaza, 1302 Baji Rao Road, Pune 411 002
8 Camac Street, Kolkata 700 017
Ashok Rajpath, Patna 800 004
Chowk, Varanasi 221 001

Printed in India

by RP Jain at NAB Printing Unit,
A-44, Naraina Industrial Area, Phase I, New Delhi–110028
and published by JP Jain for Motilal Banarsidass Publishers (P) Ltd,
41 U.A. Bungalow Road, Jawahar Nagar, Delhi-110007

For My Friend

SHIRISH SULE, *M.D.*

Contents

Preface

> Do not accept what you hear by report, do not accept tradition, do not accept a statement because it is in our books, not because it is in accord with your belief, nor because it is the saying of your teacher. Be lamps unto yourselves. Those who now or after I am dead shall rely upon themselves only and not to look for assistance to anyone besides themselves it is they who shall reach the topmost height – Gautama Buddha.

Buddhism is a religion, but not a dogma. Its agnosticism and rational outlook has attracted many western scientists. There is abundant literature on similarities between Buddhism and science.

Two revolutionary theories were born in the twentieth century. Relativity theory brought about radical changes in the scientific concepts of space, time and gravitation. Quantum theory was more shocking, it was weird and so bizarre that it dazzled contemporary physicists. This micro world within our classical world was truly mysterious where the laws of science appeared to be violated and many classical concepts in science seemed to lose meaning.

Western scientists and scholars soon discovered that there were many similarities between RQ (Relativity-Quantum) theories and eastern mysticism. Much has been written by both western and eastern scholars on parallelism between RQ theories and eastern mysticism. In Buddhist logic they found a doctrine called *catuṣkoṭi* which was astonishingly similar to a quantum phenomenon called matter-wave duality. It refers to the strange behaviour of light and subatomic particles like electrons : light behaves sometimes as a wave and sometimes as a stream of particles, and electrons, normally conceived as particles, sometimes display wave properties *catuṣkoṭi* and matter-wave duality both seemed to violate the most sacred Aristotelian laws of thought; the law of identity, the law of excluded middle and the law of contradiction.

Most commentators on science do not seem to have realized that now they confronted a new riddle :

(1) Buddhist teachings were similar to the principles of science.
(2) There were parallels between eastern mysticism and RQ theories. The most singular discovery was that Buddhist logic had a mystical school whose teachings violated the three immutable laws of thought, but which seems to endorse the schizophrenic behaviour of the actors in quantum world.

How do we solve this conundrum of parallelism? Isn't it ironical that the credo which scientists looked upon as a model of scientific religion harboured dark mysteries? Or had they found in Buddhist logic solutions to quantum puzzles and a path to New Science? Do we need a different quantum logic to deal with modern science?

This book analyzes these two apparently contradictory parallels

(i) that between Buddhism and science and (ii) that between eastern mysticism and modern science.

In this work Buddhist logic and quantum world are the principal areas of investigation. My focus on Buddhist logic and quantum theory stems from the fact that they are the most important areas for comparison. But you will also find many references to other eastern philosophies on the one hand and relativity physics on the other.

In order to fully understand the nature, degree and limitations of parallelism, we have not only to analyze the basic concepts in science but also apparent contradictions in Buddhist philosophy.

What's more, the well-established laws of deductive (western) logic need to be reexamined for their correct interpretation. This is what this book attempts to do.

Every author who selects an interdisciplinary topic, faces the problem of the reader's prerequisites. After much deliberation, I thought it would be proper to assume that the reader is familiar with western logic and high school mathematics. At some places I have included important mathematical equations used in physics for the purpose of completeness. I have explained the meaning of these equations in a simple language. It is not necessary for the reader to remember the formulas or know the method of their derivation.

Finally, in the title the term *Buddhist Logic* was purposely chosen. The word "logic" is flexible. In the narrow sense it means what Aristotle thought were the fundamental laws of thought. In a broader sense, especially with reference to Buddhism, it connotes epistemology and even metaphysics. The title suggests that the book incorporates these three branches of philosophy, but emphasizes that it also discusses logic in the narrow sense. This is the area which is generally ignored by analysts who explore similarities between Buddhism and modern science.

Pronunciation of Sanskrit / Indic Phonemes and Words

1. Sanskrit vowels are pure such as are found in French, Italian and Spanish. (a, i, u, ṛ, ḷ) are short while (ā, ī, ū, ṝ, ḹ, e, o, ai, au) are long.
2. A dental consonant is one in which the tip of the tongue presses against the upper teeth.
3. A retroflex sound is pronounced with the tongue-tip curled back.
4. An aspirate is a consonant followed by the sound of "h", e.g. gh in doghouse.
5. It is necessary to know the sounds only to recognize their basic differences. It is not necessary to pronounce the words exactly as Indians do, unless one is learning Sanskrit or an Indic language.
6. Some Indic languages have also borrowed certain sounds from Dravidian languages. These are omitted to avoid complications.

a	p*u*n
ā	f*a*rm
ai	*ai*sle (approximate)
au	c*ow* (approximate)
b	*b*ear
bh	aspirated b as in a*bh*or
c	*ch*est
ch	aspirated as in chur*chh*ill
ḍ	*d*en, but retroflex
d	*d*en but dental similar to th in *th*en

ḍh aspirated ḍ resembling dh in a*dh*ere
dh aspirated d
e pl*ay*
g *g*o
gh aspirated g, as in do*gh*ouse
ḥ (slight aspiration of the preceding vowel)
h *h*im
i *i*n
ī s*ee*
j *j*et
jh aspirated j as in lo*dgeh*ouse (approx)
k *k*ill
kh aspirated k similar to kh in wor*kh*ouse
ḷ a short vowel resembling lry in reve*lry*
ḹ similar to ḷ, but longer. Usually not found in the text
l *l*ip
ṃ (nasalization of the preceding vowel)
m *m*eet
ṅ si*ng*
ṇ a*n*d
ñ ni*na* (girl child) as in Spanish
n *n*ever
o n*o*
p *p*en
ph aspirated p similar to ph in u*ph*ill
ṛ short retroflex vowel slightly resembling short " i" in the third syllable in *ability*
ṝ similar to ṛ, but longer
r *r*un, but more audible than in English resembling that in Italian
ś *sh*e
ṣ as in *sh*e but retroflex
s *s*it
ṭ *t*ip, but retroflex

t	wa*t*er, but dental
ṭh	aspirated ṭ similar to th in an*th*ill
th	aspirated t similar to th in *Th*ailand
u	p*u*t
ū	r*u*de
v	*v*ery
y	*y*es

Abbreviations

CCD	Common Conceptual Denominator (philosophy)
GUT	Grand Unification Theory (physics)
JTMF	*Jaina Theory of Multiple Facets of Reality and Truth (Anekāntavāda)*, ed. by Nagin J. Shah
Kārikā	*Mūlamadhyamakakārikās de Nāgārjuna avec la Prasannapadā (commentaire de Candrakīrti),* ed. by Louis de la Vallée Poussin
NB	*Nyāyabindu* by Dharmakīrti
NBT	*Nyāyabinduṭīkā* by Dharmottara
NK	*Nyāya-kaṇikā* (Reprint from *Paṇḍit*)
NVTT or Tātp	*Nyāya-vārtika-tātparya-ṭīkā* (Vizian)
PNT	*Pramāṇanayatattvāloka* by Vadideva Suri
PRM	*Pramāṇamīmāṃsā,* ed. by Sukhlal Sanghvi, *et.al,* Singhi Jaina Series no. 9, Bombay 1931
RQ	Relativity-Quantum (physics)
Śāstra	*The Mahā-prajñāpāramitā-śāstra of Nāgārjuna,* tr. by Kumārajīva
SBT	*Saptabhaṅgītaraṅgini,* ed. with Hindi *Ṭikā* by Thakura Prasad, Rayacandra Jaina, Shastramala No. 4, Bombay 1905

Symbols

	invariable concomitance (Buddhist logic)
$\Rightarrow$	material implication (western logic)
$\wedge$	and (conjuction, western logic)
$\equiv$	identity, similarity, equivalence, etc. (western logic, mathematics)
$\sim p$	not p (western logic)
$\forall$	universal quantifier (western logic)
$\exists$	existential quantifier (western logic)
$\varepsilon, \in$	membership of a class (western logic, mathematics)
R	relation (western logic)
A, E, I, O	universal affirmative, universal negative, particular affirmative, particular negative (Aristotelian / western logic)
ϕ	the null class (western logic, mathematics)
$f(x)$, f_x, etc.	function of x (mathematics), propositional function (western logic)
h	Planck's constant (physics)
ν	frequency (physics)
ω	angular frequency (physics)

Part I

Identity and Diversity

1

Introduction

The twentieth century witnessed the emergence of two revolutionary theories in physics, relativity and quantum theories. They not only shook the fundamental concepts in physics, their impact was truly seismic and was felt in every branch of human knowledge. I have called this phenomenon RQ effect (R for "relativity" and Q for "quantum"). RQ theories threw up many mysteries which could not be explained by contemporary science. In fact, even the fundamental laws of deductive logic appeared to be violated. Of these two theories quantum theory is more puzzling and leads to a bizarre subatomic world. This mystical quantum world has attracted many western intellectuals including scientists, philosophers, religious scholars and sci-fi writers. Many eminent scholars have found a number of parallels between eastern mysticism and RQ theories, especially the quantum phenomena.

There is abundant literature, technical as well as popular, relating to RQ mysteries and eastern mysticism. Some of the eminent commentators who have contributed to this literature include Roger Penrose, Fritjof Capra and Deepak Chopra.

This book critically examines in what sense eastern philosophy and mysticism is analogous to RQ conundrums. For several reasons my focus is on logic. I have chosen Buddhist logic as the principle area of investigation. The mysteries relating to other areas are dealt with only briefly. First, while there are many excellent critiques that have explored other branches of eastern philosophy, logic, especially Buddhist logic, has not been paid adequate attention. Secondly, violation of (deductive) logic is much more perplexing than violation of physical laws. The latter are subject to revision as science progresses. For instance, scientists once treated energy and matter as entirely different; but Einstein's relativity showed that they are interconvertible and his equation $E = mc^2$ could be empirically verified. However, such assertions as "x is both A and not-A" looks logically absurd because it violates the well-established law of contradiction which was formerly treated as one of the laws of thinking innate to the human mind. Such apparent violation occurs in multi-valued truth systems of logic which differ from our bivalent logic (true / false).

In Buddhist *catuṣkoṭi* there are four truth values while in Jaina *saptabhaṅgī* there are seven truth values. While some commentators mention these facts they do not seem to have analyzed *catuṣkoṭi* or *saptabhaṅgī* vis-à-vis quantum mysteries in depth.

Thirdly, when we contend that in the quantum world the laws of western classical logic, viz. the law of identity, the law of excluded middle and the law of contradiction are violated, we have first to analyze these "foundational" laws *de nouveau* to ascertain what they actually mean and to ensure that their usage is uniform.

For example, the words "identity" and "identical" are used in several senses. Such semantic ambiguities can lead to dubious parallels between quantum phenomena and eastern philosophy.

Ostensibly both Buddhist and Jaina philosophies have multi-valued truth systems, but there is a difference between how the logicians of these two systems interpret logical deadlocks. Jaina scholars prefer interpretations shared by common people, steering clear of mystical areas, while Buddhist logicians often tread the apparently mystical or transcendental terrain . This is why Buddhist logic has to be analyzed in depth.

While Buddhist logic and quantum theory are the principal areas for comparison, I have discussed many other topics such as "thought experiments", similarity between relativism and Einstein's relativity, and a number of apparently mystical concepts which arose in the wake of RQ shock and which cannot be divorced from these two theories.

But as we begin to compare the two apparently mystical areas of Buddhism and quantum world, we confront a paradox or rather a puzzle within a puzzle. Scholars usually consider Buddhism the most "scientific religion", it appears to stand closer to science than to religion because of its rational outlook and agnosticism. This necessitates a thorough comparison between Buddhism and science. This exercise should provide us a greater insight into the nature of connections we intend to find out.

2

The Riddle

2.1 Logical Confusion

Kumaran and Rajan, two students of a well-known school, once saw a small animal in the school compound. It looked like a cat, possibly sleeping, but there was something strange about its abnormally large face. "It's a cat", said Kumaran. "No, it's not", countered Rajan. They argued with each other for ten minutes, but could not decide who was right. They decided to consult their science teacher. The teacher was quite popular and friendly. He followed the two students to inspect the quadruped. When he saw the animal he, too, was a little confused. "Looks like a cat, but the face..., no it cannot be a cat," he said to himself. "Sir, is it not a cat?" asked Kumaran. "It's not a cat", said Rajan emphatically. The teacher's knowledge of zoology did not seem to be much more advanced than that of his students. "Hmmm...", he said. A teacher cannot display his ignorance. His face became grave. He cogitated for five minutes and added, "Well, there is some substance in what both of you contend". He concluded "That creature is either a cat or not a cat".

I do not know how the students reacted, but their teacher was absolutely right. He was merely stating a well known principle of logic :

a is *B* or not *B*

For example,

A human being can fly or cannot fly.

There is no third possibility.

This is called the law of excluded middle or *exclusi tertii principium.* In ordinary language, we say, "A third is not given" or *tertium non datur.*

A closely related with this law is the Law of Contradiction, viz.

a cannot be both *B* and *not-B*

For example, a figure cannot be both a square and not-square.

All of us accept these laws of logic as absolute truth. In accepting these laws we recognize that predicates B and not-B are mutually exclusive options which exhaust all possibilities. These laws appear obvious and were once called the laws of the mind or the laws of thought.

2.2 *Catuṣkoṭi*

In some Buddhist schools of logic and philosophy instead of the two-fold assertion, a four-fold assertion is accepted as a valid law of logic. It is called *catuṣkoṭi.*

In simple language it can be stated as

a is *B*

or *a* is not-*B*

or *a* is *B* and not-*B*

or *a* is neither *B* nor not-*B*

The first two options appear quite natural to us and exhaust all possibilities. The third and fourth options appear impossible; they violate the laws of contradiction and excluded middle. A careful examination even suggests *catuṣkoṭi* makes *a* semantically indeterminate. In short it violates the very first law of Aristotelian logic, viz. *a* is *a* or the law of identity. A concrete example of *catuṣkoṭi* is :

Quindo is a dog

Quindo is not a dog

Quindo is a dog and not-dog.

Quindo is neither a dog nor not-dog

We would certainly reject the third and fourth options as nonsense.

However, in matters not relating to the phenomenal world, we either accept or tolerate the violation of the two-value truth system. A spiritualist or a mystic can make such statements as

1. I am God and I am not-God
2. God is neither merciful nor not-merciful

Since the statements belong to the transcendent, one may refrain from making any comments on them. Nevertheless to scientists *catuṣkoṭi* appears mysterious if it is used with reference to the material world. Most of us feel that the third and the fourth options of *catuṣkoṭi* merely suggest that these statements are made by a person who cannot describe his experiences which are usually called "spiritual", "mystical", "revealing", and so on.

Buddhist logic also differed from the classical Indian logic embodied in *darśanas.* This often led to heated debates between Buddhist and Hindu scholars. We will find later that Buddhist logical and dialectical views have been interpreted at different levels and raise questions similar to those in quantum theory in physics.

Jainas, too, have a system similar to *catuṣkoṭi.* It has seven options instead of four and is called *saptabhaṅgī.* Such systems are called multi-valued (truth) systems in logic. It would be worthwhile to recall that the doctrine of *catuṣkoṭi* can be traced to Gautama Buddha's attitude towords speculative philosophy. It is well known that he refused to answer a few questions which he considered useless from the view-point of ethics. His main goal was alleviation of human suffering. Nevertheless these philosophical questions are important for us. Some of them are :

(1) Is the world eternal?
(2) Is the world noneternal?
(3) Is the world finite?
(4) Is the world infinite?
(5) Do the body and soul constitute one entity?
(6) Is the body different from the soul?

(7) Does a realized or liberated person continue to live after his (mundane) death?
(8) Does a realized or liberated person cease to live after his (mundane) death?
(9) Does a realized or liberated person live and not live after death?
(10) Does a realized or liberated person neither live nor not live after death?

While Gautama's silence has been interpreted in many ways leading to different schools of Buddhism his refusal to answer such metaphysical questions appears to indicate his agnostic attitude towards the transcendent. You can also observe that the last two questions which appear senseless and self-contradictory, are a pointer to the logic of *catuṣkoṭi,* at least in the matters pertaining to what is transcendental or indescribable or indeterminate. In Buddhism such indeterminate knowledge is called *avyaktāni*.[1]

Anyone who has some acquintance with eastern philosophy cannot but observe that matters related to the transcendent are broadly handled in three ways. Most people follow religious philosophy as a matter of faith. There is a small minority among intellectuals who reject traditional philosophy. But most intellectuals perpetually live in a dilemma whether they should accept tradition or not. We generally find that the intellect-belief confrontation then leads to the world of contradiction where positive and negative appear to coexist (through not at the same moment and same place) and need to be reconciled. *Catuṣkoṭi* in Buddhist logic, *saptabhaṅgī* in Jainism, Dialectics of the East as well as West display some areas of conflict. We shall see how the scholars in the past dealt with such ambiguities, and how we can address the problem in post-RQ era.

2.3 Relativity and Quantum Theories

In the twentieth century emerged two revolutionary theories in physics – relativity theory and quantum theory.

Einstein proposed the Special Theory of Relativity in 1905 and General Theory of Relativity in 1915. For the time being we may merely state the essentials of Einstein's theory :

(1) There is neither absolute time nor absolute space.

(2) The velocity of electromagnetic waves of which the "visible" light occupies only a small range of frequencies is a universal constant denoted by c, about 186,000 miles per second. This is based on the Michelson-Morley experiment in 1887.

(3) Under certain circumstances matter can be converted into energy and vice versa.

(4) Time, not being absolute is now given the status of the fourth dimension. Any event recorded by an observer needs to specify four coordinates (x, y, z, t). Scientists now prefer to talk of space-time instead of space (x, y, z) and time (t).

(5) In presence of a gravitational field the space-time becomes "curved".

To put it simply the behavior of a body in space-time with a gravitational field depends *inter alia* on the pattern of the field.

However, it is the quantum theory which is important for us for the time being.

Newton thought that light consisted of a stream of particles. However, in order to explain some phenomena such as interference Huygens maintained that light consisted of waves. The wave theory had an upper hand for a considerable period of time. The correct form of the electromagnetic waves was expressed by James Clerk Maxwell in 1865. His equations contained a constant c which was later identified with the velocity of electromagnetic radiation. Michelson-Morley's experiment mentioned above confirmed that this c is nothing but the velocity of light which is constant for all observers.

Einstein and later Poincaré suggested that electromagnetic waves did not require for propagation any medium such as the mythical ether.

In 1900 Max Planck suggested that electromagnetic radiation is absorbed and emitted in discrete packtes of energy, called quanta. Symbolically,

$$E = h\upsilon$$

where E is the energy, υ the frequency of the wave and h is "Planck's constant". But if electromagnetic radiation is a wave how can energy be absorbed or emitted in discrete bundles? Even a student of elementary physics would expect that as wave, the radiation should transmit energy continuously and not in "packets".

In 1923 French physicist de Broglie conjectured that even entities usually called particles should sometimes behave like waves just as light (usually treated as waves) behaves like a stream of particles called photons. His guess was confirmed subsequently. These waves are called matter waves.[2]

The upshot of this history of physics is that an entity has a dual nature : it may sometimes behave like a wave and sometimes as a particle in motion. However, this dual nature is observable only in the micro world or the sub-atomic world. This world involves light and other electromagnetic radiation and "elementary particles" such as electrons, protons and so on. We thus face a riddle in physics : why should tiny entities behave in a dual fashion? How can we explain this dichotomy which is similar to the inconsistency in *catuṣkoṭi*, the quaint logical system we mentioned earlier?

How can we describe the nature of light?

Can we assert that light is neither made of particles nor is it a wave?

Can we assert that light is both matter and wave?

Does light obey the four-valued system of *catuṣkoṭi*?

In fact, this riddle is compounded by other strange phenomena observed in the quantum world.

In 1929 Werner Heisenberg a German physicist formulated the uncertainty principle. According to this principle you cannot measure both the position and momentum of an elementary particle accurately at the same time. If you concentrate on one parameter, say, position, to reduce the error of measurement, you find that there is a greater error in the measurement of the other parameter (momentum in this case) and vice versa. What's more, this error cannot be attributed to limitations of the instruments used. This error is inherent in the very nature of our universe.

The quantum world appears quite strange compared to the macro world which we perceive without the aid of any instruments. Certainty is replaced by probability. The laws of logic and epistemology appear to be violated. We will discuss the quantum world in greater detail later, but it is necessary to list some of the consequences which are not limited to the world of physics and even science :

(1) In the quantum world the laws of logic cease to operate. This is especially true of the laws of identity, excluded middle and contradiction.

(2) The quantum reality is quite different from the reality we perceive in our everyday life.

(3) In uncertainty found in the micro world, some scientists perceive characteristics attributed to intelligence and consciousness.

(4) Mysticism and spirituality seem to have some place in the quantum world.

(5) Many scientists have turned to eastern religions and philosophy where they find a parallel between the quantum world and such concepts as Brahman, *māyā,* yin-yang and so on.

(6) The quantum theory and relativity theory have become veritable gold mines for science fiction writers who can create incredible fantasy worlds.

These two revolutionary theories have created shock waves in almost all fields of knowledge and have impacted human life significantly. We may call this phenomenon "RQ effect".

A thorough discussion on RQ effect would fill hundreds of pages and is beyond the scope of this book.

As mentioned in Introduction, our agenda is more modest. We will critically analyze the two mysteries, viz. (1) Buddhist logic which seems to violate the classical laws of logic, as also multiple levels at which Buddhist thinkers apply their heretical theories (2) the weird quantum world which displays matter-wave duality and its characteristic uncertainty alien to our perceptual (macro) world. We will address the following questions raised by these two riddles :

1. Can we have different logical systems, their validity depending on circumstances?
2. Can there be different logical systems all of them valid at different levels?
3. What is the meaning of uncertainty in the quantum world?
4. Is there a connection between those two mysteries in the world of logic and the world of quantum physics?
5. The erratic behavior of elementary particles resembles uncertainty inherent in human mind and its choices. Does it merely reflect duality in general? To be more specific, is there something mental in the quantum world?
6. Are the quantum phenomena dependent on the mind of the observer?
7. Can we reconcile these two apparently parallel mysteries to the accepted criteria which determine what is science and what is not?

There are many quanta-related mysterious results and "thought experiments". We will try to find out if they can be demystified. As mentioned earlier, relativity theory throws up fewer challanges. Here we shall investigate if Einstein's relativity is in any way connected with relativism (non-absolutism) in Jaina and Buddhist philosophy.

But before we try to answer these questions, we will have to reexamine many basic concepts in logic, theory of knowledge or epistemology, metaphysics or the nature of reality on the one hand and the concepts in physics such as matter, wave, individuality, space and time, energy and so forth.

The process will involve comparison of many modern concepts in logic and science with similar concepts in Buddhist and other Indian philosophical systems as well as traditional western theories.

3

Identity

3.1 The Law of Identity

The strange quantum world, which we will describe in detail later appears to violate three important Aristotalian laws : the law of identity, the law of excluded middle and the law of contradiction. It is necessary for us to thoroughly understand these laws and their implications. In this chapter we concentrate on the first law.

While the law of identity was accepted by philosophers as well as scientists, in practice the word "identity" was not used in the same sense. A few versions of this law are listed below :

1. If a proposition is true, it is true.
2. An object is equal to itself.
3. No two things are equal.
4. Every meaningful expression (concept, judgement, etc.) must be used in the same meaning.[1]
5. What is, is.

Symbolically, it is usually expressed as A = A

Ostensibly A can be anything, a thing, proposition, set, adjective, adverb and so on. This equality appears tautological and does not throw much light on the concept of identity in the sense in which the word is used in practice. Perhaps a better equation is

A = B

where " =" means identity and if every proposition which is true of A is also true of B, and vice versa. Of course A, B are symbols indicating something else, they are not the first and second letters of the Roman alphabet.

3.2 Individuals

Suppose A or B (which is nothing but A) is an individual. To simplify matters suppose A is Gandhi, then the law of identity

Gandhi = Gandhi

where Gandhi refers to Mahatma Gandhi, seems obvious. This is subject to proviso : both sides of the equation should imply "Gandhi at a certain moment". We cannot say that the infant Gandhi at one year is identical with the Gandhi at fifty. He certainly has changed during 49 years. His appearance, his attitudes and even the molecules in his body are not the same. But Gandhi's biographer would use the word "Gandhi" to refer to the Mahatma irrespective of his age. It is here understood that there is some assumption that despite several changes in his body and mind we can trace a unique entity called Gandhi by the biographer.

This is the case of a proper noun in which you can at least abstract a unique individual. Let us take another case. You utter the word "dog" three times on a certain day. There are two possibilities. You may be referring to the same dog Winky which you own. But out of context "dog" would mean any dog. A proposition about Winky need not be true of any dog.

We use common nouns or general terms to identify any member of a class defined on the basis of some common properties or relations. In such cases one dog would be identical to another when we are discussing dogs in general, i.e. a particular species of animals.

In science we usually employ common nouns. A scientist studying the properties of an element will not differentiate between one atom of the element from another atom of the same element. He would not assign proper names Tom, Dick and Harry, etc. to different atoms. In rare cases, at the micro level, he may concentrate on a particular individual.

When we study the macro world, we often concentrate on a specific individual say X. Even in such cases as mentioned earlier X at a certain time is not X at another time but the scientist will ignore this aspect unless the time factor is relevant.

3.3 Other Existents

The concept of identity is not confined to things; it may be used in case of other existents such as adjectives, adverbs and so on. If you say these two colors are identical without using any instrument, you are merely saying that they are indistinguishable.

Of two specimens of sound occurring continuously for one minute you may say their pitch and loudness are identical, if such is the case. You may also add that they have run for identical time intervals.

In practice the law of identity is used to identify an element of a class or set defined intensionally. For example, we may divide all employees in a firm on the basis of their monthly salaries into, say, three classes :

A ($<$ Rs. 10,000), B ($\geq$ 10,000 but $<$ 20,000), C ($\geq$ 20,000). We may have the following statistics.

Class	*Number of employees*
A	10
B	8
C	2

Each class consists of employees having a common characteristic, viz. their salaries are in a given range. Employees belonging to two different groups cannot have this common characteristic. Most classifications in science are of this kind in which we wrongly perceive identity where only some characteristics are common. This is the relation of equivalence which we will study later.

The following illustration will elucidate how the concept of identity varies :

E1.

(a) Let ABC and XYZ be two triangles on a flat surface. Their corresponding sides and angles are equal. Are these triangles identical? As individuals ABC cannot be identical with XYZ. These triangles are congruent. However, if we are considering a class of congruent triangles, we may call them identical, keeping in mind what we mean by identity.

(b) We have a set of balls; 3 white and 5 blue. How can we introduce the concept of identity? If the white balls have exactly the same color, size, material, etc., *qua* individuals they are not identical since they occupy three different portions of space. The same argument applies to the blue balls. This view is held by many philosophers such as Wittgenstein. However, Russell does not seem to agree with this view. Actually his view leads to a problem of enumeration and numerical diversity.If we follow Russell, white counting the balls all white balls will be considered as one unit and all blue balls... will constitute another unit, giving us two balls in all instead of eight. This view considers that two things occupying different space portions are identical if they are otherwise indistinguishable. This does not appeal to our common sense. We do not consider two things as one if they are separated though they may look identical. Russell's argument does not appear convincing.[2]

(c) It is easy to see that the phrase "identical twins" is a metaphor, since despite considerable similarity such twins are two different individuals.

(d) When an anthropologist studies man as a type of animals he will usually consider all humans under observation as identical but will establish subclasses such as "males", "females", etc. when necessary. In this case males will be considered identical *qua* men and females will be identical *qua* women.

(e) Suppose you meet a college friend Chan accidentally at a function. It is more than thirty years since you met him last time. He looks so different that you do not recognize him easily. However, once his identity is established you will introduce him to other friends as Chan and not as "Chan minus the hair on the head plus twenty kilograms of fat".

(f) For a certain purpose you may classify your employees in two groups S and T; those having height less than or equal to 5'7'' (S), and those who are taller than 5'7'' (T). For convenience you may call those employees belonging to the same group "identical". After two years you repeat the process and find that one Jack who was an "S" has become a "T". Certainly S who is in his fifties has not become taller in the last two years. You realize that you are now using more accurate instruments to measure the height than you used last time. This shows that the concept of identity in practice is subject to the degree of accuracy that can be attained by the instrument used to measure the relevant property.

(g) An example similar to (b) can now be considered. You see three colors at three different places . They all appear the same as far as the shade (blue) is concerned. What is the concept of identity in this case? Remember, in (b) above we spoke about balls which we view as "things". A color is not an object or a thing. It is an attribute of another entity, say, a file, a wall or a chair. Russell suggests that we can say that these colors are identical if they are indistinguishable from one another. In other words, we do not treat these three "blues" as distinct existents. We would rather say they are instances of the identical color "blue X" which is a "universal" that defines the class "blue of shade X".

However, if we are considering three "patches" of blue where the number of patches is important, then we would say there are three patches at different locations having identical color "blue".

Similarly if you see three cars running in different directions, but with the same speed you could say that there are three moving cars with identical speed. If the speed happens to be 50 miles per hour, you could even add "These are three instances of the identical speeds".

To summarize, the law of identity should be interpreted contextually. In case of specific individuals such as Thames, Ganges, John Wike, Ramu S., etc. the law merely asserts the obvious : A is A at any given moment. A will not remain A next moment. When the law is used in reference to general terms "cat, "dog", "boy", etc. the law of identity merely implies "any cat" "any dog", etc. unless constraints are imposed depending on the circumstances.

I personally feel the law of identity when not used in the strict sense such as "John at five p.m. today", has vague and misleading connotations not befitting the word "identity". In practice the law of identity is used for creating classes based on similar attributes or relations and all the members of a class are considered undifferentiated only in the limited sense of having the same attributes. Though we may for convenience say these entities are "equal" or "identical", these words convey different meanings depending on the particular case under consideration.

Our analysis of "identity" is not yet complete, because we have to consider other related concepts such as numerical diversity, individuation, discontinuity, classes and sets. But before we discuss these topics, we must briefly say something about how we acquire knowledge.

4

Knowledge, Universals and Particulars

4.1 Epistemology and Metaphysics

Everything we can learn about nature may be called knowledge. This is a very wide definition because nature includes our senses and mind. We can thus speak of the knowledge of the arts, science, religion, society and so forth.

Knowledge has also been defined as the product of material and intellectual activity of people. This view reflects that aspect of human society which is called culture.

Knowledge is sometimes divided into "scientific" and "pre-scientific" categories. The former includes what is called theoretical knowledge and empirical knowledge.

The branch of philosophy which discusses the theory of knowledge is called epistemology, a term coined by a Scottish philosopher J.F. Ferrier in 1854.[1] Epistemology discusses such topics as the relation of subject and object, the relation of knowledge to reality, limitations of acquiring knowledge, criteria for valid and invalid knowledge, etc. Epistemology is closely related to another branch of philosophy, called ontology or metaphysics which is concerned with existence, being and reality.

4.2 Analytic-Synthetic Dichotomy

There has been a controversy between two schools of philosophers; rationalists and empiricists. The rationalists hold that true knowledge can be gained only from the mind or from deductive logic. The role of experience, according to them, is triggering off the concepts or innate ideas. On the other hand, the empiricists contend that sense experience is the only mode of acquiring knowledge. Of course, between the extreme rationalists and empiricists there are many shades of epistemologists who acknowledge that both logic and experience are necessary, but differ as to their relative importance. This has a bearing on how a concept is formed. This controversy is also closely connected with what is called the problem of universals, to be discussed later.

This controversy is often called Analytic-Synthetic Dichotomy. The following illustrations will elucidate the dichotomy :

E1 Consider the following statements :

(a) The animal you see is either a dog or not a dog.
(b) A tiger cannot be both an animal and a not-animal.
(c) A lion is a mammal. An ant is not a mammal. Hence an ant is not a lion.
(d) A human being cannot live for more than 300 years.
(e) The sun rises in the east.
(f) Humans cannot fly.
(g) A dog has three eyes.

These statements are called "propositions". A proposition is a statement which is either true or false.

In E1, (a) through (f) are true propositions, while (g) is false. These propositions, however, fall under two broad groups. To the first group belong (a) through (c) whose truth or falsehood is obvious. In the second group are (d) through (g) whose truth or falsehood contains an element of uncertainty. The propositions in the first group are such that once you know the meaning of their words and symbols, your conclusion follows automatically. These are called logical (deductive) or analytical statements. Incidentally (a) is the law of excluded middle and (b) the law of contradiction.

In the second group are those statements whose truth or falsehood can be known only through observation. For example, we feel (d) is true because in human memory no person has ever lived for that long. Nevertheless we cannot be "cent percent sure", because there might have been an unrecorded case of a person who lived beyond 300 years in the past. It is also possible that medical advances may enable us to live for more than 300 years in the future. A similar argument can be made in case of (e) A celestial accident may occur in the future which may tear the earth away from the sun's orbit and there will not be the usual sun-rise. These propositions are called "synthetic".

The first group contains the statements from mathematics or deductive logic earlier called the laws of the mind. The second group contains those statements whose truth or falsehood is only probable. For example the truth of (e) has a very high degree of probability, and we may say it is almost certain. As we know the truth of the second group is determined by general induction. Many philosophers like Ayn Rand consider the analytic-synthetic split as artificial.

4.3 Hume and Kant

Philosophers have used many terms to distinguish these two groups. The statements belonging to the first are called analytic, a priori, rational, logical, etc. while those belonging to the second group are known as synthetic, a posteriori, empirical, inductive and so on. However, the words belonging to the same group are not exact synonyms and may have slightly different meanings.

Philosophers have also used the terms "rational epistemology" and "empirical epistemology" to indicate the knowledge pertaining to these respective groups.

David Hume (1711-1776) had suspected that a relation such as 2+2=4 is not of the same type as "when a ball A hits a ball B, A causes B to move". Their contradictions elucidate the point succinctly. The statement $2+2 \neq 4$ is self-contradictory, while "A does not cause B to move" may be false but is not self-contradictory. However, Hume was not able to provide a satisfactory explanation of the difference. You will appreciate that the first statement is mathematical (and hence logical) but the second involves a causal connection or a "factual truth".

It was Immanuel Kant (1724-1804) who analyzed the situation further. He contended that in a true statement of the subject-predicate type the predicate is either implied in the subject term or excluded. In the former case, the judgement is analytic. For example, a proposition "A square is not circular" is analytic. We also call such a statement tautological.

A "synthetic" proposition, on the other hand, is one whose truth depends on extralinguistic facts, its truth has to be ascertained through observation from the external world. "The sun is a star" is a synthetic statement whose truth can be determined only empirically. Historically, analytic and synthetic statements have been associated with theoretical and practical knowledge.

An "a priori" judgement is one which is independent of our sense experience. *A* "posteriori" knowledge, on the other hand can be obtained, only from sense experience, Kant maintained that "analytic a priori" and "synthetic a posteriori" are not the only types of knowledge. He suggested a third type, "synthetic a priori". According to him a true proposition may have a predicate which is neither included in the subject, nor dependent on experience. The third type is reflected in such statements as :

(1) Every event has a cause.
(2) 7+5 = 12

He even went further and asserted that synthetic a priori statements are found in such areas as ethics and epistemology.

Based on the concepts "a priori", "a posteriori", "analytic" and "synthetic" we can have four combinations, viz. analytical *a priori*, analytical "a posteriori", synthetic "a priori", synthetic "a posteriori". It is usually believed that "analytic a posteriori" statements cannot exist, leaving the three possibilities contemplated by Kant.

4.4 Russell

In effect Kant was suggesting that logical and mathematical truths could be of different nature. Peano, Frege, Russell and Whitehead in the 20th century have brought logic closer to mathematics.

Russell has almost succeeded in proving that all mathematics is symbolic logic. According to him, "by the help of ten principles of deduction and ten other premises of general logical nature (for example, 'implication' and 'relation') all mathematics can be strictly and formally deduced; and all the entities that occur in mathematics can be defined in terms of those that occur in the above twenty premises".[2]

4.5 Plato on Universals

The dynamics of concept formation is closely related to what is called the problem of universals. When we see an object, it appears as an individual. When we encounter a number of objects we tend to classify the objects on the basis of similarities. Thus we may assign the pen to the class of "writing instruments". An individual which we recognize as a pen then becomes a particular of this class. Of course, an individual may belong to more classes than one. All particulars (such as "chairs") having common properties belonging to a class ("chair") collectively constitute the universal. However, to determine the relationship between the individual, particular and universal is not easy. Even the idea of the universal may vary from one philosopher to another. Broadly speaking, four or five schools may be identified.

According to Plato we can understand the world only on the basis of what he called "ideas". These may be called forms, principles or universals. Plato thought that our knowledge of concretes depends on the Ideas which are innate to us. For example, if you did not have the Idea of "dogness" you would not have the knowledge of a dog when you see a concrete or a particular representative. Plato believed that the archetype of an Idea was known to us before our birth and when we see a particular, our memory is linked with it and the particular is identified or classified.

Plato believed that these Ideas were logically prior to their concretes. This was not all, he thought they were more real than their concretes. If we see a number of dogs, we can find some differences. The reason lies in the fact that these particulars are only imperfect imitations of the perfect Idea.

Platonists thus appear to believe that universals exist as realities in some other dimension and the concretes we come across in this world are only poor imitations whose knowledge we acquire through the archetypal universal.

Plato's philosophy is treated as "idealism". Nevertheless in concept formation, those who agree with Plato are called "extreme realists" because for them the universals actually exist in another dimension and are more real.

4.6 Aristotle

Aristotle opposed the notion of the eternal "idea". The universals according to him did not have a separate identity or existence. For him it is through the particulars that we make abstractions.

Aristotle maintained that Plato ignored a basic fact, viz. experience which was epistemologically important. He also contended that the Plato's concept of eternal Ideas belonging to another world was metaphysically unsound.

It is difficult to see how these ontologically different existents (universals and particulars) belonging to different worlds could have any connection. However, Aristotle did accept the notion of abstraction qua universals but asserted that they exist only in concretes. For him, too, the universals were discovered and not invented, but he denied the two different types of existents postulated by Plato.

He also believed that a natural thing was a dynamic entity in space and time in the sense that its essential development is internally directed, though there may be accidental changes brought about by external forces. He believed in the "final cause", a principle according to which an object can be fully comprehended. For example, to know a tadpole is to comprehend that it is a potential which will become a frog. However, he does not recognize that this directive principle inherent in every object is a divine design. He regards the teleology as immanent.

Those who broadly agree with Aristotle's conception of acquiring knowledge are called "moderate realists" who believe that the common qualities found in concretes are metaphysical essences.

It must, however, be emphasized that Aristotle believed that since there were millions of final causes, there has to be the first cause, the "unmoved mover" or God. It appears that despite Aristotle's argument regarding the "immanent teleology", he believed in the ultimate purpose attributed to God.

4.7 Roscellinus

Roscellinus (1050–1122) may be called a typical representative of extreme nominalism in epistemology. Extreme nominalists maintain that only particulars or concretes are real. The universal is a mere name, a common term used to designate particulars which are grouped arbitrarily based on perceived similarities.

There are a number of shades in nominalism. For example, Abelard (1079–1142) who was Roscellinus' student did not agree with his teacher's extreme views. He accepted that a common noun like "dog" did imply a universal concept. According to him this concept had two sides. First, "dog" was a confused or blurred image abstracted from various dogs one sees. Second, it also implies an abstraction which makes the dog different from a "nondog". He recognized that a concept was an abstraction of common features, but maintained that this abstracted meaning was born of the psychological process. He, however, did not equate abstraction with the psychological process. He agreed that concretes were real but abstractions resulted from a mental process that isolated common characteristics that were extra-mental.

George Berkeley (1685–1783) may be cited as another nominalist. His philosophy called "subjective idealism" incorporates three fundamentals tenets. First, the existence of a concrete object is dependent on mind. Second, concrete objects are essentially mental in nature. Third, all valid ideas are particular and not universal. It is the third principle which aligns him with nominalists.

William Ockham (1285–1349) was another nominalist who contended that universals are only common names which exist in the mind. Curiously his brand of nominalism led to a very important principle of "Ockham (Occam) razor". He deprecated the use of the plethora of explanations used to describe universals, essences and equivalent notions. It complicates philosophy and introduces terms that are superfluous. Maintaining that we gain knowledge from our immediate experiences of concretes, he advocated the rejection of statements referring to inexperienced entities. His principle also implies that an entity need not be added to a model unless it is absolutely required. In modern language this means that if we can describe a phenomenon with the help of n parameters x_1, x_2,....x_n and it is found that two of them can be completely described in terms of n-2 parameters, then these two parameters are superfluous and can be dropped. Incidentally this shows how epistemology and ontology are interwoven. While "nominalism" may be called an epistemological doctrine, "Ockham's razor" is an ontological principle.

4.8 Locke

It is interesting to consider Locke's solution to the problem of universals. On the one extreme lies William of Champeaux who adhered to extreme realism asserting that universals exist independent of particulars. In the middle is Abelard's moderate realism, viz. the universals are present only in particulars and grasped by us through abstraction. On the other extreme is Roscellinus who considers the universal as a mere name.

Locke's views are known as "conceptualism". Locke stands between Abelard and Roscellinus. He stresses on particular ideas of the mind; neither on particular objects nor on common properties of the objects. He maintained that our immediate knowledge is confined to ideas. According to him a word is a symbol for an idea. Thus when we say "dog" there is an implicit understanding that this word stands for the abstract idea "dog". In other words concepts exist in our mind as ideas not as images.

He argued that the origin of ideas lay in our experience. He rejected the notion of innate ideas. If the ideas were innate they should be the same for all human beings. In that case there would not be any philosophical controversies on such views as "Nature abhors vacuum" or "whatever is, is; whatever is not, is not".

He distinguished between knowledge and pseudo-knowledge. According to him all ideas stem either from sensation or reflection. First, the external objects give us such simple ideas as yellow, white, cold, soft, hard and so on. Second, we have ideas of higher order when our mind reflects on simple ideas. These "operations of our minds" give rise to such concepts as perceiving, thinking believing etc. The higher ideas are thus an interplay between the simpler ideas and mental operations.

Locke's philosophy implies that our knowledge is limited since ultimately it is based on experience. Thus he rejects the idea of the infinite space because our mind cannot "pass over" such a thing. The infinite space is a mere repetition of the idea of space we know. Similarly all our arguments about God are meaningless.

Locke's views had a profound impact on his successors – in the study of philosophy, epistemology was made prior to metaphysics. For example, before we answer questions relating to the relation between the word "dog" to dog qua object we have to consider the relation of the word "dog" to our idea of dog.

4.9 Russell's Views

Russell's views seem to indicate his agnostic approach to the problem of universals. In his paper "On the relations of universals and particulars" he maintains that the dualism between universals and particulars is ultimate. His earlier views reflected in this paper can be summarized as follows :[3]

> We can divide all entities into two classes – particulars and universals. Particulars are those entities which enter into complexes only as subjects of predicates or the terms of relations. For example, in "A is white" and "B is the father of C", A,B,C are particulars. In the first sentence, A is a subject. In the second, B and C are the terms which indicate a relation. If the particulars belong to the world which we experience, they exist in time and cannot be at more than one place at one time. For example, if Tommy and Jersy are two distinct dogs, at any given instant they cannot occupy the same portion of space.
> Universals can occur as predicates or relations in complexes. In "A is white", "whiteness" may be treated as a universal. In " B is the father of C", "father" is a universal. Universals do not exist in time, what exist are the particulars such as A. Universals have no relation to one place which they may not have simultaneously to another place. For example, whiteness may exist in two different places at one time.

In his paper cited above he held the view that some relations in space such as "A is to the left of B" implied numerical diversity (between A and B). But these particulars could have the same predicate "white". As to predicates they are indistinguishable. Hence "whiteness" should be treated as the universal while A and B are particulars.

However, Russell seems to have changed his views subsequently and abandoned the opinion that "there are any spatial or temporal relations which always and necessarily imply diversity". [4]

In his subsequent work he uses the concepts of "events" and "complexes of compresence" instead of objects and particulars.[5]

He seems to have come to the conclusion that the theory which asserts particulars is not wrong, but it cannot be proved to be right.

So the theories which assert and deny particulars are equally tenable. He feels however, that the latter theory has the merit of being logically parsimonious.[6]

In the next chapter we shall see how some epistemologists handle the problem of universals and treat the controversy related to it as redundant.

5

Perception and Concept Formation

5.1 Introduction

In the last chapter we saw how various schools compete with one another to explain the formation of a concept through particulars and universals. For some philosophers there is no need to assume the universals with respect to a group having common characteristics. According to them, the notion of the universal is not only redundant but irrational. It implies that a group has some unique inherent characteristic such as "catness" or "dogness", etc. while in reality we can classify objects on the basis of different criteria : shape, size, color, use and so forth. This gives rise to innumerable classes which intersect each other.

Epistemologically, it is the similarity of different aspects which is the major determinant of classification. A growing infant does it unconsciously, while adults may classify objects consciously or unconsciously.

According to the objectivists an infant learns by the process of "integration and differentiation". Suppose the child comes into contact with many tables and chairs. He perceives similarities and differences in respect of their characteristics. For example, a table has a flat top and four legs. A chair has a seat and a back. He observes that smaller things are kept on the tables and people occupy the chairs. The child integrates the pronounced features of the tables which gives him the concept of "table". Similarly the most common characteristics of chairs leads him to the concept "chair". His rudimentary classification into "table" and "chair" involves differentiation. He perceives, though he may not be able to articulate, that there are differences within the same group as regards color, shape, use, etc., but these differences are minor compared with a difference between any chair and any table.

This process of differentiation and integration continues. The child observes that the tables are not identical : some are small, some have a large top, they are also used for different purposes. The child is thus able to differentiate the subsets of the tables and learns that the "dining table" is different from the "writing table" and the table used for displaying curios. He similarly discovers the subcategories of the chairs : reclining chairs, folding chairs, small chairs for children and so on.

The child also proceeds in another direction. He comes into contact with different types of furniture in addition to chairs and tables; sofas, cots, cupboards and so forth. Most of them are movable and used for sitting, storing, sleeping, etc. The process of integration helps him to gain the concept of a superset which he subsequently learns to call "furniture". The process of differentiation enables him to isolate furniture from other household items such as doors and windows which the adults call fixtures. The process of differentiation and integration leads to sets, subsets and supersets.

However, this process is not unidirectional. There is abstraction based on shape, size, color, etc. which leads the child to distinguish not only white, black and red colors but also "white chairs", "black chairs" and "red chairs".

Integration and differentiation is also operative in the area of adverbs. The child learns to distinguish slow and fast, left and right, up and down and so forth.

Unlike the adult the child's classification is almost unconscious. His learning involves abstraction and further abstraction of abstractions. As he grows he builds a complex web of concepts.

The process continues when he becomes an adult when he is also able to "design" classes consciously.

5.2 Sensation, Perception and Concept

A sensation is usually treated as a psychical phenomenon which appears when an object influences our sense organs : eyes, ears, skin, tongue, etc. Without the brain we would not have sensations. However many epistemologists and psychologists treat an isolated sensation as momentary which is not integrated into the memory. It is believed that for an infant a sensation is an undifferentiated chaotic experience.

The objectivists believe that the acquisition of knowledge really begins with percepts. A percept is a bundle of sensations automatically retained and integrated by the brain. It is the percepts which appear self-evident whether they are visual, tactile or auditory.

An *existent* is anything that exists. It may be a thing (which is recognized by a proper name or class-name) or an attribute (like shape, color which is recognized by adjectives) or action (running, walking, etc. usually indicated by verbs).

An existent is a concept. In the process of learning it undergoes different stages. When the infant becomes aware of objects it is called "entity". When the infant is able to recognize this entity as separate from the rest of his perceptual field, the concept is called "identity". When the child is able to grasp the characteristics of an object and compare it with other objects, he reaches the third stage of the concept, viz. unit. At this stage he sees a unit as a unique thing whose characteristics he can compare with those of other units.[1]

It must be realized that concept formation is facilitated by our consciousness which is an active process capable of differentiating and integrating various characteristics as mentioned earlier. It would be appropriate to mention here that mathematicians sometimes define a class (or a collection) "extensionally" or by "enumeration". For example, I may declare that {2, 5, Gandhi} is a class. This method sharply differs from the above process of classification and subclassification which is coextensive with our learning. This method is used in defining classes intensionally as we shall see later.

Since it is the units which help us in comparing and relating one existent with another, the concept of unit is treated as a bridge between metaphysics and epistemology.[2] It is a bridge between "what" and "how".

5.3. Measurement

According to the objectivists cognition involves two areas; conceptual and mathematical, where by mathematical is meant that which is related to measurement.

Strictly speaking, measurement need not involve numbers : numerical measurement is only a sophistication introduced by us. The minimum apparatus that is needed for rough measurement is the concept of order such as less than, or greater than, heavier than, etc. If we have, say, sticks of different lengths we can arrange them in order starting with the shortest stick and ending with the longest.

However, numerical measurement enables us to take a quantum jump. We can select a standard, say, a particular stick, the man's foot and so forth. The length then can be measured in terms of these "yard sticks". In the modern era we have various standards. In case of length there is an inch, a foot, mile, centimeter, meter, etc. For weight we have standards like a gram, kilogram, pound, tonne and so on. In some cases it is difficult to establish a scale based on standards. Some qualities like love or hate cannot be measured explicitly but can be guessed in terms of the order relation. If A loves B, C, D,..., etc. he can arrange these intensities of love in order.

One should think of measurement in a wider sense to include non-numerical measurement which is facilitated by the order relation. We mentioned earlier that when the infant reaches the third stage he can identify and compare existents qua units. This is the conceptual stage. When a concept is clothed with quantitative dimension, measurement, we take another leap forward. With measurement, especially numerical, our knowledge can encompass the range which is many billion times the range of perception. To take an example, mere perception may enable us to identify a decagon but only a supermind could say that "this polygon has 2000 sides" merely by looking at it. Measurement and language help us understand even the numbers and the degree of quality or action which we cannot perceive or even create ourselves.

We can not only understand the idea of "as slow as a snail" or "as fast as a tiger" but can fully comprehend "the speed of .001 centimeter per hour" or "the speed of one billion miles per hour", whether such a speed is attainable in our physical world is a different matter. For example, as the knowledge of physics stands today, no signal of any kind can travel faster than light.

Philosopher Protagoras maintained that "Man is the measure of all things" this is usually interpreted to imply relativism or subjectivity. Rand aptly provides a novel interpretation : man *is* the measure, epistemologically but not metaphysically.[3] Man is the user of the objective methods to probe into the universe.

5.4 Concept Formation

The process which starts at the level of sensation and culminates in the formation of concepts is extremely complicated involving comparison, analysis, synthesis, abstraction, idealization and generalization. The most important characteristic involved in concept formation is abstraction. But the process does not end when a concept is formed; there is further abstraction of abstraction. It must be pointed out that the hierarchy of concepts is dependent on the level of knowledge we possess at any given time. Our ancestors 500 years ago would not have been able to "abstract" what we can today and our descendents 500 years hence will be able abstract what we cannot even imagine.

Abstraction is a never-ending process. Moreover our epistemology is "open" in the sense as we explore the world more and more, the older concepts are modified and abstraction undergoes fine-tuning. We shall in a later chapter show how abstraction can be depicted, albeit approximately, as a logical system.

Rand defines a concept as "a mental integration of two or more units which are isolated to specific characteristic(s) and united by a specific definition".[4]

Consider a library in which thousands of books are stocked in shelves and are easily accessible. There are also numerous chairs and tables. It is extremely easy for us to isolate common characteristics, integrate them into conceptual units and differentiate one unit from the other. This abstraction should lead at the first, to the broad categories – table, chair, book, shelf, etc. Let us concentrate on one such category, "book". There are thousands of members in the library belonging to this concept. But the books are not exactly similar, they differ in size consisting of length, breadth and thinckness. These dimensions are measurable by the units of length. However, in the concept formation at the first level these measurements are dropped. This only means that the concept "book" has the measurements of length, but they may have many values (theoretically, any value). Similarly tables in the library may have tops with different colors, but this measurement will be dropped in the concept of "table". A table will have a color but it can have any color.

A distinguishing characteristic or the set of characteristics which isolates a concept and makes it different from other concepts is called Conceptual Common Denominator (CCD), not a popular term, but nevertheless a useful term employed by the objectivists.

When we consider the concept "motion" the essential characteristic or CCD is "the change of position continuously in finite time" with respect to an observer. However, we drop the measurements like the size of the body, its color, use, etc. which are not relevant. A moving body can have any size, weight or color. The concept of "edible" has the CCD "fit for human consumption". Such measurements as taste, color, price, etc. are dropped.

It is necessary to realize that CCD is a commensurable characteristic essential in the formation of a concept. We recall how Pythagoras thought that the length of the diagonal of a right angled triangle, each of whose sides is 1, is "incommensurable". The famous Pythagoras theorem is

$$z^2 = x^2 + y^2$$

where z is the hypotenuse and x, y are other two sides of a right angled triangle. When $x = 1 = y$, we get

$$z^2 = 1+1= 2$$
$$z = \sqrt{2}$$

Since the Greeks were not familiar with irrational numbers, Pythagoras called this length "incommensurable". Epistemologically, he was right – the CCD of a rational number is that it can be expressed as p/q where p and q are integers. Obviously $\sqrt{2}$ cannot be expressed this way, and hence is not commensurable with rational numbers.

Consider the concepts "in", "above", "below" which are prepositions. Consider specifically "above". This is a relational concept expressed by "x is above y", and can be ostensively defined. Incidentally "below" is a relation which is the converse of "above". Relations will be discussed at length in a later chapter. What is important to realize is that other measurements of x and y, size, color, shape, etc. are dropped.

The adverbial concepts such as "fast", "slow" can be easily understood. For example, in "walking slowly", "slowly" involves an essential measure of the already mentioned concept "motion". In practice, however, "slow" and "fast" are relative terms and have to be defined in relation to some average speed which partitions "high" and "low". Language plays an important role in the area of concepts. While the formation of concepts is not dependent on language, language introduces precision and also increases the range of our knowledge.

5.5 Important Concepts

We can briefly discuss a few important concepts such as Existence and Consciousness.

Existence

Existence may be called a primary concept whose common characteristic is shared by all things. Unfortunately, the word "thing" itself leads to controversies. Some philosophers may attribute existence to those things which are in reality and assert that such things as mermaids, unicorns, fairies, etc. do not exist. Some philosophers such as neorealists include the imaginary beings among existents.

Existence has also been defined as "the whole diversity of mutable things in their concatenation and interaction".[5] Most philosophers agree that essence and existence are inseparable.

According to the objectivists, "Existence exists" is the full description of existence. We cannot question why existentialists treat nonexistence or nonbeing as a valid concept. They may retort "why should an existent exist?" In a narrower sense, the existentialists treat existence as the kernel of human ego.

Nonexistence, according to the objectivists, is not a concept at all. Nonexistence is a derivative of a certain object. It is the absence of a concrete.

In existentialism nonbeing or nonexistence is important. Nonbeing may even be treated as logically prior to being.

In the eastern mysticism nonexistence is sometimes treated as a distinct concept. For example, *śūnya* (zero) or void, paradoxically has an immense creative potential. In *vaiśeṣika* one of the orthodox Indian philosophies claiming allegiance to the Vedas, nonexistence is treated as one of the seven categories (*padārthas*).

Consciousness

Consciousness is awareness. It is through consciousness that we perceive existence. It is also regarded as the aggregate of mental processes which enable us in the cognition of the external world as well as our personal being.

One may think of the ascending scale of consciousness possessed by living organisms. Man undoubtedly has the most highly developed consciousness. While consciousness is "of" something, only a human being is believed to be conscious of his own consciousness. Consciousness is usually treated as active while some existentionlist posit two parts : active and passive.

The objectivists consider "content" and "action" – content of awareness and action in regard to the content – the fundamental CCD of consciousness. According to them only the human consciousness is able to reach the conceptual stage. The animal conciousness functions only at the perceptual level.

Consciousness, it must be remembered, is a *sine qua non* of knowledge. While we may have computers and robots to help us in acquiring knowledge, they are ultimately the creations of our consciousness. Without consciousness epistemology cannot exist.

It is necessary to remember that in philosophy there is no standard nomenclature. In this chapter we have used the words "unit", "percept", "concept", etc. as the objectivists use. The meaning of such words may differ from one school to another. When used out of context these concepts must be properly conveyed either through definition or through a reference to the appropriate school of thought.

5.6 The Web of Abstractions

Concept formation involves abstraction, but the process of abstraction continues vertically as well as horizontally forming a complex web of interconnecting concepts. This also leads to the classes of classes on the basis of different criteria called "differentia" or the distinguishing characteristics.

At the lowest stage the formation of wider concepts is comparatively simple, based on perceptual concretes. We have already discussed the transition from the concepts table, chair, stool, sofa to a higher concept, viz. furniture. We are familiar with the words "species" and "genus" in biology. These are extremely convenient in the terminology of epistemology. In the above example, the table, chair, sofa, etc. can be treated as "species" while they all belong to the "genus" furniture. In the other direction the concept "chair" may be subdivided into "chair without arms", and "chair with arms". These two subdivisions then become the species and "chair" now becomes the genus. But there is also a horizontal expansion, a chair may have a cushioned seat or be without a cushioned seat. These new subdivisions are the species of the genus "chair" but based on different differentia.

Take the concept of "man" qua species, it belongs to the genus mammal, while qua genus it has species – male and female (one subdivision), or child, adolescent, youth, adult (second subdivision), or Caucasian, Negro, Mongolian, etc. (third subdivision), or Indian, Pakistani, Sri Lankan, Englishman, American (fourth division) and so on. In the first subdivision, the differentia is sex, in the second it is age, in the third it is race, in the fourth, citizenship. It is interesting to observe that in the process of integration of concepts, a concept is treated epistemologically as if it were a single notional concrete while metaphysically each unit stands for a number of concretes. Concept formation has another useful aspect, we can recognize new concretes which have been already conceptualized. This ensures a smooth transition from the past to the future. Without the hierarchy of concepts, we would find the world of the future very strange, especially when we move from one place to another, one town to another and one country to another. There is a misconception that as we move to the higher concept, the cognitive content decreases. This is not true. For example, if we did not have more knowledge we would not ascend from the concept of man to the concept of mammal. This misperception arises on account of the fact that higher conceptualization involves greater abstraction. It must be borne in mind that when we go from the species to the genus, the latter subsumes the knowledge of species plus the knowledge of their common characteristics.

As we move higher in the hierarchy of concepts, we gain more extensive knowledge. As we go down and create subdivisions, we gain more intensive knowledge. When we make man the genus and the citizenship as differentia for subdivision we need the knowledge of what "citizenship" means and the various sovereign states which are different political units.

5.7 Definition

One often encounters definitions in various branches of knowledge, especially what are called sciences. While in logic, mathematics and physics it is easy to define a concept or a word, philosophy which analyzes concepts usually does not define terms. This leads to an epistemological difference in science and philosophy. Like God, the mathematician may say, "let there be the null set", and that is the end of it; the null set is treated as an axiom. The philosophers, however, prefer to analyze the concept of the null set which is a collection containing no objects. It may consider such questions as "Can there be a null set?" "Is it possible to reach the concept of the null set in different ways?"

While definitions make a concept or word definite, it also introduces rigidity.

Definition is usually a laconic and logical description of a thing, or the meaning of a word or concept stating the distinctive properties and also limitations.

A definition can consist of symbols or words which have already been defined. One of the important types of definitions is the one through genus. For example, "Iron is an element (genus) whose atomic weight equals...".

Definitions are subject to rules : the rule of proportion between what is defined and what is defining, the rule that there should not be a vicious circle, the rule that there should not be contradiction and so forth.

The objectivists, unlike other philosophers, consider "definition" an important element of their epistemology. This is possibly because they do not consider logic and empiricism as two distinct sources of knowledge. According to them definition is not a description, "it implies but does not mention all of a concept's units".[6]

If in the formation of classes there appear to be more than one characteristic, we use the essential characteristic (CCD mentioned earlier). For example, man may be defined as a "featherless biped". The definition implies all other characteristics of "man". This enables us to go either vertically upwards or vertical downwards. Treating "man" as the species we may ascend to the genus "animal". Again, treating man as the genus we descend to species with the differentia "occupation"– doctor, engineer, housewife, farmer, etc. In these cases the genus and species are both abstractions showing that these illustrations exemplify "abstraction from abstraction".

Epistemology is open in the sense, with new discoveries we may have to rearrange our concepts. Suppose at a later date we find that a certain tribe living in a remote inaccessible area on earth are featherless bipeds with three eyes, we will have a subdivision of man – (1) man with three eyes, and (2) man with two eyes.

Some discoveries in quantum physics have baffled scientists. It is found that elementary particles like electrons have dual nature; that of a material particle and that of a wave. There is no reason to believe that this is a mysterious phenomenon. What is needed is a reclassification of our concepts. We may use the terminology of the objectivists who employ the generic term "existent" to encompass "thing", attribute and action. We may treat thing as a genus under which are the species (i) particle or object (ii) wave (iii) "wavicle". Here we have created a new species that may be called wavicle, which, like the electron, has a dual nature.

It would be interesting to summarize how the problem of the universal leads to the notion of concept formation.

Plato believed in the existence of "prototypes" of particulars in, as it were, a different world. Aristotle treated the common property or "essence" as metaphysical, relegating consciousness almost to the position of non-existence. In reality we find that the common characteristics are epistemological and cannot be divorced from human consciousness.

The schools on the other side of the spectrum; nominalists and conceptualists, exalted consciousness to the unnecessary height, which often made knowledge highly subjective. The objectivists take the middle course and consider concepts as the product of human consciousness interacting with the facts of reality.

6

Individuals and Classes

6.1 Classes and Sets

We may resume our discussion on identity and a few related concepts, viz. individuation, sets or classes and numerical diversity. These are important in the quantum theory where we find strange phenomena : a particle may suddenly appear from nowhere or an elementary particle may suddenly disappear; a particle and its antiparticle may coalesce, one particle may appear to be simultaneously at two places and so on. The micro world will be discussed later. Here we are analysing our concepts which human beings picked up from the external macro world. Aristotelians laid emphasis on subject-predicate relationship in a sentence. But modern logic studies three different types of algebras or calculi, viz. propositional calculus, calculus of classes and algebra of relations. This is recognition of the fact that every proposition is not of subject-predicate type.

We mentioned earlier that we may identify an individual through classification in which the individuals in the same class have a common property or relations. This method of collecting the individuals having common properties is employed even by uneducated people though in a crude way. Mathematicians have a wider concept of a class or a set.

A set is a collection of things. In other words individuals or things need not have common properties. These individuals are specific and are not class names. Consider the following collections :

E1

A = {0, 1, 2, ...}
B = {a, 2}
C = {The tower of Pisa, Qutub Minar, New York}
D = {2, 3, 5, 0, 3}
E = {happiness, fast}
F = {0, 1, 4, 9}

A is a class of natural or whole numbers (from which 0 is sometimes omitted). They certainly have some common properties and A is a homogeneous set. This set has infinitely many elements. B is a set having only two members but they do not have a common property. It is a heterogeneous set. C, again, is a set having three elements. Many students have a feeling that a set is a heap of things, which is erroneous. The elements may be widely separated as in case of C. D is not a set; "3" appears twice and should be counted as one element. E is not usually treated as a set since they do not consist of "things". In a special case when the given adjectives are to be counted E may be called a class. F is a finite class having a common property. They are squares of the first four elements of the set of natural numbers. The relationship between a set and its elements is denoted by "∈" thus

2 ∈ B above.

The method of denoting the class by the above method is called extension. Logicians and even mathematicians are usually concerned with "intensional" definition. This reflects the fact that they are more interested in the homogeneous sets defined on the basis of common properties. For example,

A = {x : x is a natural number}
F = {x : x is the resident of London}
and so on.

6.2 Numerical Diversity

Clearly, we call a thing an "element" when it appears as a unit or individual. If there are two blocks of the same size touching each other, from a distance they would appear as "one". A closer examination would indicate that there are two objects and not one object. *Qua* set, a distant observer would consider it as a singleton or a one-element set. A closer scrutinity would reveal that it is a set of two elements. Similarly what appears as one will appear as many if we use a microscope. The main test to determine "not one" or numerical diversity is whether there is perceived discontinuity either in space or time.

When a musician plays an instument with a rapid movement, we feel the music flows continuously. If he slows down considerably the successive notes may be heard as discrete elements which can be counted. I repeat that what we call a unit or "one" is a discrete entity. Whether there is one or many ultimately depends on perceived discontinuity.

There is another problem releated to counting. A woman carrying a baby may be treated as a collection of "two", but for practical purposes, the duo may be treated as "one", e.g. when the baby does not need a ticket in a bus or train. These are practical problems of counting which can be solved by convention or custom.

Two sets are called equal only when they contain the same elements. For example,

$\{2, 3, 7\} = \{7, 2, 3\}$

In other words the order in which the elements appear is immaterial.

A set B is called a subset of set C if every element of B is an element of C. We denote this relationship by $B \subset C$. B is a proper subset of C if it is a subset of C, but B is not equal to C. For example,

$\{2, 3\} \subset \{2, 3, 4\}$

{2, 3} is a proper subset of {2, 3, 4}. Again, a set A is a subset of A itself but not a proper subset.

There is a notional set containing no elements, called the "null set" or "empty set", denoted by ϕ. It is necessary to remember that there is only one null set. The null set D in the class of dogs is not different from the null set of the class of stones.

6.3 Addition of Individuals

Suppose a class or a set is extensionally defined

A = {x, y, z)

It means A consists of elements "x and y and z". But this "and" has a peculiar significance. Suppose x, y, z all are red in appearance then we can say x is red, y is red and z is red. Collectively we can say x and y and z are red. Now consider the statement :

"x and y and z are three" which is true collectively, but we cannot assert x is three, y is three and z is three. This is unlike the previous case where the predicate is a quality of each element.

Russell calls this "and" implied in a set addition of individuals.[1] This is, of course, subject to the proviso that in case of a one-element set the question of addition does not arise.

6.4 Class Concept

We have used the terms "set" and "class" as synonyms. Mathematicians sometimes use these terms with a slightly different connotations. For our analysis this difference is not relevant.

In logic where classification is important the intensional definition of a class is natural. In this method, every class is based on what Russell calls "class concept".[2]

Consider the following propositions :

(a) Mandela is human

(b) Mandela has humanity
(c) Mandela is a man

The first proposition is of the subject predicate type, the second expresses a relation between two terms, the third contains an article "a". These propositions convey the same truth based on the class concept "man" or "human race". In (c) we find a direct statement that Mandela is a member of the entire class generated by the concept "man". However, from the class-concept we can generate saveral classes such as "all men", "humans in Europe", "Humans who lived on 1-1-1900".

6.5 Relations and Equivalence

The classical theory of logic ignored a very important type of proposition in which two or more existents are "related". It was preoccupied with the subject-predicate type. The theory of relation is extremely important in science when a structure is to be analyzed. We will need the theory of relations when we analyze certain concepts in Buddhist and Jaina logic.

Consider a set of three human beings {a, b, c}. This is an enumeration of a class which does not tell you much about the three persons. However, if you are told that *b* and *e* are the daughter and son of their father *a*, the set appears "structured". We can think of several relational sentences : a is the father of b and c, b is the daughter of a, b is the sister of c and so forth.

Given two elements, x and y of a class if there exists a relation R between them, we write xRy. For example, in the set of human beings "offspring of" is a relation. Given a relation R, a converse relation R^{-1} automatically follows. For example, if xRy is "x is an offspring of y", then $yR^{-1}x$ means "y is the parent of x". Note that in a set it is not necessary that every two elements should be related for a given R. For example if R is "divides" in the set of integers, then 2R10, 6R18 but 7 and 18 are not related. The relation we just mentioned is called "binary relation" in which only two elements are involved in R. In xRy, x is called the "referent" and y is known as "relatum".

Russell attaches a sense to a relation. Thus xRy is a relation from x to y. The converse relation $yR^{-1}x$ is from y to x.

Modern mathematicians usually define a relation in a set. The older logicians considered two classes – domain which consists of all referents and codomain consisting of all relata. The logical sum of the domain and codomain is sometimes called the "field". One can also conceive of relations involving more than two terms. For example, "a, b, are father and mother of c" is a "triadic relation" and can be written as R(a, b, c).

Types of Relations

(1) A relation R in a class S is called reflexive if for every element *a* in S aRa holds good. "Equality" in numbers, "has the same height as" or "earns the same salary as" are all reflexive relations. There are a few borderline cases which we sometimes face. In the set of lines, is the relation "parallel to" reflexive? In such cases we may redefine our concept of the given relation to include reflexivity. Thus taking a broader view of parallelism, we may say that a line is parallel to itself.

(2) A relation will be called one-one if for a given referent *a* there is one and only one relatum, and every relatum is associated with only one referent.

For example, among married couples "spouse" is a one-one relation in a monogamous society. We shall call a relation one-many when a referent can have more relata than one. Where polygamy prevails, "husband of" provides an example. A relation will be called many-one if a relatum can have more referents than one. In a society which practices polyandry, "husband of" is a many-one relation. In the same society "wife of" is one-many.

(3) R is symmetric if aRb implies bRa. The relation "brother" in the class of the sons of the same parents is symmetric. However, R is not symmetric if the class is extended to

siblings, because if b is a female, bRa will not be true. Such a relation which is not symmetric may be called not-symmetric or nonsymmetric.

(4) R is asymmetric if aRb implies bRa cannot hold good. "Greater than", "less than" are asymmetric relations. Note the distinction between "nonsymmetric" and "asymmetric". In case of the former, aRb does not prohibit bRa though it does not guarantee bRa. An example is "brother" among siblings.

(5) R is called transitive if for any a,b,c of the class, aRb, bRc implies aRc. "Greater than", "equal to" exemplify transitivity.

(6) R is a strict order or simply an order relation if R is asymmetric and transitive. "Less than" is an example. In case of human beings "descendent of" is also an order relation

(7) R is antisymmetric if aRb and bRa imply a = b , In case of numbers, "≤" and "≥" are antisymmetric.

(8) R is a partial order relation if it is reflexive, transitive and antisymmetric; "≤" and "≥" are partial order relations.

(9) R is aliorelative if it is not reflexive. "Brother" is an aliorelative relation.

(10) If R is an order in set S and a, b are distinct elements, then S is called totally ordered if aRb or bRa.

E1

(a) In the set of real numbers "divides" is a relation which is reflexive, nonsymmetric and transitive, and also antisymmetric.

(b) In the class of human beings, the relation "sibling" is aliorelative and symmetric.

(c) The relation "equal" in the class of real numbers is reflexive, symmetric and transitive.

(d) In the set of points on a line "left of" and "right of" are (strict) order relations.

(e) The relation "square of" in real numbers is aliorelative, asymmetric and not transitive.

(f) The relation "diversity" is interesting. It is aliorelative because *a* cannot be diverse from *a*, symmetric but not transitive.

The following result can be easily proved.

If R is transitive then it is aliorelative if and only if it is asymmetrical.

Intension and Extension

The manner in which relation was defined above is called "intensional" in which a relation is explicitly mentioned. However, some mathematicians define a relation extensionally. If A and B are two classes then (a, b) where a $\in$A and b$\in$B is called an ordered pair. The class of all such pairs is the Cartesian product A×B. We also define

(a, b) = (c, d) if and only if a=c, b=d

A relation R is defined as the subset of ordered pairs constituting A×B. For example,

A = {0, 2, 3}, B = {2, 1}

then the subset

{(0, 2), (0, 1), (2, 1)}

may be called a relation. This looks highly artificial and one is at a loss to know why it should be called a relation. However, the intensional definition can also be expressed as a set of couples (x, y) which satisfy the relation R, i.e. xRy.

A relation can also be defined extensionally in a set A in which case it is a subset of A×A. Our earlier discussion on extension and intension with reference to classes also applies to relations to some extent.

Equivalence

In chapter 3 we saw how the employees of a firm were classified according their salaries. Similar classification is possible when a relation is given provided it is an equivalence relation. A relation is called equivalence if it is reflexive, symmetric and transitive Equality in algebra, congruence and similarity in geometry (e.g.

triangles), parallelism in case of lines are a few examples, of equivalence. There are a few border line cases which can be easily handled by re-defining our concepts. For example, in case of lines is parallelism reflexive? Can we say, "is a line parallel to itself?" We may define parallelism to connote reflexivity. If we assert that a line is parallel to itself, no contradictions arise and the relation appears to be equivalence without ambiguity.

Consider the relation R where aRb means "the couple a has the same number of children as the couple b". A survey on population studies furnishes the following data for a village :

	No. of children	No. of couples
A	0	2
B	1	20
C	2	35
D	3	22
E	4	11
	Total	90

Clearly R is an equivalence relation. In fact the data is classified on the basis of R. There are five classes A through E such that (i) all couples in that class have the same number of children and (ii) Two couples in different classes cannot have the same number of children. These classes are called equivalence classes generated by R. You may use this statistics to identify the class to which a certain couple belongs. If the given couple belongs to D, it can be identified as "couple D" for a specific purpose. The label D is a method of identification by equivalence classes. Two couples in the same groups may be treated as indistinguishable or identical for some purpose. Identity here has only a limited scope : it shows that two identical couples have a common property, viz. they have the same number of children. As mentioned earlier the word "identity" is misleading without the context. In the present case we could say that all the couples in the same group have an identical property. What is true of identity is also true of other mouns and adjectives such as "similar", "same", "equal", "congruent", etc. The relevant concept (e.g. 'equivalence' in the above data) should be properly defined.

6.6 Definition and Equivalence

According to Rand a definition "is a statement that identifies the nature of the units subsumed under a concept". Let us go back to the process of differentiation and integration we discussed in chapter 5. We saw how the child develops the concept of "furniture". An adult would define furniture as household movables used for sitting, sleeping, supporting, etc. These common characteristics constitute the "differentia" of the definition of the concept "furniture". The existents qualifying as furniture also have a Common Conceptual Denominator or CCD which a child perceives. In other words, a definition is a linguistic expression of CCD.

Consider the set of objects called "furniture". It consists of (usually) mutually exclusive subsests — tables, chairs, cots, etc. each subset having a separate CCD. Each subset differs from other subsets. In fact, these subsets are similar to equivalence classes of a given set. In an equivalence class all elements have a distinguishing property or an equivalence relation. In the logician's parlance the set "furniture" is called the "genus" while the equivalence classes tables, chairs, etc. are the "species" of this genus. This similarity is approximately depicted below :

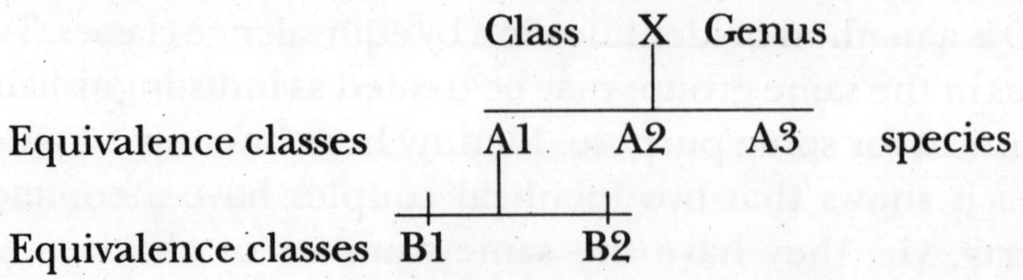

Fig. 6.1 Species and Genus

The words genus and species are, of course, relative. Differentiation helps us expand downwards. In the figure 6.1 A1 which was a species earlier becomes a genus with its species B1, B2, etc. The Concept "table", for instance, would lead to sub-concepts "dining table", "writing table" etc. Similarly integration will help us move upwards. X can be integrated with another class, say, Y on the basis of common characteristics. X, Y now become species and their superset becomes a genus.

We should, however, observe the limitations to the analogy between equivalence classes and the objectivist's approach. In mathematics X can be arbitrary since its elements need not have any common characteristics, which will halt our journey upwards. However, when X is defined intensionally we can usually move vertically upwards as well as downwards.

6.7 Chain

The concept of a chain or a totally ordered set is extremely important in mathematics and science. If in an ordered set, any two elements are comparable the set is called a "totally ordered set" or a "chain". The definition is equivalent to the assertion that if *a* and *b* are two distinct elements of the set either aRb or bRa. We can use the concept of either partial order or strict order. A chain is also called a series a very convenient term, now reserved for a sum of terms. The serial relation is equivalent to the existence of the law of trichotomy.

a	b	c
1,	2,	3
1^2,	2^2,	3^2....

are all examples of chains. Points on a line, instants with respect to an observer are all serial relations forming a chain, with suitably defined order. For example, in case of instants "before" or "after" will generate the strict order and a chain. Note that in a chain an elements cannot occur twice. For instance 1, 2, 3, 3, 4.. is not a chain, but a sequence. A chain which has a beginning but which is endless is called a progression. Thus 1, 3, 5 ... is a progression, but ....-2, -1, 0, 1, 2... is not.

6.8 Numerical Equivalence

When we say that India is more populous than say Russia what do we mean? The assertion involves such concepts as equal, more and less in respect of the individuals belonging to two classes.

Suppose there are three classes :

A = {a, b, c}, B = {7, 3, d}, C = {0, 1, 9, x}

As educated people we can at a glance assert that A and B have the same number of elements, but they have fewer elements than C. A and B can have any type of elements the classes have identity in one respect, the number of elements they contain or what the mathematician would say, "A and B are numerically equivalent" or "A and B are similar". In a way, "three" is the measure of both sets A and B. This number three can be regarded as a measure of numerical contents of the elements which are distinct according to our criterion of "perceived discontinuity", mentioned earlier. Is there a principle behind the numerical measure? Certainly there is. When numbers were not invented people used this principle of "one-one correspondence". Even today those who do not know counting use it.

Suppose with every element of A we associate one and only one element of B. The following is one of the possible arrangements :

A	B
a	7
b	d
c	3

You will observe that there is a perfect match, none of the elemens of A or B remain without an association. This principle is called "one-one correspondence". Those who do not know counting may not be able to say that the cardinal number of A and B is three, but most of them will recognize that A and B have the same number of things. If you try the same method of one-one association between A and C or B and C, you will find one of the elements of C remains unpaired showing that C has more elements than either A or B. For example, in the following correspondence the element of C remains unassociated :

B	A	C
3	b	0
7	a	9
d	c	1
		x

and you can say that C has more elements than A or B. Notice that elements of two sets can be matched in many ways. For example, you can try other combinations between A and B and you will find there are a number of possible arrangements. Similarly, there are many arrangemens between A (or B) and C. In every case you will have the same results – A and B are numerically equivalent but each of them has fewer elements than C.

There are many ways of defining or constructing natural numbers 0, 1, 2, ... Pehaps the best approach was suggested by Frege and further developed by Russell. From what we discussed above, we can say that the cardinal number of all similar classes is the same. One of the ingenious definations of the cardinal number is :

The cardinal number of a class A is the class of classes similar to A.

This definition may appear queer to you, but if you introspect a little you will find that the advantage of this nominal definition lies in making the (cardinal, natural) number a class (of all similar sets)

For example, A and B above have the same cardinal number, viz. three. Hence they have the same cardinal number "which is the class of all trios".

But how do we get "three" as the cardinal number of A or B? We assume that the cardinal number of the null set is zero or 0. Similarly we can easily define the next number called its successor s(0) which is one or 1. If n is the number of a class X, take any *a* not belonging to X then the cardinal number of X ∪{a}is the successor of n or s(n). The above developement is not rigorous but you can see that it will lead to natural numbers

0, 1, 2, ... n, (n+1), ...

We will not discuss the theory of numbers in greater detail. We must however, observe that this construction is related to many concepts; number, unit, individual, next number, numerical diversity and so on which are useful for the study of physics especially in quantum physics.

6.9 Reality and Relations

There are a few philosophical problems connected with the concept of relation, which may be briefly discused.

(1) Bradley has questioned the reality of relations. According to him if aRb, then R itself must be related to a and b, we then will have to write RR1a and RR2b. This argument can be repeated : R1 has a relation with R and a, R2 has a relation with R and b, and so forth which leads to an endless regress. Russell has, however, dealt with two types of endless regresses : objectionable and harmless. When a relational proposition aRb does not include in its *meaning* any relation of a or b to R, the regress is harmless. Hence Bradley's objection may be ignored. [3]

(2) Is relation "internal" or "external"? Consider the human body. Its organs are related either spatially or functionally and it would be correct to say that the relation in this case is internal because the hand, nose, etc. cannot be treated as separate entities, though they may be treated as logical terms. It would be appropriate to say that the parts of an

organic whole or a man made object are internally related. But what about the relation between a house in Mumbai and a building in New York? They can be related spatially. In fact any two objects *a* and *b* can be arbitrarily related by defining (a,b) as the instance of a relation. As we mentioned earlier, the extensional definition appears artificial. Common sense tells us an object in Mumbai and an object in New York are usually related only spatially. In such cases the relation has to be treated as external.

There are some philosophers as well as scientists who believe that the universe is an organic whole. They may either argue on the basis of God and teleology or determinism. Given the present state of the universe the future state, according to determinists, is predictable if the universal laws are unchanged. Any view which treats the universe as a connected whole will also hold that no two objects are unrelated and the relations are internal. This controversy between the "internal" and "external" view of relations cannot be resolved.[4]

However, epistemology always takes into account the known connections and in practice, the scientist will formulate his laws or models based on the known connections.

(3) Two types of relations are sometimes distinguished : logical and causal. For instance 2<5 is a logical connection while "A kills B" may be treated as leading to a causal relation between A and B. The physical laws are described in terms of parameters that are causally related. However, for those who treat the universe as an organic whole or a grand design, there appears to be fusion of these two relations. Thus for the determinist any two events A and B has the unique determinate relation. Similarly the teleologist would argue that there is a unique teleological relation between A and B.

Part II

Buddhist Logic

7

Śākyamuni's Teachings

7.1 Moral Philosophy

Gautama Buddha (ca 563–483 BCE) the founder of Buddhism was Prince Siddhartha of Śākya clan before he became an ascetic. Though a spiritual Master, Gautama's main goal was to teach people how they can come out of their suffering. As far as possible he avoided speculative metaphysics. The word "Buddhist Logic" would therefore perplex the common person – why should the great healer be interested in logic? Their perplexity would lead to astonishment if they were told that Buddhist Logic is not only logic in the sense in which we normally use the word, but includes epistemology and even ontology or metaphysics. It includes many topics on which Gautama preferred to remain silent.

Whether it is religion or philosophy the original teaching or the doctrine appears to grow rapidly as time passes. Scholars of every generation write their own commentaries not only on what the Master said or wrote, but also on commentaries already written by previous generations of scholars. This involves interpretation and reinterpretations of words and expressions of the Master and other commentators. In case of Buddhism you find that Gautama's silence on many metaphysical questions was interpreted in several ways. There are mainly two reasons why the original credo, however laconically expressed, continuously gains mass and grows into a giant mountain having many peaks. These peaks are the schools of the original doctrine. Every society changes as time passes and the commentator has to reconcile social change with the original philosophy. The commentator cannot afford to openly defy the Master nor can he halt social change. Hence he tries reinterpretation in a subtle manner. Second, sooner or later, the followers find a need to connect the original principles with other branches of knowledge, logic; epistemology, metaphysics and even science and technology. However, every scholar sees to it that the original central credo of the Master remains sacrosanct and is not challenged openly. Buddhism is no exception to this rule of expansion. This is despite the fact that Gautama exhorted his followers to find for themselves the truth of his teachings through their own experience. He did not want them to blindly accept his teachings.

Those who want to study Buddhist logic should therefore remember that every Buddhist who contributed to this area always had to guard the original principles.

It is instructive to briefly recall these principles :

First, Gautama was a social reformer, a teacher of moral and ethical principles and of course, a healer. Basically, he was not a metaphysician. In the first chapter we mentioned his silence over metaphysical questions, which indirectly suggests that Buddhism is agnostic.

Second, he taught what are called the four noble Truths :

(i) Suffering exists
(ii) There is cause of suffering
(iii) There can be cessation of suffering
(iv) There is a means to stop suffering.

His prescription to come out of suffering was a path consisting of eight disciplines; right views, right resolve, right speech, right conduct, right livelihood, right effort, right mindfulness and right meditation.

Dvādaśanidāna

Though Buddhism does not believe in either the ego or soul, it believes in a cycle which has a semblance of rebirth. This cycle is called *dvādaśanidāna* and pertains to human suffering. It consists of twelve links. The links are : ignorance (*avidyā*, a), past impressions (*saṃskāras*,s), initial consciousness (*vijñāna*, v), the body-mind complex (*nāmarūpa*, n), six cognitive senses including the mind (*ṣaḍāyatana*, sa), contact of the senses with the object to be cognized (*sparśa*, sp), previous sense experience (*vedanā*, ve), thirst for enjoyment (*tṛṣṇā*, t) mental clinging (*upādāna*, u), will to become (*bhāva*, b), birth (*jāti*, j), old age and death (*jarāmaraṇa*, jn) which ends at the starting point (*avidyā*). If we start from the birth (j) the cycle can be shown as j →jn → a → s → v → n → sa → sp→ve → t →u → b→j

We may use " → " for "cause" so that j causes jn, etc.

A few links appear strange. Consider *upādaṅa*→ *bhāva* →*jāti*. Given the causal cycle we can understand that if one has a will to become, one would take birth; but who is the "one"? Remember, Buddhism does not recognize the soul, ego or an individual as an entity which would retain its identity after death. Ostensibly according to commentators it is the consciousness that flows in the cycle.

If we maintain the continuity of consciousness, memory in it would have to be retained along with consciousness. This would ascribe an "identity" to the consciousness. And this is nothing but ego which Buddhism denies. Again, the cycle assumes the doctrine of *karma*. According to Tigunait, "the impressions of past *karmas* are responsible for driving consciousness to move the wheel of life... Ignorance is the main cause of imprinting the impressions on the screen of consciousness".[1]

The entire explanation of the cycle is applicable to the moving consciousness from which emerges the identity of the sufferer. But such identity is denied by Buddhism.

If we follow the eight-fold path prescribed by Gautama, we can be liberated from this cycle, *avidyā* disappears and we attain the state of *nirvāṇa* in this very life. We become *arhat*, a venerable person. A liberated person can continue to live and guide the community. He is, however, detached and does not expect any returns for his work.

Repeated cycles appear to be the fate of a person who clings to desires. But who is that person? Fortunately, this problem of identity pertains to the transcendent and we can exclude it from Buddhist logic. But this cycle is central to Buddhist doctrine of liberation, or *nirvāṇa* which is linked to Gautama's main goal of alleviation of suffering. We will try to reconcile this apparent contradiction later when we discuss Buddhist dialectic.

7.2 Other Principles of Gautama Buddha

According to Gautama everything has a cause and there is no accidental origination. This theory is called the Theory of Dependent Origination *(pratītyasamputpāda)*.

A corollary of this theory is that nothing is permanent. We live in the everchanging world. This is called the Theory of Universal Change. This doctrine leads to the notion of momentariness (*kṣaṇikavāda*). We shall see later that the ultimate reality for Buddhists consists of a chain of insubstantial momentary beings.

Gautama does not believe in the soul. *Anātman* is the word used for the absence of soul. He regarded every human as a mere assemblage of five states or *pañcaskandhas* which are always changing. These *skandhas* are form (*rūpa*) or material body, feelings (*vedanā*) which include pain, pleasure, etc.; past impressions (*saṃskāras*) which we have already come across, consciousness (*vijñāna*) and, of course, perception (*sanjñā)* which includes comprehension.

7.3 Buddhist Schools

As explained earlier the original words and even the silence of the Master are interpreted in different ways, subsequently leading to many branches of an original philosophy. Scores of schools exist in Buddhism. The main schools are (1) *Śūnyavāda* or *Mādhyamika* founded by Nāgārjuna (first century CE) (2) *Vijñānavāda* (subjective idealism) propagated by Asaṅga, Vasubandhu, Dignāga and Dharmakīrti. This school is also known as *Yogācāra* (combination of yoga and good conduct or *ācāra*) (3) *Sautrāntika* (Representationalism) based on *Sūtrapiṭaka* or the original Pali text. (4) *Vaibhāṣika* or Direct Realism.

Hīnayāna or "small vehicle" is the word used for orthodox schools such as *Sautrāntika* and *Vaibhāṣika. Mahāyāna* ("great vehicle") is a heterodox or liberal school which includes *Śūnyavāda* and *Vijñānavāda.*

While Buddhism almost disappeared in India, it spread to other countries. Hīnayāna to Ceylon (Sri Lanka), Indonesia, Burma (Myanmar) and Thailand. Mahāyāna went to northeast, Tibet, Mongolia, China and Japan.

While Gautama himself was agnostic, he was deified by his devotees later. He was regarded as a Supreme Being having a transcendental status. This innovative elevation of Śākyamuni is called *dharmakāya* or the *dharma* body of Buddha. Another view regarded him as God controlling the phenomenal world. This view is called *sambhogakāya.* His followers also see him at another level where he is the historical Buddha. This is an incarnation of *sambhogakāya* and this state is called *nirmāṇakāya,* consisting of *pañcaskandhas.* At this level he appears in several forms as spiritual guru helping others attain liberation.

Most readers are likely to be familiar with what is contained in this chapter. The main purpose of this introductory chapter is to identify the original kernel of the doctrine introduced by the founder himself. The subsequent accretions were added by later commentators, apparently using rationalizations to keep the central doctrine intact.

In this book the word "logic" is used in different senses : (i) deductive logic (ii) deductive and inductive logic (both in western sense) (iii) logic and epistemology (iv) logic, epistemology and ontology especially with reference to Buddhism. Usually the right meaning will be clear from the context.

8

Development of Buddhist Philosophy

8.1 Three Stages of Buddhist Philosophy

The history of Buddhist philosophy is divided into three periods of five hundred years each from 500 BCE to 1000 CE, we can only make a very brief survey of these periods, highlighting matters relevant to our purpose.

First Period

This period in which Gautama Buddha's teachings were dominant has the following characteristics:

1. The philosophy was basically a moral philosophy. As Stcherbatsky points out, ordinary life was considered a condition of degradation and misery (*duḥkha*).[1] Suffering could be overcome by following Gautama's eight-fold path.
2. There is no ego, no self, no soul and no personality (*pudgala*). What we call personality is only a flow of ever changing elements.
3. The external world, too, consists of momentary flashes of efficient energy, a flow. There is no substance.
4. The flow of moments is subject to the theory of causation – "this being; that arises". The laws were partly physical and partly moral since it contained the notion of cause as well as retribution.
5. The illusory matter was the result of these energy moments which operated in mutual cooperation.

Second Period

1. Gautama's conception of liberation (*nirvāṇa*) seems to have been re-interpreted. Liberation which was a matter of personal attainment was converted into the doctrine of Universal Liberation of every life. This process led to a new outlook. As Stcherbatsky rightly points out, "It (Buddhism) forsook the ideal of a human Buddha who disappears completely in a lifeless *nirvāṇa* and replaced it by the ideal of a divine Buddha enthroned in a *nirvāṇa* full of life".[2]
2. Buddhist philosophy/religion is usually treated as pluralism in the first period. In the second period it became monistic, possibly under the influence of Advaita school of Vedānta.
3. The universe was regarded as One whole and even identified with Buddha's cosmic body.
4. In the earlier period the existence of elements (though not substantial) was accepted. In this period scholars denied existence of ultimate reality of elements.
5. The earlier doctrine of Causality, viz., all real elements are interdependent had to be modified. This is a difficult task since the elements are now unreal. A strange rationalization was employed to retain the doctrine. "All elements are unreal because they are inter-dependent".[3] This leads to one motionless reality, consistent with monism.
6. But the new thought also led to a dichotomy – there are now two truths or realities, the illusive and the ultimate one. Both realities had their own place; for ordinary people the mundane (illusive) reality is real. For saints who grasped the reality through intuition, there is the higher reality or truth.

7. Logic was banished and mysticism was glorified.

Nāgārjuna, Deva and Bhavya were some of the great thinkers belonging to this period.

Third Period

This period is dominated by Asaṅga, Vasubandhu, Dignāga and Dharmakīrti.

There were many revisions of Buddhist philosophy. The most important changes may be mentioned :

1. The importance of logic rose to a dizzy height in this period.
2. Introspection was considered a valuable source of knowledge. This was a reaction to the extreme skepticism of Mādhyamikas.
3. However, introspection and consciousness were elevated to such an extent that Buddhism appeared to be moving towards idealism. It was even asserted that knowledge is necessarily mental.
4. Ideas were divided into three categories – 1) totally fanciful (*parikalpita*), 2) relatively real (*paratantra*) and, 3) absolutely real (*pariniṣpanna*). The status of real was given to 2) and 3). In the second period ideas were treated as unreal (*śūnya*) because they were relative (*paraspara-apekṣa*)[4]

Now, idealism recognized two realities, relative and absolute. The universe or the real world was nothing but all possible ideas, products of introspection and thinking. Concurrently consciousness began to be regarded as a depository or storehouse (*ālaya-vijñāna*), a theory which lost its importance in the second half of this period. According to Stcherbatsky the period is characterized by freedom of thinking.

8.2 Nāgārjuna (ca 150–250 CE)

Nāgārjuna is one of the most brilliant Buddhist philosophers. Unfortunately his biography is shrouded in mystery. There are many controversies regarding his birth, authorship of some books, his hometown and so on. Many scholars are not sure if there was only one Nāgārjuna or many different Nāgārjunas, all Buddhist philosophers. We need not discuss these controversies, but confine ourselves to major contributions made by the author(s) Nāgārjuna.

Nāgārjuna is believed to be the founder of Mādhyamika. It was Kumārjīva who introduced Nāgārjuna and his philosophy to China.

Nāgārjuna is believed to have been born a Brahmin in South India.

K. Venkata Ramanan has classified his work in six categories : [5]

1. His critiques on other schools such as *Madhyamaka-śāstra* or *Mādhyamika-kārikā, Vigrahavyāvartani,* (Repudiation of contests), etc.
2. Expository texts such as *Pratītyasamputpāda-hṛdaya-śāstra, Yuktiśāstra,* etc.
3. Commentaries and records of oral instructions (*Upadeśa*) such as *Mahāprajñāpāramitā-śāstra, Daśabhūmi-vibhāṣā-śāstra,* etc.
4. Devotional songs *Lokātīta-stava, Dharmadhātu-stava,* etc.
5. Letters such as *Suhṛllekha and Ratnāvalī.*
6. Some of the works whose authorship is regarded as doubtful, e.g. *Sūtrasamuccaya.*

Unfortunately, Nāgārjuna is better known as a dialectician. Stcherbatsky's following comments are not very flattering :

> ... two tracts by Nāgārjuna : Repudiation of Contests and Dialectical splitting (of every thesis). Both contain the exposition and vindication of that unique method of conducting a debate which consists in proving nothing positive, but in applying the test of relativity to every positive thesis of the opponent and thus destroying it dialectically. [6]

This reminds one of the Sophists of western philosophy.

For us Nāgārjuna is perhaps the most important philosopher. First, his logic of *catuṣkoṭi* is central to our search for linkage between Buddhist logic and quantum riddles. Second, he was renowned for his concept of "functional relationship" which we will consider later. Third, his exposition on *śūnyatā* and other thoughts show how Buddhist notion of love and compassion can find a place in Buddhist logic. Finally through *śūnyatā* he also made an attempt to bridge the mundane with the transcendent.

Two of his works *Suhṛllekhā* and *Ratnāvalī* have puzzled Buddhist historians. The former was written for a Sātavāhana king and the latter for the Śaka Satrap of Ujjaiyinī. The contents appear to suit two different temperaments, one for Hīnāyana adherent and the other for Mahāyāna believer. What's more these recipients were rivals for the control of the west coast of India. Although Ichimura contends that this is not impossible.[7]

8.3 Nāgārjuna's Philosophy

Nāgārjuna tried to reconcile different schools of Buddhism, each claiming that it alone represented Gautama's teachings. In his works he lays considerable emphasis on non-contentiousness (*anupalambha*). Most schools seem to have forgotten the founder's message that one has to be aware of the fact that the same truth can be formulated from different viewpoints. Their claim to exclusiveness reflects the common person's tendency to seize and cling to the relative as absolute. Such clinging gives us a false sense of security leading to frustration.

According to Nāgārjuna, the right knowledge (*dharmāṇam bhūtapratyavekṣa*) consists in understanding that the determinate is dependent on the independent ultimate reality. Nevertheless he warns us that "while the indeterminate reality is the ground of the determinate entities, it is only the ultimate nature of the latter themselves and not another entity apart from them".[8]

According to Nāgārjuna *śūnyatā* is not nihilism; it is relativity and conditionedness.

In fact a person who understands *śunyatā* as conditionedness should also understand the further truth that conditionedness of the conditioned is not unconditioned (*śūnyatā-śūnyatā*).

Mādhyamika or Middle way seeks to provide insight (*prajñā*) into what the nature of reality is; the relative is not the absolute. *Nirvāṇa,* the goal of the serious Buddhist cannot be attained unless the ultimate truth is realized. But before the aspirant reaches this stage she has to first undergo the process of understanding the mundane truth connected with concepts and conceptual formulations. When Nāgārjuna says that "Everything holds good in case of one who is in agreement with *śūnyatā*"[9] he is referring to the principle of comprehension or *prajñā,* the insight one has into not only *śūnya* but also *śūnyatā-śūnyatā* which opens the door for reaching the ultimate reality.

Here it would be appropriate to mention that words having apparently different connotations are often equated. For example, in Kārikā *pratītyasamputpāda* (conditioned origin), *śūnyatā, upādāya-prajñapti* (derived name) and *madhyamā-pratipat* (Middle way) are declared as synonymous.[10]

8.4 Kuan-yin Bodhisattva

Kuan-yin Bodhisattva is the iconic figure in *Mahāyāna,* revered next only to Śākyamuni. Originally called Avalokiteśvara in India he epitomizes supreme virtue of love and compassion. In fact he symbolizes two virtues – love and compassion on the practical side and *śūnyatā* on the theoretical side.

Bodhisattva is one who has chosen the path of Buddha in order to help all beings to be free from suffering. The dual virtues mentioned above are prerequisites of a Bodhisattva. A Bodhisattva has an insight into the basic nature of *śūnyatā* (emptiness), whatever is, is devoid of its own nature.

Mahāyāna scholars mention three motivational contexts of love and compassion – 1) love and compassion motivated by the similarity with otherselves, i.e. other human beings (*sattva-ālambana*), 2) love and compassion motivated by the similarity of psychophysical elements or five *skandhas* (*dharma-ālambana*), and 3) love and compassion devoid of any motivation.

There are two negations that came to be recognized by Buddhists. We have already mentioned the first. In *Hīnayāna* the Self was denied (*anātman*). This made a person an aggregate and components. The second negation was highlighted by *Mahāyāna* thinkers who denied reality to even the aggregate of *skandhas.* Thus the human was first reduced to *skandhas* and by second negation *skandhas* disappeared (*dharma niḥsvabhāvya*) leading to unreality of *dharma (dharma-śūnyatā)*. The motivational contexts mentioned above run parallel to dual negations. An ordinary aspirant has to pass through these two negations and two motivational contexts. Buddhas do not need any motivational context because they are always in contemplation of the insight of ultimate emptiness or *śūnyatā.* Bodhisattva has a middle position – he has already outgrown the first motivational context and now relies on the second.

It is impossible to elaborate the concept of Kuan-yin Bodhisattva here, though it is important for those who want to fully understand the development of Buddhist philosophy. The following remark by Ichimura highlights the connection between love and insight :

> Although the locus of Kuan-yiṇ is in the human world, his love and compassion seems to be consistent with the transcendent love and compassion of the Buddhas, for whom the abode is non-duality based on the dual negation of this world and the other world. The ultimate purpose of Buddhist love and compassion is to help to reach an understanding of four holy truths in terms of Non-self and śūnyatā so that each individual helps one's self rid of ignorance and realize emancipation.[11]

We shall see later how Buddhist spirituality finds a place in Buddhist logic and Dialectic.

9

Momentary Beings and Causation

9.1 *Kṣaṇikavāda*

Buddhism regards knowledge as valid when it is used in action that is successful. According to Dharmakīrti, "All successful action is (necessarily) preceded by right knowledge, therefore we are going to investigate it".[1] This is not the pragmatism of western philosophy. It merely reflects the Buddhist theory that every event has a cause. If we diagnose the cause properly we can use the knowledge to reach the desired goal. Of course, the goal can be negative in the sense that we may want to avoid something.

There are two broad cases of successful actions. First, we may act automatically in which case the reflex is an instinctive behavior. Second, our action may be discursive which uses knowledge stored in memory. Buddhists concern themselves with the second type which, unlike the first, is amenable to analysis.

According to Dharmottara anything that leads to right knowledge without contradiction is a source of knowledge.[2] In view of the theory of causation the source is also the cause leading to efficacious action. In choosing a certain action to achieve a goal even ordinary people use right knowledge. Hence according to Dharmottara knowledge used in science is not different from that used by common people in everyday life.[3] While Buddhist philosophers try to confine themselves to the reality perceived by everyone, insight and mysticism often crop up in the works of some scholars. For example, Candrakīrti recognizes the existence of a transcendental source. According to him mystic intuition is required to cognize such a source.[4] However, under the influence of Dignāga most Buddhist scholars came to believe that the ultimate reality cannot be divorced from logic.

In chapters 3 and 6 we briefly discussed the problem of identity, individuation and numerical diversity. It is interesting to see how these notions can be handled in Buddhist epistemology and ontology.

The world of Buddhists is dynamic, ever-changing and impermanent. It consists of a series or rather multiple series of events or moments. The sensible world consists of sensibilia which are momentary flashes of energy.[5] Nothing exists permanently. The so called eternal entities like time, space, soul, God are myths created by philosophers belonging to other schools. Every being we perceive is momentary. All these moments are, of course, efficient in accordance with the doctrine of causation. According to Kamalaśīla these moments are discrete. This is the ultimate reality. It is the flow of discrete moments which when acted upon by our mind projects the empirical world which we perceive. It is necessary to remember that the doctrine of momentariness is valid in both realities, transcendental and empirical. Both a point-instant and its image are momentary.

Such a series of moments is often likened with a field or force, universal flux or, to borrow from Greek ontology, "a flow of external becoming".[6] Another *darśana,* viz. *Sāṅkhya* has similar views on the flow-like cause, but *Sāṅkhya* contends that in series representing the chain of phenomena, the elements form a continuous flow or if there are discontinuities, they can be ignored, so densely packed are the elements. However, *Sāṅkhya* treats this flow as waves or periodic variations – a mere pattern having a base of solid matter which is undifferentiated, eternal and all-pervading.[7] Buddhists, on the other hand, treat the series of moments as discontinuous, though the gaps may be infinitesimally small.

For Buddhists these moments are dimensionless. They are point-instants because time and space are one and the same. What's more, they cannot be separated from "objects".

Realists often argue that the things we perceive appear to exist for some duration, though the intevnal may be small. Similarly, we perceive that an object has extension. This seems to contradict the theory of momentariness. Buddhists reply that there are imperceptible changes in all things; the world we see is a construct of the intellect, an interpretation of what ultimate reality is, viz. a series of moments. Neither point-instants nor the objects we perceive have either duration or extensions. A moment or its projected entity is an instantaneous being, the next moment is *eo ipso* different from this moment. Existence is synonymous with a moment. If we postulate that a thing has a duration or extension it would follow that the causal moments are identical which is absurd.[7a]

According Buddhists existence is efficiency and efficiency means change. Stcherbatsky points out that "the terms existence, efficiency and change are connected by 'existential identity' (*tādātmya*) that is to say they can be without contradiction applied to one and the same point of reality, to a real fact". [8]

9.2 Two realities

Buddhists face the same dilemma as all philosophers who postulatc "ultimate reality" "thing-in-itself" or simple invisible "real" noumenon. When different observers perceive a thing the process of perception and inference appears similar except for variations which arise due to the observers' positions and other conditions. When millions observe a TV program, we have no doubt that they are perceiving the same sequence of events.

There is some common attribute present in all humans which enables them to perceive or even react to a stimulus in a similar way. Hence despite our philosophical views we behave in the world assuming that other humans have the same kind of perceptive ability. For us there is some reality in the external world shared by all of us but which is different from the philosopher's ultimate invisible reality. All philosophies that believe in the ultimate reality have to create a hierarchy of realities with various degrees of authenticity.

For Buddhists, therefore, there are two realities created for convenience; the first is pure sensation created by the point-instants. The other is the conditional or empirical reality the objectivised world in which we live. This is the phenomenal world of space and time. The former is of course the reality of a higher order and the latter an illusion which is given the status of reality for convenience. There is, of course, another category of absolute unreality, God, soul, afterlife, etc. We will discuss this topic at length later.

9.3 Existential Identity

We mentioned "existential identity" (*tādātmya*) a little while ago. Since words "identity", "identical", etc. are important for us, the notion of existential identity needs to be elaborated.

Consider the following argument :

a) Whatever exists is subject to momentary change.
b) For example, a jar which in ultimate reality is a point-instant.
c) The cosmical ether is believed to be motionless.
d) Hence the ether does not exist.

This deduction is analytical (*svabhāvānumāna*) because the predicate in (a) is implied in the subject. But we should remember that (a) is a premise.

According to Stcherbatsky, who borrows mainly from Dharmakīrti the connotation of "existential identity" is much wider and encompasses the following facts : [9]

a) Whatever has an origin is always changing.
b) Whatever is produced by causes is impermanent.
c) Whatever is variable in dependence on a variation of its causes is subject to momentary change.
d) Whatever is produced by a conscious effort is impermanent.

Thus all entities which are existentially identical have these common characteristics, though these entities may have different extensions. For example, a jar produced by a potter through efforts can be characterized as variable, a product, as having an origin, as changing, efficient, and existent.[10]

Closely related to existential identity is the notion of non existence. Realists recognize not only different categories of existence but also the categories of "meaning".[11] For some of them non-existence can be valid since it can be produced by its own causes. For Buddhists however, non-existence cannot exist "... existence alone can have cause, non-existence cannot be produced".[12]

We must realize that according to Buddhists the ultimate reality consists of instantaneous moments, which appear and disappear. Buddhists can accept the argument that one thing is replaced by another, but cannot agree that there is anything like non-existence in toto.

Buddhists' views on a falling body or rising smoke is immensely appealing to some physicists. A falling body is accelerated under the gravitational field. Buddhist scholars argued that the falling body was changing every moment, rather the body lasted only for a moment only to be replaced by a new body. It would be worthwhile to quote Stcherbatsky, "It is clear that the fundamental elements of matter are rather forces or momentary quanta of energy than substantial atoms".[12a]

Early Buddhists based their theory of momentary existence by induction or through observation and hence called this principle a posteriori. However, later Buddhists thought that the principle was a priori. There was no need to prove either an empirical object or its noumenon had momentary existence. What appears has to vanish. They were often asked by realists to explain the fate of the jar when it is hammered and broken to pieces. Buddhists' answer was that the momentary change was a priori, a necessity. A jar hammered is a special cause. The jar would in any case change from moment to moment. A special cause is neither a necessary cause nor is it a priori.

9.4 The Law of Otherness

Whatever exists, exists separately[13] from other existing things. In what sense is a thing different from others? It is the point-instant which is unique. The "law of otherness" implies that every point-instant is "individuated". Three determinants – time, space and quality characterize individuality. A blue ball is different from a red ball of the same size and material. Two absolutely indistinguishable balls are different if they are located at different places. But time is the greatest of the criteria of "otherness". An object at the same place becomes another object next moment. Buddhist scholars sometimes use the law of otherness to prove momentariness which means the order "from point-instant (premise) to law of otherness" is reversed to "from law of otherness (premise) to point instant".

We may summarize as follows – The world of Buddhists is dynamic. There is nothing static and nothing substantial. A point instant is the unique momentary being in ultimate reality which is projected as a momentarily perceived object in the empirical world. It is our mind which constructs the empirical phenomenal world.

9.5 Causation

The doctrine of Dependent Origination suggests that a point-instant depends on all the point-instants preceding it. This leads to a paradox. All point-instants are instantaneous, they have no time to create anything. Hence stricly speaking though the point-instants in a series are interdependent, we cannot use the term "cause", A point-instant emerges but not "caused" by the preceding members. This leads to the notion of functional dependence of the point-instants within the series. The correct description of a sequence A, B, C, D, ..., etc. is that every momentary being is a cause itself or is an efficient moment; we cannot say, for example, that C is caused by A, B; we can only say C appears after A, B and before D. The order implies funcional dependence.

The crux of the matter is that since ultimate reality consists of a sequence of instantaneous beings, improper use of the word "cause" would suggest a material substance continuously changing. Since Buddhists do not believe in matter, they have to live with the paradox : moments appear in accordance with the causal law. They just emerge according a functional formula, but are not "caused" in the usual sense.

9.6 Multiple Causes

Buddhists were aware that an event is the result of multiple causes and not just one. In fact many scholars thought that there are infiniely many causes. It is worthwhile to know what Rahula thought :

"Every variety of cause
which brings about the glittering shine.
In a single eye of peacock's tail.
Is not accessible to our knowledge.
The Omniscient knows them all".[14]

This leads to a view comparable to that in modern science, viz. the entire universe is a connected whole and changes from one state to another involving all these interdependent elements.

Nevertheless, Buddhists are also aware that in practice all parameters are not equally important and the minor ones can be ignored, say, for a scientific prediction.

9.7 Special and General Theories

We mentioned earlier in chapter 7 that the twelve-link cycle raises certain questions. This cycle and the conception of rebirth is based on Gautama's moral philosophy. In fact the doctrine of Dependent Origination relating to this cycle is also called the Special Theory of this doctrine. Gautama says, "I declare that there are voluntary deeds and there is a reward, but the perpetrator of these deeds does not exist at all. No one there is who assumes those elements, who is the bearer of them, who throws them out and assumes a new set of them".[15] Gautama was aware of the criticism that was levelled against his twelve-link cycle – Who is responsible for attracting the law of *karma*? Who is rewarded? Who is punished? There are many maxims in support of this strange Buddhist doctrine. "This being, that appears" and "They appear not out of oneself, or out of another self nor at haphazard, they are not really produced, they appear in apparent apperations".[16]

Mahāyāna thinkers seem to have differed from this principle and there was a change of meaning of interdependence which was interpretated as relativity and even unreality of the separate elements. But as we pointed out earlier, this new interpretation was pushed through the back door. Every adherent of Buddhism staunchly supported the doctrine of Dependent Origination as the central theme of Buddhism. The following two quotations from two renowned scholars would indicate how a doctrine can be interpreted in two unidetical versions.[17]

Nāgārjuna after praising Gautama says :

> I salute the Buddha who has proclaimed the principle of Dependent Origination according to which there is no plurality, no differentiation, no beginining and no end, no motion neither hither nor thither.

Śāntirakṣita who belongs to the later period of Mahāyāna says :

> I salute the Buddha who has proclaimed the principle of Dependent Origination according to which everything is kinetic, there is no God, no Matter, no substance, no quality, no (separate) actions, no inherence but the strict conformity between every fact and its result....

Later we shall see how Nāgārjuna used the concept of interdependence to refute Naiyāyikas' logic.

Dependendent Origination thus becomes a perplexing term : it implies causation but not in the sense in which the western scientists use the term. Stcherbatsky borrows from Buddhist literature to elucidate this dilemma. If we ask the Buddhist logician what is meant by "operation" of a cause producing its effect and what is meant by "dependence" of the effect on its cause, the logician is likely to provide the following answer :

> We call dependence of the effect upon its cause the fact that it always follows upon the presence of that cause and we call operation of the cause the fact that the cause always precedes its effect. The cause is the thing itself, the bare thing, the thing cut loose of every extension, of every additional force.[18]

We may conclude this chapter with the following observation :

1. When Buddhists speak of "causes" they mean functional interdependence of point-instants each of them efficient.
2. When we discuss Buddhist science later, we will have to recall that the phenomenal world is a conditioned world and no part of it can be described in isolation because the conditioned world and interdependence are two sides of the same coin.

10

Perception in Buddhism

10.1 Sense-perception

Buddhist logicians usually recognize two sources or kinds of knowledge; direct perception (*pratyakṣa*) and inference (*anumāna*). Dharmakīrti calls that, "cognition *pratyakṣa* is free from constructive thought and non-delusory".[1] Dignāga, too, subscribes to this division. However, words such as sense perception, perception, sensibility, inference, construction and so on are not used uniformly by translators and some elucidation is necessary. Sense-perception is the word often used for *pratyakṣa* which implies the role of pure sensibility. Unfortunately since Buddhists believe that the ultimate reality is a sequence of instantaneous moments which are transcendent, its impact on the senses is just a flash and there is no real perception of an empirical image. Another Buddhist definition of perception is quite laconic – perception is sensation followed by conception.[2] Conception in this context means nothing but the image.

In this book we shall use sense perception to mean pure sensation that signals the presence of something. It is the sensational core of what we generally call perception. In fact Dharmakīrti tells us that the direct perception is free from constructive thought and "constructive thought is the cognitive dawning of an image able to coalesce with verbalism".[3] His assertion clearly distinguishes the sense-impact, which is unutterable, from its image which can be verbalised (utterable).

We shall often use the word perception in ordinary sense, i.e. we perceive a thing when sense-perception is clothed with total construction of an image that appears in the empirical world. When quoting Dharmottara, Stcherbatsky maintains that perception is a source of knowledge whose function of making the object present in the ken is followed by the construction of its image, he is referring to the sense perception and not fully ripened perception.[4]

We should remember that the real source of perception is the instantaneous being in the transcendent. This leads to some puzzles when we try to describe perception – what ordinary people perceive. It is not easy to build a theoretical model that connects the transcendent with empirical reality. Since Buddhism asks you to find the fact yourself, Dharmakīrti decided to find out what the point-instant means. The only method we can use in such a search is introspection. Dharmakīrti observes :

> That sensation is something quite different from productive imagination can be proved just by introspection (*pratyakṣeṇa*). Everyone knows that an image is something utterable (capable of coalescing with a name). Now if we begin to stare at a patch of color and withdraw all our thoughts to a condition of rigidity (and become as though unconscious), this will be the condition of pure sensation.[4a]

If we then (awakening from that condition) begin to think, we notice a feeling remembering that we had an image, (a patch of color before us) but we did not notice it whilst we were in the foregoing condition (we could not name it) because it was pure sensation. Kamlaśīla endorses Dharmakīrti's opinion and says, "At the very first moment when an object is apprehended and it appears in its own absolute particularity, a state of consciousness is produced which is pure sensation".[5]

In chapter 5 we described how according to Rand perception takes place. Dignāga's thoughts parallel the objectivist's "unintegrated perception" when he says, "A man who is absorbed in the contemplation of a patch of blue, perceives the blue, but he does not know what kind of object it is".[6]

10.2 Illusion

According to Dharmakīrti, constructive thought is the cognitive dawning of an image which is able to coalesce with verbalism. But is every cognition thus constructed valid knowledge? It is necessary that perception is not distorted by any eye-disease or any other ailment or external conditions which cause illusions. However, the concept of illusion is not free from controversy.

In a way every empirical image is a transcendental illusion. What is an illusion and what is not depends on the commentator's view as well as the interpretation of sensibility, sense-perception, perception, etc.

It would be worthwhile to mention Dharmakīrti's four-fold Direct Perception which is free from constructive thought. It is not clear whether the four steps are sequential or he merely mentions four different methods of cognition. Unfortunately his words lead to several interpretations. This is what he says :

1. Sense-organ cognition.
2. Mental perception which is generated by the immediately preceding condition, viz. the cooperating sense-organ cognition as an object which immediately follows its own (partite) sense object.
3. Introspection (which is of every thought and mental).
4. Yogin's cognition born of the vivid fulfillment from contemplating the true end.[7]

What Dharmakīrti here describes is the pure sensation.

In view of interpretative quarrels Dignāga dropped non-illusiveness. He does recognize the sources which lead to illusions, but prefers to treat them separately. His criterion is simple; only the pure sensation is free from illusions because it is neither wrong nor right. Dharmottara's views on illusion are perhaps most lucid and acceptable :

> The causes of illusion are various. They may lie in the external object or in the observer, they may be called forth by a disease of the sense-organ or they may be entirely psychical as the visions of mentally diseased people. But in all cases of illusion sense faculties one involved; they are in an abnormal condition.[8]

10.3 Intuition

According to Stcherbatsky "perception" should be interpreted as direct knowledge or intuition. Sense perception is only one variety of intuition. Thus according to Dignāga perception of a patch of blue is a moment of pure sensation followed by the construction of the image by intellect. Stcherbatsky calls it mental sensation (*mānasa pratyakṣa*). Using Stcherbatsky's nomenclature, the process of direct perception for ordinary people is Pure Sensation–mental sensation–construction–understanding.

Saints' perception works in a different manner. There are no intermediate stages of sensation and construction, they have what is called intelligible intuition (*yogī-pratyakṣa*).

As mentioned earlier, Dharmakīrti uses the introspection in his four fold direct perception. According to him all consciousness and mental phenomena are "self conscious". Knowledge is self-luminous and does not need an agent.

Dharmottara emphasizes introspection by analyzing sense perception and subsequent construction. When we perceive an image of the object, we are aware of our own self, but that awareness is present even when there is no object and no construction.

Many Indian schools of philosophy explain cognition using such concepts as organ, ego, consciousness, sixth sense and so on. Hīnayāna discards many of these concepts but retains consciousness, organ and object. For the sixth organ, (inner sense), mental phenomena are "objects" (*viṣaya*). It is nothing but a passing pure consciousness. It cognizes mental phenomena directly and external objects indirectly with the cooperation of five outer senses, according to the law of dependent origination.

Dignāga rejects this theory. According to him, "No objects are the feelings, no sixth sense is the intellect".[9] He agrees that all cognition consists of two parts, subject and object, but denies that the former is further divided.

10.4 Judgement

Since Buddhist scholars posit that ultimate reality consists of instantaneous moments, each moment having no extension, no time duration, absolutely unconnected, indivisible, transcendental and so on, they find it difficult to connect this transcendent with what we perceive or empirical reality. How can we build a bridge connecting these two dissimilar realities? The projection of these ultimate moments into empirical phenomena is believed to be facilitated by what is called conformity (*sārūpya*) or correspondence. This may be called according to Stcherbatsky a similarity between things absolutely dissimilar. Fortunately, the law of causation connotes functional interdependence and this does not require that the effect should be similar to the cause.

The psychological solution to the above mentioned problem is as follows : In terms of the sequence of moments, the first moment is "pure sensation". This is followed by a moment of mental sensation or "intelligible intuition". The second moment may also be called the moment of attention. This is believed to be the moment when the object is "present". The third moment sees the entry of intellectual construction and fading of the sensation. This gives rise to the image. Unfortunately the second moment is transcendental. It cannot be proved empirically in a manner the first moment was verified by Dharmakīrti.

Despite the holes in this theory, an ostensibly plausible explanation was provided by Jñānagarbha and others. The main argument runs as follows :

> An intelligible intuition is pure intuition which makes it homogeneous with pure sensation. Again, being intelligible it must

be homogenous with intelligible conception. However, since there is functional dependence between the moment and its image two pure intuitions cannot exist simultaneously. Hence it is assumed that the intelligible intuition arises at the moment the outer sensation having achieved its function disappears.

10.5 Understanding

The intelligible intuition sets in motion the process of understanding : the dichotomy between the subject and object. Stcherbatsky calls it transcendental apperception. It is believed that the mind runs through manifold of sensuous intuition till after many "misses" it finds the right conception.

When we identify the perceived object we might judge, say, "This is a dog" Here "this" is the incognizable sensational core and "dog" the conception identified by the class name. Knowledge perceived thus is the union of sensation and conception. This often raises a question whether the conceptions are innate in the human mind or learned later. Certainly our mind is not "tabula rasa" at birth. As to which abilities or potentials we are born with and which abilities are acquired later is a scientific question which modern geneticists are trying to solve. What we know at present is that our body-mind complex is the result of both heredity and environment. A judgement is a synthesis of sensation and construction.

It is assumed that judgements can be classified because they are nameable. Dignāga constructed a table of categories relating to reality which is nothing but a classification of names (*nāma kalpanā*), viz. proper names, class names, adjectives, verbs and substantives. Proper names however, are believed to be general names and not personal names. Kamalaśīla observes :

> Although the words like *dittah* are generally admitted as to be proper names, but, since they have a continued existence from birth upto the moment of death, they are not capable of designating (a real individual) which changes every moment and is a real thing (in itself) having nothing in common with other things. The object they are intent upon and which they designate is (also) a class, inhering in a

> Thing which is characterized by the limits of an enduring (lapse of) time.[10]

Remember that in Buddhist logic, nothing is permanent. It is on account of synthesis between consecutive moments that there is a semblance of a durable object such as cat, dog, etc. According to Vācaspati Miśra :

> When the cognizing individual thinks that he perceives by his senses an image which he has really constructed himself, he simply conceals, as it were his imaginative faculty and puts to the front perspective faculty....[11]

10.6 Concepts and Names

A concept comes into existence when we are able to verbalize an experience. We may say expressibility is the mark of a concept. Sensations on the other hand are unutterable. For this reason a concept is closely connected with the theory of names. Dignāga rightly observes, "The names have sources in concepts and the concepts have their source in names".[12] Dharmakīrti even contends that the narrow association of conceptions with words can be proved by introspection (*pratyakṣataḥ*) just as pure sensation was demonstrated by him.

10.7 A Model for Perception

In Appendix II of *Buddhist Logic,* Vol.II Stcherbatsky presents a genesis of mental sensation with diagrams. The first diagram represents the early Abhidharmists' views, and the second reflects the influence of Mahāyāna thinkers especially those belonging to Sautrāntika-Yogācāra.

Unfortunately, perception in Buddhist logic has roots in the transcendental chain of moments. We do not know the ontology of these moments. Nevertheless, we may treat them as mere parameters such as we use in physics – photons, matter, field, electrons, and so on. So long as these concepts do not violate our established scientific theories we can retain them if they help us understand the phenomenal world.

We can modify the Mahāyāna model and present a plausible picture starting with pure sensation and ending with what we call cognition.

In the figure shown below x_1, x_2,..., etc are the first, second,... moments in ultimate reality. For the human observer they appear as y_0 (void), y_1, y_2, etc. These y's are the images of x's in the objective world. We can assume a functional relationship between x's and y's and write y = f(x)

$y_1 = f(x_1)$, $y_2 = f(x_2)$ and so on.

Moments of the object Moments of consciousness y_o, y_1, y_2, y_3

Moments of the object	Moments of consciousness
	y_o (void)
x_1 ———	y_1 (pure sensation)
x_2 ———	y_2 (mental sensation)
x_3 ———	y_3 (*savikalpa* cognition)

The first moment x_1 produces y_1 which is pure sensation; x_1 is also called *ālambana pratyaya.* It is also the substrate (*upādāna*) of x_2 (*ālambana*) whose image is y_2 or mental sensation. The further images $y_3 = f(x_3)$, etc. are *savikalpa,* fully constructed images.

Note that there is a time lag between the source-moment x_n and its the image moment y_n. (x_n is contemporaneous with y_{n-1}). For example, in case of "seeing" it shows the time required by the electromagnetic waves to reach the eye followed by the time required for electrical/chemical impulses to reach the brain.

Actually there is what is called cooperaion between x and the predecessor of f(x). For example, y_2 is produced by x_2 in cooperation with y_1 which is called the substrate cause (*samāntarapratyaya*) of y_2.

These consideration leads us to assume that y depends on whatever is contained in its pre-image x and we can write y = f(x).[13]

Images y_3 onward are called *santāna.* Although x's are transcendental moments, cognition invests them with a temporal position. Hence we can take x_1, x_2, x_3... as a temporal (discrete) series having 1-1 correspondence with y_1, y_2,... If we define R, R' as the order relations "occurs before" in x series and in y series respectively then it can be proved that yRy' if and only if xRx' where y, y' are images of x, x' respectively.

Both these series x and y are ordered series and the above statement merely means that the temporal order is preserved in image formation.[14]

10.8 Similarity and Dissimilarity

We have seen earlier that Buddhist logicians often face the problem of connecting the similar with the dissimilar. When structures are transmitted through various media they can retain the quality of similarity. For example, an audio or video input at a TV station may be first converted into electrical impulses, then electromagnetic waves through space. At the receiveing end the sequence is reversed and you see the output in the audiovisual form though you may be hundreds of miles away form the TV station. Throughout the journey the input may undergo qualitative changes, but the structure remains similar. This preservation of structures is called isomorphism. When you finally receive the TV transmission you see the structure which is not only isomorphic but qualitatively similar.

However, since Buddhists claim that the original chain of moments is in the transcendental sphere, building of a consistent model is a little difficult, because these moments are not structured. Nevertheless since in the empirical space-time all the spectators see an assemblage of things or a drama or a TV program in almost the same (though not identical) way, we may assume that each moment holds some potential (something transcendental) which is projected as an image after interacting with the human mind. Since all perceivers see things in a similar fashion we may safely assume that the transitions from the moments in the ultimate reality to the images perceived by different people are similar. It is safe to assume that there is isomorphism of some kind. Two points need to be noted :

1. Due to the defective eyesight or any other illnesss or outside agency perception may be grossly distorted.
2. The potential which inheres in moments resembles the concept of "entelchy" of Aristotle. For example, an acorn will grow into an oak tree according to the inherent potential unless the growth is hampered by external circumstances.

We may summarize as follows :

There are two kinds of knowledge according to Buddhists, *pratyakṣa* (direct perception) and inference. What we call perception in ordinary language is the perception (cognition) in the empirical world. This involves a process starting from a momentary being in ultimate reality followed by pure sensation, a mere flash, mental sensation construction, conception, understanding, judgement, etc. The stages in the sequence may appear different either because nomenclature is not uniform or there is no unanimity among Buddhist logicians about the entire process of understanding. Vācaspatimiśra's quotation is worth remembering, "judgement (or decision), conception (or synthesis) and necessity (or apodictic necessity) are not different things".[15] We may conclude that most of the process of perception is mental construction; the external stimulus is just a trigger.

11

Inference

11.1 Vasubandhu's Criterion

The second method of cognition according to Buddhists, is inference. Suppose there is fire on the mountain, one observer may see it directly while to another observer the fire may be hidden. If the latter sees the smoke, he may judge that there is fire because wherever there is smoke there has to be fire. His knowledge is inferential, through a mark (*liṅga*) "smoke". Inference is thus the cognition of nonperceived object through a perceived object. In perception there is synthesis of a sensation and a conception. In inference there is synthesis of a sensation and two conceptions.

Inference has three terms; the logical subject, the logical predicate and the mark or reason. In the above illustration the mountain is the subject. However, according to Dignāga, the mountain is a mere mental construction and hence the true subject is the point-instant of the ultimate reality. The predicate in the illustration is fireness though it appears as a substantive "fire". The third term is the mark, viz. smoke.

Dignāga compares perception and inference in a lucid manner. According to him there are only two sources of knowledge – perception and inference – and corresponding to them only two classes of objects, viz. the particular and the universal. The universal is cognized by inference whereas the particular is grasped by the senses.

It must be remembered that Buddhists do not regard inference as a deduction from other premises, rather it is a method of cognizing reality.

A source of valid knowledge is defined as a first moment of cognition which does not contradict experience. Even in direct (perceptual) judgement knowledge is mixed with imagination and memory. Inference is till more remote seeking cognition of an object through its mark. This has led many scholars to declare that inference does not yield authentic knowledge. Dharmottara maintains that "inference is an illusion ; it deals with non-entia which are its own imagination, and wrongly identifies them with reality".[1] Despite such scepticism most commentators including Dharmakīrti and Kamalaśīla admit that though we do not cognize the ultimate reality, we cognize its empirical representation.

Vasubandhu is credited with creating the renowned "three aspects of logical reason". These aspects are endorsed by Dignāga and Dharmakīrti. With the appropriate linguistic technique of using the particle "just" the three aspects are presented as follows :

1. The presence of the reason in the subject "just", i.e. never absence.
2. Its presence in similar instances "just", i.e. never in dissimilar, but not in the totality of the similar.
3. Its absence from dissimilar instances "just", i.e. never presence.

Its laconic variety is :

1. In subject wholly.
2. In similar only.
3. In dissimilar never.

E1.

(1) Trees are sentient beings.

Because they sleep at night.

This argument attributed to Jaina scholars is fallacions since the reason is not wholly present in the subject. Only a few trees close their leaves at night giving the appearance of sleep.

(2) Words are non-eternal.

Because they are produced at will.

This is a correct inference although the reason "produced at will" is not present in all non-eternal cases. Note that the second rule does not require the presence of reason in all similar classes. At the same time it is never present in eternal entities.

(3) Words are produced voluntarily.

Because they are impermanent.

The inference is erroneous. The mark (impermanence) is present in lightning, etc. (which are impermanent but not voluntarily produced). On the other hand, it is not present in space which is eternal. Thus the presence of the mark in one part and absence in another of the dissimilars should prompt us to reject the inference since it violates the third test.

11.2 Kinds of Mark

According to Dharmakīrti there are three kinds of marks, viz. negation (*anupalabdhi*), identity (*tādātmya*) and causation (*tadupatti*). Consider the arguments :

On some particular place there is no jar.

Because it is not perceived although the conditions of perceptions are fulfilled.

The proviso of the conditions for perception given is important. For example, a blind person cannot perceive the jar although it is present. Similarly if a screen is placed between the observer and the jar, the jar will not be visible. As to how we come to a negative assertion depends upon the antecedent state of our mind. If we are asked "is there a jar on the table?", we imagine a jar in that place and the negative answer would follow on realizing its absence. However, there is a second case where you are asked "is there anything on the table?". You might automatically say "there is nothing". What you mean, of course, is there is nothing that can be seen by the average human eye. These two negatives, "not-jar" and "nothing" are in fact epistemologically quite different. The first is easy to prove. The second "nothing" implies that you are asserting there does not exist a, there does not exist b, ... where a, b, ..., etc. are all imaginable entities in the universe, infinite in number.

The second kind, viz. "identity" is not used in the sense A = A, but in the sense of A and B have some common attribute or A is the subset of B .

Consider :

This is a tree

Because it is Aśoka.

Your conclusion is based on a particular, but the fact remains that Aśoka trees are a subset of all trees.

The third kind involves the concept of causation and ultimately depends on the principle of Dependent Origination. The example of fire-smoke given in the beginning falls under this category. The reason in this case is "concomitance". The cause p(fire) and effect q(smoke) should both appear in similar cases. This is shown as conjunction p.q.

The essence of inferential judgement is beautifully captured by Dharmottara :

> The predicate (in a judgement) is either affirmed or denied... When it is affirmed through a mark, this mark is either existentially identical with it or when it is different, it represents its effect. Both possess the three aspects.[2]

The principle of dichotomy completely separates affirmation (*vidhi*) from negation (*anupalabdhi*). Affirmation as mentioned above can be either based on identity (*tādātmya*) or casusality (*tadutpatti*).

The question now arises whether the above classification is exhaustive and the classes mutually exclusive. The principle of dichotomy ensures that the main divisions are exhaustive and exclusive based on the law of contradiction and excluded middle. But are divisions identity-casuality exhaustive? The answer to some extent depends on the concept of "analytic" and "synthetic" statements or judgements which we discussed in chapter 4 with reference to western logic. Buddhists have a slightly different views on this division. According to Stcherbatsky, strictly speaking even the judgements called analytic are also synthetic because "understanding itself and its function the judgement is nothing but synthesis".[2a] The concept of Aśoka is synthesis and so is that of a tree. Their union is also synthetic. The same reasoning applies to fire and smoke. Quoting Kant, Stcherbatsky asserts that the intellect can dissolve only where it has itself previously united. The Buddhist argument runs as follows :

Identity according to Buddhists is an identity of objective reference. There are two concepts but the same reality. If you are talking about a particular Aśoka tree you have two concepts "tree" and "Aśoka". But both refer to the same reality, the particular under consideration. On the other hand, suppose you are showing your garden to a friend and tell him, "See, this is Aśoka". After half an hour after inspecting various trees and flowers you may happen to be near the same Aśoka. But if your intention is to let your friend have some knowledge of Buddhist logic, you may tell your friend, "this is an Aśoka tree". Your friend is likely to reply "but we saw it before". Your reply would be "everything exists momentarily. The Aśoka you saw half an hour ago is not the same Aśoka as you see now". Here the concept (Aśoka) is the same but realiy is different though the difference may not be discernible. For Buddhists the term analytic is used when there is synthesis of two different concepts. The term synthetic is to be applied to the synthesis of two different things.

11.3 Concomitance

The most puzzling aspect of Buddhist theory of inference is concomitance.When there is conomitance of p and q, it is understood that both p and q occur. Invariable concomitance would mean when p occurs, q also occurs and vice versa. However theoretically, concomitance can be interpreted in several ways, viz.

1. Whenever p occurs q also occurs.
2. Whenever q occurs p also occurs.
3. p is the cause of q.
4. q is the cause of p.
5. p need not be the cause of q.
6. q need not be the cause of p.
7. There is a common cause r of both p and q.
8. There is only a functional relationship between p and q.
9. The temporal order is important, i.e. p.q and q.p are not the same.
10. The temporal order is not relevant, i.e. p.q = q.p.

According to Dharmakīrti :

> A dissimilar locus is not a similar locus, namely, other than it, opposed to it, or its absence" which in turn can be interpreted in many ways.[3] How do we interpret "opposed to it"? The commentator further says "This is the formulation of result-reason. In the absence of a fire, there would be no smoke. But there is (smoke)".[4] However, some commentators use contraposition -q . -p for *vyatireka*[5] (dissimilar classes) and not -p.-q implied by Dharmakīrti, in his first sentence. Again, Dharmakīrti is more cxplict – Here "there is no smoke because there is no fire".[6] He also implies that concomitance connotes causal relation when he says, "... or else because of arising from the thesis entity (as a given thing)".[7]

It looks that concomitance means "invariable association" at least at the empirical level. Fortunately, in Buddhism all events can be traced to the microscopic level where causality reigns supreme thanks to the doctrine of Dependent Origination. The last moment contains the entire complex of causes and is responsible for the "image" at the empirical level.[8]

11.4 Instinct, Environment and Learning

A problem similar to the one faced by western intellectuals confronted Indian philosophers. How do we learn? Is it on account of experience or some innate abilities? The modern scientist's answer is the safest – Our instincts or the genetic composition are the instruments we have when we are born. We learn through experience using these basic instruments. Unlike realists who stressed the importance of experience through which we gain knowledge almost by accident, Buddhist logicians believed that there is a set of principles which are innate to human beings. These are the laws which help us in cognition and interpretation of events. This is precisely why all humans have similar though not identical idea about the various aspects of the phenomenal world.

We may recall the views of western philosophers of the concepts such as, "a priori", "a posteriori", "analytic" and "synthetic" knowledge in chapter 4. Such mathematical truths as 7+5=12 appeared perplexing and Kant created a new category "synthetic a priori". Dharmakīrti did not need a new type. He would call this in fact analytical, i.e. founded on identity of reference. His reasoning was that the statement merely referred to a collection (what we call twelve objects) and showed one way of distributing the collection. Thus the identity of reference would justify several alternate equivalents 7+5 = 5 +7 = 3 +9, etc.

12

Syllogism

12.1 *Pañcāvayava*

Syllogism is of great importance in Buddhist logic for several reasons. On the one hand it affords us an opportunity to compare Buddhist method of presenting inference with western syllogims. On the other hand it shows how Buddhists reduced the number of steps in the traditional Indian syllogism typified by *pañcāvayava* or "five limbs".

At the outset it must be clarified that syllogism for the Buddhist logician is not a source of knowledge. Through this method a person merely conveys inferential knowledge to another. Dharmakīrti defines syllogism succinctly in *Nyāyabindu*. "A syllogism consists in communicating the three aspects of the Logical Mark to others".[1] These aspects are the minor and major premises of Aristotalian model, and conclusion.

Let us start with how syllogism in Nyāya looks like :

1. Statement (*pratijñā*)
   There is fire on the mountain
2. Reason (*hetu*)
   Because there is smoke above
3. Example (*udāharaṇa*)
   Where there is smoke, there is fire;
   Anvaya : as in kitchen
   Vyatireka : unlike on the lake

4. Application (*upanaya*)
   The hill is having smoke
5. Conclusion (*nigamana*)
   Therefore, the hill is having fire.

In Aristotle's or even the modern western syllogism this argument would appear as

1. Major : Where there is smoke there is fire
2. Minor : There is smoke in the mountain.
3. Conclusion : Hence there is fire in the mountain.

The concept on which Indian syllogism is based is the relation of concomitance (*vyāpti*) between reason (*hetu*) and conclusion (*sādhya*). The western syllogism, on the other hand, is based on entailment or implication – the conclusion is almost tautological. The Indian method lays great stress on instantiation. In *udāharaṇa*, the logician furnishes a dual evidence of common experience. *Anvaya* supplies the positive evidence or correct concomitance while the negative evidence is supplied by *vyatireka* where conditions are not suitable for correct conclusion.

We can use conjuction to denote concomitance. Thus p.q will indicate "p and q" and its equivalent contraposition will appear as -q .-p (not q and not p).

It is convenient to indicate "x having smoke" and "x having fire" by p(x) and q(x). These are called propositional functions of the variable x. For specific instances we can use letters such as h (hill), α (kitchen), β (lake) instead of x. For example, p(h) will mean fire on the hill. This is a proposition where the variable is converted into the constant h. Symbolic representation of *pañcāvayava* is given in Appendix.

12.2 *Trairūpa*

Dignāga established a rule for inference called *trairūpa* according to which inference depends upon the characteristics of the classes to which the above variables belong. The conclusion is – (i) correct when concomitance is in respect of the members of the same class (*sapakṣa*), e.g. kitchen, hill (ii) wrong when concomitance is in respect of dissimilar (*vipakṣa*) class, e.g. lake. This is equivalent to saying that concomitance of the contraposition is valid.[1a]

Dignāga argued that these two tests involving similar and dissimilar classes ensured that the argument is applicable to the substratum which belongs to the *sapakṣa* (hill h in this case). Dignāga's model incidentally eliminated two limbs from the Naiyāyika's *pañcāvyava,* viz. *nigamana* (which is repetition of *pratijñā*) *upanaya* (which is redundant since *hetu* is already mentioned). Subsequently even *pratijñā* was considered superfluous. The goal of syllogism is to convey an already established inference to the common person. Buddhist logic depends on the individual's experience, and the common people already know from experience the relationship between smoke and fire. Dignāga's theory reduced syllogism to only two steps[2] :

1. *Vyāpti* : Whenever there is smoke there is fire.
   Anvaya : As in a kitchen where their concomitance is observed.
   Vyatireka : Unlike in a lake where neither is found.
2. *Hetu* (implying *sādhya*): There is smoke which implies fire.

Its symbolic expression will be found in Appendix.

This reduction led to heated debates between Naiyāyikas and Dignāga. Buddhist logicians always remind us that in an argument, words and expressions should have the same meaning for both adversaries.

Naiyāyikas considered the specific case (hills) important and hence insisted that *pratijñā, sādhya* and *hetu* which mentioned the specific case could not be dispensed with. Dignāga, on the other hand, was thinking in terms of classes and their relationship.

Dignāga furnished three reasons to support his thesis against Naiyāyikas :

(1) When the concomitance of p and q is known universally, q should be implied in p(h) or hetu.

(2) When q is found universally in a *dṛṣṭānta*, the *pakṣa* in question (hill) should be the object to be cognized.

(3) If the object of an inference is the relationship between hill and fire in q(h), there is no element here capable of making an inference possible, nor is there anything to be inferred. Hence the connection between the *dharmin* h and *dharma* q need not be mentioned nor should it be accompanied by *hetu.*[3]

It must be borne in mind that syllogism is a communication of valid knowledge. It is inference "for others" in contrast to inference for one-self. The dynamics of attaining knowledge in the case of oneself is a natural process of inferring while in knowledge for others the flow of the argument is opposite. This can be elucidated by the following (omitting *anvaya-vyatireka* for convenience) :

1) Inference "for oneself"
   i) There is fire on the hill
   ii) because there is smoke as, e.g....
   Syllogism "for others"
   i) Whenever there is smoke there is fire, e.g...
   ii) There is such smoke on the hill
   These involve a Causal Relationship

2) Inference "for oneself"
   i) Spoken words are impermanent
   ii) because they are the result of "production", e.g....
   Syllogism "for others"
   i) Whatever is the result of production is impermanent, e.g...
   ii) Such are the spoken words
   These involve Identical Reference of two concepts – "impermanence" and "production"

3) Inference
   i) There is no book here.
   ii) Because we do not perceive any as we do not perceive flower in the sky.

   Syllogism
   i) Whenever we do not perceive a thing, we deny its presence, e.g. a flower in the sky.
   ii) At this place we do not perceive a book.

This example is based on Negation.

You will realise that in the above, "inferences" shows how the investigating mind naturally behaves, while in syllogisms there is a formal approach "which is most suitable in science and public debate".[4]

12.3 Induction in Buddhism

Since our principal areas of investigation are Buddhism and modern science, a few words on induction are necessary.

In western science induction is a *sine qua non* of scientific investigation. It connects particular instances and a general law which we know is always probabilistic. Scientific predictions are deductions based on a scientific law.

What is the status of induction in Buddhist logic?

It is easy to see that Buddhist syllogism contains both induction and deduction. *Anvaya* and *vyatireka* contribute to establish a general rule or major premise. Without instantiation there is no syllogism or inference.

Moreover the test for establishing an inference, seems to be rigorous especially in case of those Buddhists who insist on instantiations, *anvaya* as well as *vyatireka*. The first is the method of agreement (*sādharmya*) and the other the method of disagreement (*vaidharmya*). Most western authors includeing Stcherbatsky equate these methods with position and contraposition, i.e. p.q and -q.-p.

In Buddhist syllogism both induction and deduction are present. According to Stcherbatsky, "In order to safeguard against incomplete induction, the examples must be positive and negative. That is to say, that the joint method of Agreement and Disagreement is applied".[5] According to Dharmakīrti :

> The essence of a logical reason must be shown to represent, the first an effect (from which the existence of *necessary* cause is inferred), the second, a necessarily coexisting attribute which alone is sufficient for deducting (the consequence). When the reasons are so represented, it is then shown that 1), wherever smoke exists fire exists also, like in the kitchen, etc; there is no smoke without fire, as in the pond and in all dissimilar cases 2) wheresoever there is production, there is change like in a jar, etc; if something is changeless it is not a product like space. It is indeed impossible otherwise to show the existence of the reason in similar and its absence from all dissimilar cases....[6]

Most commentators like Dignāga and Stcherbatsky consider two methods equipollent; one method is positive while the other is negative.

The three kinds of syllogisms, viz. through cause, through identity (analytical) and through non-perception can be expressed using both the methods of agreement and disagreement. All these types incorporate both induction and deduction. The crux of the matter is there is interdependence of variables.

For example, in the causal category, the same syllogism can be expressed in two ways :

Agreement

Wherever there is smoke, there is fire, as in the kitchen.

Here there is smoke.

There must be some fire.

Difference

Wherever there is no fire there is no smoke, as in water.

But here there is smoke.

There must be some fire.

Western logicians have tried to fit Buddhist logic into the

classification in Aristotelian logic. Stcherbastky thus calls these positive and negative methods the figures of Agreement and Difference because they depend on the form. However, because of equipollency, he considers any one method sufficient, the other method follows by implication :

1) Whatever is not perceived, though conditions of perceptibility have been satisfied, is absent.
   On this table the book is not perceived.
   Hence the book is absent.
2) Whatever is present, is necessarily perceived if all conditions of perceptibility are realized.
   On this table no book is present.
   Hence the book is absent.
   These are the arguments based on nonperception – (1) uses the method of Agreement (2) the method of Difference.

(3) Whatever varies being functionally dependent on variation of its causes is noneternal like pot, etc.
   The sounds of speech are variable. Hence they are non-eternal.

(4) Whatever is eternal is not variable in functional dependence on a variation of its causes, e.g. space.
   But the sounds of speech are variable.
   Hence they are not eternal.
   These are analytical deductions based on Agreement and Difference.

12.4 Russell's Postulates of Induction

It would be pertinent to briefly describe Russell's Postulates of Induction which most western physicists implicitly use. Unfortunately they do not seem to be aware that these postulates are necessary for validating a scientific method. These postulates will be recalled later when we discuss the field theory.

We shall consider these postulates briefly. The importance of these postulates lies in the fact that they are a bridge between common sense and science. While the student of science may not be taught these epistemological premises science uses them implicitly. If any scientific theory violates them, in all probability it is invalid. There are five postulates and they will be called the postulates of induction.

Modern scientists and philosophers prefer to replace the concept of substance by "event". One of the compelling reasons is that ever since the relativity theory was firmly established, the boundaries between matter and energy have become blurred, since under certain circumstances, one can be converted into the other.

An event may be defined as any happening which occurs at a certain place and time with respect to an observer. An explosion, lightning, an accident, watching a star are all events.

Suppose you are watching a cricket match and perceive a series of appearances which you interpret as the ball which is rolling on the ground after being hit by a batsman. Actually what you are seeing is a series of events e_1, e_2, e_3 .... at times t_1, t_2, t_3 .... What is the reason to believe that these events constitutes a "thing" or a ball? There is no logic behind it. The only reason is that from experience you have found it convenient to group a certain series of events into a thing, it fits admirably into the world in which you live. This principle is the postulate of semi-permanence which may be stated as follows. If there is an event *A*, it very frequently happens that there is another event close to *A* in time and space, very similar to *A*. A series of such similar events we call a thing. In the present case you call it the cricket ball which is rolling on the ground. However, once the identity of a thing is established, it is not necessary that the events characterizing the thing should all be close to one another. For example, you may recognize a friend even when you see him after many years.

The second postulate has to do with cause. The concept of cause is primitive and pre-scientific. You see a boy lift a brickbat and after a few moments receive a blow on the head. You conclude that the boy is the cause of the injury. You are a diabetic and need a daily injection of insulin. You forget to take the injection on three successive days. You feel uncomfortable and the blood test shows that the blood sugar has shot up. You attribute it to the missing injections.

The concept of cause, however, is an embarrassment to science. If an event of type *A* is always or usually followed by an event of another type *B*, we usually assume that it is the cause of *B*. But this may be misleading. If you find that your postman always delivers your letter at 5.30 p.m. and your husband returns home from office at 6 p.m., you do not conclude that the frail postman is causing the movements of your muscular husband.

There is also the problem of multiple causes. Suppose an intoxicated man jumps through the open window of his apartment on the first floor, falls on the ground and breaks his neck. What is the cause of his injury? Is it the open window, the liquor he has consumed or the gravitational force?

The concept of cause is replaced by another and more satisfactory concept called causal line. The second postulate or the postulate of separable causal lines states that, it is very frequently possible to form a series of events such that, from a few members of the series, something can be inferred about other events in the series. A causal line is the series of the events connected in this way. What makes such an inference possible is called a "causal law".

Let us go back to the cricket match you were watching. You identify the ball as the series of events e_1, e_2,... at times t_1, t_2..... From a few members of the e-series you can know something about other events. The e-events constitute the causal line. Two events in this line are related in such a way that the prior event can be called the cause of the later event. But the first event does not entirely determine the second, because there is also the effect of the environment – also of causal nature – on the causal line itself. To understand this, suppose a fielder is chasing the ball. His movements give rise to another causal line. When the fielder stops the ball, the two causal lines have interacted.

The second postulate involves separability of causal lines. A given event can be a member of two lines. For example, when you are watching the ball or the the series of e-events, the light ray *(AB)*, consisting of photons from an event, say, e_2 reaches your eyes and causes, the perception of e_2-*AB* and e-series are two causal lines, e_2 being the common member. *AB* itself consists of several closely separated events which are similar to each other. (see fig.)

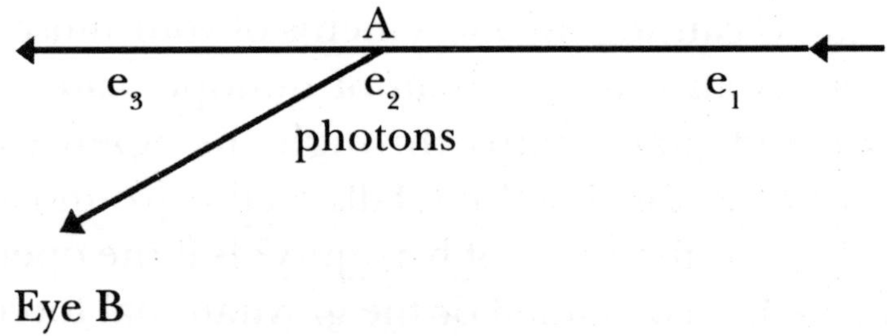

Causal Lines

The second postulate implies that an event is frequently one of the series of events which has always an approximate Law of Persistence or Change. The postulate is general and applies to other branches of knowledge as well as physics. For example, it implies that the cricket ball rolls on the ground preserving its shape and colour, a photon travels with the same velocity and direction, a mango seed when planted grows into a tree and yield mangoes, and so on. The first law of motion in physics states that a body continues to be in the state of rest or uniform motion unless it is disturbed by outside causes. A little thought will convince you this is only one case of the postulate of separable causal lines. We must, however, mention that the postulate does not attempt mathematical precision, and leaves this question to the respective branches of science.

The concept of causal lines can however be valid only if it is assumed that space and time are continuous. This takes us to the third postulate or the postulate of spatio-temporal continuity. If we assert that there is a causal connection between two events *A* and *B*, there should be a continuous causal link between *A* and *B*. This postulate abolishes the notion of "action at a distance" which at one time seriously blocked the progress of physics.

It must, however, be observed that this postulate can be used when a causal law is presupposed. For example, if you see *A* in London on a certain day, and another person resembling *A* in New York a week later, you cannot infer that *A* traveled to New York (as you did) unless you first verify that the person you saw in New York is really *A*.

The fourth postulate is called "structural postulate." Going back to the cricket match, there are thousands of spectators who are watching the match. They are located at different distances and in various directions with respect to the "centre" where the match is being played. Their perceptions are similar, not identical. But we have no doubt that they are observing the same event. What this means is that the structures which reach these spectators have causal lines which have a single origin having the same structure.

The last postulate is about analogy which we are omitting.[7]

13

Logical Fallacies

13.1 Classification

We have seen that there are three rules of valid inference :

1. Reason should be present in the subject of the conclusion.
2. It should be present in similar instances only.
3. It should be absent in all dissimilar instances.

When any of these rules is violated fallacy occurs. However, it is impossible to infringe the second rule without violating the third. This means we classify fallacies based on the violation of (1) and the violation of (2) or (3).

Since the minor premise has a reference to reality, its violation is called "unreal reason" (*asiddha-hetv-ābhāsa*). The major premise requires necessary dependence of the reason in the consequence. When such reason is absent there follows a fallacy of "inconsistency". (*anaikāntika-hetv-ābhāsa*)

You will recall that in Aristotelian classification there are four *figures* depending on the position of the middle term. Moreover, there are nineteen *moods* based on the quality and quantity of its constituent propositions. As we know a proposition is of four types; A, E, I, O you can try several combinations of these types. Theoretically we get 4 × 4 × 4 = 64 combinations of which only 19 are valid considering other compatibility rules. Some of the well known moods are AAA (Barbara) from the First Figure and EAE (cesare) from the Second Figure.

Indian logicians are equally at home with permutations and combinations. Dignāga prepared a table on the basis of the presence, part presence and absence of reason in similar instances and dissimilar instances. Of nine (3×3) combinations seven turn out to be fallacious. If we consider the other variable "reality" (real, unreal, partly real) we have 9×3= 27 combinations.

Dignāga's overzealous followers found that based on different criteria, the table of reasons could be expanded *ad infinitum.*

13.2 Dignāga's Hetucakra

With a slight modification Dignāga's table of reason can be elegantly depicted as follows: Each box in figure 13.1 represents two letters; the first letter is for similar instances and the second for dissimilar instances. A, S, N stand for "all", "some", "no". Thus the first row first column, is AA or "all similars and all dissimilars".[1]

AA	AN	AS
NA	NN	NS
SA	SN	SS

Fig. 13.1 Hetucakra

It is clear that there are only two cases AN and SN which are totally correct, the rest are fallacies of uncertainty. Of these the first and the third columns contain "inversions" NA and NS showing maximum deviation and are called *virudhha-hetv-ābhāsa.* The top in the first column is the case of "overwide" (*sādhāraṇa-anaikāntika*).

The central box NN is "overnarrow" (*asādhāraṇa-hetv-ābhāsa*). The remaining, SA, AS, SS are overlapping and are called *asiddha-vyatirekin.*

If we also consider another variable, reality, we will again have only two cases of reasons which are totally correct (consistent as well as real), viz. ANR, SNR (R for "real") The remaining 25 cases are fallacies.

However, most logicians consider Dignāga's compact classification most useful. It consists of four classes as follows :

A reason (1) right, i.e. real and consistent (2) unreal, or (3) inverted, or (4) uncertain, i.e. inconsistent and non-concomitant

Modern western logic has actually dispensed with many Aristotelian methods of classifying moods, fallacies, etc. But habits die hard and our colleges continue to adhere to Aristotelian approach despite superfluities and errors contained in it. Historically, Buddhist logic adopts a similar path creating a plethora of subdivisions of correct reasoning and fallacies. We shall adopt the broad criterion of validity following Dignāga though occasionally we may use subdivisions if they are historically important.

In the following, a few illustrations are furnished. Two points of comparison between Aristotelian and Buddhist syllogisms must be noted. First, western syllogism is based on material implication, while Buddhist syllogism uses concomitance. Second, a western syllogism may be valid though its premises may be false. This need not be the case with Buddhist logic.

13.3 Examples of Fallacies

E1

Whatever exists is a noneternal Ens.

(1) The chair exists.
Hence it is a noneternal Ens.

(2) Whatsoever dose not exist is not an Ens.
The chair does not exist.
Hence it is not an Ens.

(3) Whatever exists is an eternal Ens.
The chair exists.
Hence it is an eternal Ens.[2]

The syllogism (1) is correct; (2) is fallacious (unreal) since the chair does exist. In (3) the syllogism is fallacious because the major premise is wrong; there are things (like the jar) which exist but are not eternal. There is no concomitance.

(4) A substance whose properties can be apprehended anywhere is ubiquitous, like space.

The soul is a substance whose properties can be apprehended anywhere. Hence the soul is ubiquitous.

According to Buddhist theory the soul does not exist. The argument is fallacious because of unreality.[3]

(5) If there is smoke there must be fire. Hence if there is fire there must be smoke.

This is the case of wrong conversion. Every fire need not produce smoke.[3a] In Aristotalian logic it is the fallacy of inverted order. (*fallacia consequentis*)

(6) Suppose you hear a cry of a peacock. There are many caves and you are not sure in which cave the peacock is present. You pinpoint the most likely cave.[4]

Major : Wheresoever there is a peacock's cry, it is present.

Minor : The cry comes probably from that cave

Conclusion : The peacock is probably in that cave. The conclusion is only probable. However, from Dignāga's first canon this is a fallacy of unreality. Note that it is not classified as a fallacy of uncertainty.

(7) Consider the following argument :

The sounds (of the Vedas) are eternal entities.

Because they are produced by causes. Whatever is a product is an eternal entity like space.[5]

This is a fallacy because there is no concomitance, the reason is absent in all similar things like space and present in all dissimilar or non-eternal objects like chairs.

(8) The sounds (of the Vedas) are eternal entities.[6]

Because they are produced at will. Whatever is produced by human will is an eternal entity.

It has the same fallacy as (1) because the reason is absent in all similar cases (eternal objects). However, this case slightly differs from (1). The reason is present in some dissimilar class like non-eternal objects such as tables but absent in other non-eternal objects like lightning.

E2

Consider the following examples :

(1) The sounds of the Vedas are eternal entities.

Because they are cognizable.

The reason is uncertain because cognizability is equally found in eternal entities like space and non-eternal objects such as telephones.[7]

(2) An example supplied by Dharmakīrti reads as :

The sounds of speech are not produced by conscious efforts.

Because they are impermanent.

The reason impermanence is partly present in similar cases (e.g. lightning), but also partly absent (e.g. space). However, the reason is present in all dissimilar cases (e.g. pots, tables, etc.). This shows the fallacy of uncertainty.

(3) The sounds of speech are produced by an effort.

Because they are impermanent.

Here impermanence is present in some contrary cases (e.g. lightning) and absent in others (e.g. space). It is present in all similar cases since anything produced by a conscious effort is impermanent. This is a fallacy of uncertainty and is similar to Aristotle's *Fallacia Consequentis* (inverted order).[8]

(4) The sounds of speech are eternal.

Because they are not limitedly extended bodies.[9]

This again, is fallacious for uncertainty. The reason is partly present (e.g. space) and partly absent (e.g. atoms) in similar cases. In dissimilar instances we find reason present in some cases (e.g. jars) and absent in others (e.g. motion).

The above four examples are often treated as four types of the fallacy of uncertain reason and are based on Dignāga's table. Their location in the squares of the table also represents various degrees of uncertainty.

13.4 Fallacies and The Transcendent

We have already remarked that Buddhism is perceived as an agnostic credo. Despite this attitude Buddhist scholars have ventured into the areas such as afterlife, infinity of space and time, etc.

Dignāga mentions a special fallacy which is not found in his table. This is in fact an antinomy. An example of antinomy is Vaiśeṣika views on universals. Some logicians treat universals as real while others think that they are unreal. The two opposite views of the same school have almost equal strength. Such opposite opinions if tried to be tabulated *á la* Dignāga, they will have two places to occupy – (1) right reason or (2) inverted/contrary reason.

Dignāga created a special category of fallacy for such antinomy. According to him antinomies arise in metaphysics and religion. "In this world the forces of direct perception and of authority of scripture is (sometimes) stronger than any argument".[10] While Dignāga was merely mentioning the dilemma, his disciple Dharmakīrti seems to have reacted violently accusing his guru of introducing a translogical problem into the domain of logic. "When the argument is founded on the properly observed.... there is no room for antinomy".[11]

Notwithstanding his criticism against Dignāga, Dharmakīrti introduced two fallacies (which are antinomical) into logic almost surreptitiously.

Consider the following argument :

The living body is endowed with a soul. Because it possesses breath and other animal functions.

According to realists this is a valid argument, there being concomitance in "a negative way" It is usually admitted that animal function is absent in objects which possess no soul. However, Dharmakīrti does not admit "purely negative" or "purely positive" reasons. His purely logical argument is that even assuming that the soul exists somewhere, there is no clear-cut classification in which the presence of reason in similar classes only and its absence in all dissimilar classes is ensured. The fallacy arises on account uncertainty.

Dharmakīrti's second type relates to the theory of Omniscient Absolute Being.

Consider :

Some human being is non-omniscient. Because he possesses the faculty of speech and other (attributes of human being).

The presence of faculty of speech has been ascertained. Moreover, the reason cannot be said to be unreal. The reason is present in case of the similar class, viz. ordinary humans whose knowledge is limited. However, the dissimilar class creates a problem. Can we assert that there is no presence of the faculty of speech among the omniscient beings? An omniscient being is a metaphysical concept. We can neither assert nor deny the existence of such a being. This category created by Dharmakīrti does not differ much from Dignāga's antinomical variety, and is thus redundant. As Stcherbatsky rightly points out :

> All such fallacies are concerned with metaphysical objects and are problematic for that very reason. They are not strictly logical, because they transfer us beyond the sphere of logic.[12]

14

Śūnyatā, Logic and Dialectic

14.1 From *Śūnya* to Infinity

While *śūnyatā* or the philosophy of *śūnyavāda* is associated with Nāgārjuna, there is no doubt that it has roots in the word *śūnya* (void) Indians have used from time immemorial. What I am suggesting is that the concept formalized by Nāgārjuna grew out of the usage of *śūnya* by ordinary people. The word has acquired many meanings and is used in different senses in various branches of knowledge. It can mean "nothing", "useless", emptiness arithmetical zero, a zero of a scale of a physical quantity, the origin where geometrical axes meet, the nihil of western philosophy, etc. In eastern philosophies and mysticism it indicates a potential infinity. In tantra, the Great Void has a status similar to the origin of the infinite.

The concept of *śūnya* is inseparable from the pairs of opposites we find in this world : hot-cold, good-bad, love-hate and so forth. It is equally connected with such concepts as conflict, and contradiction. It is not possible to discuss the general concept of *śūnya* and its plethora of interpretations in this book.[1] Suffice it to observe that Nāgārjuna's *śūnyatā* can be traced to the inevitable association of the negative with positive. In his dialectic, the negative has as much role to play as the positive.

14.2 *Śūnyavāda* or *Mādhyamika*

Śūnyavāda does not imply denial of reality, it considers the phenominal world unreal. All phenomena are momentary, the sequence of these events is an illusion. Neither the events we perceive nor our own minds are real.

Behind this illusion lies the ultimate reality which is indescribable. Let us see how *śūnyatā* enters logic :

1) Anything that is real must not have origination or must not be conditioned. But every reality we know is dependent on some conditions. Hence anything which we call real is unreal.
2) Reality cannot be called unreal because it does exist and anything that is unreal cannot come into existence.

A careful inspection of these two contradictory conclusions would lead us to the following corollaries which appear absurd.

3) Reality is both real and nonreal.
4) Reality is neither real nor nonreal.

We recall that these two corollaries constitute two of the four arguments of *catuṣkoṭi* mentioned in chapter 2. For the time being the only conclusion we draw is that reality is indescribable.

Empirical and Transcendental

The Nāgārjunian concept of *śūnyatā* can be approached in a slightly different way. *Śūnyatā* has two different meanings :

1) It characterizes what we perceive, viz. the events which obey Gautama's law of dependent origination. We may say the phenomenal world which is momentary and conditional has an intrinsic property (*svabhāva*) called *śūnyatā.*
2) *Śūnyatā* also means Absolute Truth which is unutterable or indescribable. One can feel this state when one attains nirvāṇa.

Reason and Spirituality

Sohei Ichimura in his collection of essays, *Buddhist Critical Spirituality : Prajñā and Śūnyatā* argues that while religions in general do not tolerate revision or re-evaluation of their principles and practice, Buddhism is an exception . Gautama is said to have warned his disciples not to blindly believe in whatever he taught, and he demanded them to critically examine whatever he said by their own thought and practice before accepting it.[2] This introduces elements of rationality and experience into the doctrine but as we shall see later this methodology is not the same as the western concept of empirical verification of a scientific principle.

This means that Buddhists accept *prajñā* and *śūnyatā* as legitimate epistemic sources. This incidentally creates a new dimension, the dimension of insight, in theory of knowledge.

14.3 Communication Gap

Ichimura regards the negation of reality as a bridge between two arguments which appear to contradict each other.

Consider the well-known contradiction :

According to Naiyāyikas *śabda* (vocal word) is impermanent because it is a product. *Mīmāṃsakas* on the other hand believe that *śabda* is permanent because it is audible or communicable.

The contradiction arises clearly because despite the same word *śabda* the two schools interpret its properties differently. *Naiyāyikas* who are realists believe that whatever is produced is impermanent. Mimāṃsakas, the trascendentalists, assume that *śabda* elicits the same meaning in all human minds irrespective of the time and place of utterance. According to them whatever is audible is permanent.

The contradiction in this example arises because of the communication gap due to linguistic, cultural or doctrinal differences. Strictly speaking both these arguments are valid, in the respective systems of philosophy. The apparent contradiction is due to the difference in premises (1) what is produced is impermanent (*Nyāya*) and (2) what is audible is permanent (*Mimāṃsā*).

Buddhist logicians had a different approach to this dispute. They resolved the quarrel through a dialectical method. Ichimura attributes logical deadlock to lack of meaningful communication. He calls the *Nyāya-Mimāṃsā* dispute a case of horizontal communications. But there are also cases of vertical communications. For example, the human prayer towards Kuan-yin Bodhisattva or the Christian prayer involves both material and transcendental elements. How can we know anything about such communications?[3] In case of a Buddhist prayer how can we expect human prayer (emanating from the defiled faculty) to the reach undefiled transcendental abode?

14.4 Dialectical Solution

While today's logicians would treat *Naiyāyika-Mimāṃsaka* dispute as a mere semantic confusion, Buddhist logicians solved this problem using a transcendental dimension.

The concerned adversaries were called for a meeting. The referees told both the sides that they were right as far as their own system was concerned. But the mediators laid stress on their respective reasons, viz "being a product" and "being audible" rather than the whole syllogism. The intention was to explain that the "reasons" provided by the debating parties were not identical in meaning.

However, the Buddhists went further and tried to reconcile the two syllogisms at a point where even the ostensible contradiction disappears. As keen observers they were aware that because of several biases, perceptual and conceptual discrepancies occur in the subliminal plane of consciousness. As Ichimura points out, "Even spontaneous perception is an interpretative and unconscious version of what we do after we have perceived. It follows that whatever is asserted by naming is more than likely non-existent, because whatever is designated is a result of defiled mental propensities".[4] In effect these logicians shifted the debate to a level where both assertions could be negated because their putative realities were equally illusive.

This is a dialectical approach inasmuch as the argument of negation is extra-syllogistic. Its original source can be traced to the Master's insight of *avidyā* or ignorance especially about one's self and its "belongings" (*raya-dṛṣṭi*). In the above illustration what the Buddhists did was to highlight the theoretical virtue or the insight of non-duality or the absence of reality in all things. The concept *śūnyatā* (voidness) connotes two successive negations; those of self and skandhas. The dialectical approach is believed to exemplify this concept of voidness of reality. The problem of the "vertical communication" is also solved on similar lines.[5]

14.5 Characteristics of Dialectics

Although we have used the word "dialectic", here the concept of dialectic is slippery. It has no definite meaning. Originally it meant the art of arguing. Later it came to be used pejoratively to indicate sophistical argument. Hegel's dialectic method is well known. Most western philosophers after Hegel seem to regard examination of positive and negative sides of any argument or idea as essential to dialectics.

In Buddhism we may trace its hidden presence in Gautama's agnosticism about transcendental questions, such as "Does life exist after death"?

Madhyamikas went further and pointed out that the dilemma of "yes or no" appeared in every branch of knowledge. Most of our conceptions involve contradictions. Candrakīrti maintains that in most of our thinking process dichotomy is involved, cognition and cognized, object and subject, man and woman and so forth. These contradistinctions throw up contraradictory couples., "All worldly manifold disappears without leaving any trace in the void (of relativity). as soon as the essence of all separate existence is perceived to be relative (and ultimately unreal)".[6] However, later Buddhist logicians contended that despite contradictions in most concepts, there exists ultimate reality (thing-in-itself) behind every dialectical couple.

Dignāga is one of the most important commentators on dialectics. Dignāga added one more dimension to the Buddhist concept of knowledge being direct or indirect – knowledge derived from words is not direct, but indirect. Moreover, it is negative or dialectical. According to him the senses make pure affirmation. The intellect on the other hand is always negative. Its affirmation is never pure. It affirms its own meaning by repudiating some other meanings. Thus the concept of whiteness is invariably linked with non-whiteness. The white is cognized through non-white and the non-white through the white.

Consider the concept "having an origin". To have an origin means negation of eternity and eternity means negation of origin.[7] Stcherbatsky points out the difference between Dignāga and Hegel. For the latter, negativity is the soul of the universe. Hegel's legacy boils down to logic containing negativity. The Buddhist on the other hand recognizes reality, the ultimate reality which is purely affirmative.

Dignāga's views on universals are equally important. He rejects the thesis that names indicate universals because of "infinity and discrepancies".[8] He was against the theory that the universal is a real Ens. residing in a particular and perceived directly. The universal would then reside in infinitely many particulars which one certainly cannot perceive directly by senses.

14.6 Dignāga's Theory of *Apoha*

Dignāga's thesis that knowledge produced by words cognizes reality by the method of repudiating the contrary, i.e. negatively and dialectically was strongly supported by Jitendrabuddhi.

Jitendrabuddhi explains that repudiation of the contrary (and nothing else) of each word is nothing but the very meaning of the word. Dignāga's phrase "repudiating the contrary" is, therefore, the correct expression of what Dignāga means.

He refers to two different complementary methods used in syllogism, viz. *bhāva-abhāva* which is the same as position and contraposition or *anvaya-vyatireka*. These examples or illustrations go hand in hand. We neither express affirmation nor negation alone. There is no position without contraposition and no contraposition without position. The position expresses the meaning and the contraposition its negative.

Jitendrabuddhi makes it clear that Dignāga's theory does not suggest, as some critics allege, a total denial of every reality. Stcherbatsky captures the essence of Buddhist dialectrical method succinctly. "It maintains that all concepts and the names expressing them are negative, because they express their own meaning through a negation of the contrary".[9]

15

Anekāntavāda In Jainism

15.1 Jaina Philosophy

Anekāntavāda may be called the main pillar of Jaina philosophy. In ontology *anekānta* implies that reality has many sides. An entity can possess many characteristics. It can even be contended that an existent can be predicated in infinitely many characteristics (*anantadharmātmaka*). Jaina scholars do not believe in absolutism; rather, *anekāntavāda* implies relativism. The philosophy is often cited as an epitome of tolerance, because it condemns the attitude that a particular tenet or philosophical view is the only correct view.

Syādvāda is closely connected with *anekāntavāda.* The Sanskrit particle *syāt* has been interpreted variously as uncertain or indeterminate, and is usually used as a pejorative by skeptics. However, many scholars assure us that *syādvāda* implies relative judgement. They emphasize that "every judgement is true only of a particular aspect of the object attended to and concentrated upon and of the point of view adopted".[1]

Both *anekānta* and *syādvāda* have been interpreted in several ways. To some extent it resembles the message of *catuṣkoṭi* and some thinkers have connected it with Einstein's theory of relativity as well as quantum theory.

15.2 *Anekāntavāda*

There is no doubt that a common ground exists between *catuṣkoṭi* and *anekānta*. Both Buddhism and Jainism caution against adopting extreme views. Buddha advocated the "middle way". Mahāvīra's teachings stressed the need to see the *anekānta* and avoid clinging to one particular view. However, according to Matilal there is a difference between the solutions sought by these two religions; the former (Buddhism) avoids extremism by rejecting the extremes altogether while the latter does it by accepting both with qualifications and also by reconciling them. The hallmark of Jainism is, therefore, the attempted reconciliation between the opposites.[2]

15.3 *Syādvāda*

While *syādvāda* is bracketed with *anekānta* it is often treated as a self-sufficient tenet though allied to *anekāntavāda*. It has been interpreted in several ways. A brief account of these interpretations is given below :

1) In *Āgama* texts Mahāvīra mentions two types of knowledge, *pramāṇa* and *naya*. These texts do not use the term *syādvāda*, but the word *siyā* is found in polemics to emphasize the Jaina view that reality is manifold.
2) The term *syādvāda* seems to have been used first by Siddhasena Divākara (ca 500-600 CE). But according to Atsushi Uno, it is not clear whether this author of *Nyāyāvatāra* accepted the three divisions of knowledge (*śruta*), viz.

   i. *Mithyā-śruta* or *durnaya*
   ii. *Naya-śruta*
   iii. *Syādvāda-śruta*[3]

3) Most Jaina logicians recognize the threefold division in epistemology.

i. *Pramāṇa* concerning perception and inference
ii. *Nayavāda* or the expression of the whole aspect of reality and
iii. *Syādvāda* the expression of the partial aspect of reality.

4) *Syādvāda* is sometimes treated as verbalized views of *anekāntavāda* or non-absolutism. As such, it recognizes two valid sources

i. words of reliable persons (*āpta-vacana*).
ii. *śruta* (āgama) which is in fact indirect knowledge (*parokṣa-jñāna*) that is expressed in words.

5) *Syādvāda* is sometimes identified with *pramāṇa* (right knowledge) in contrast to *naya* (right partial view) and *durnaya* (wrong partial view).

15.4 *Saptabhaṅgī*

Syādvāda has given rise to a many-valued logic called *saptabaṅgī* ("seven-fold predication" or "seven forms of judgement"). It embodies what is called "the theory of conditional predication". Each of the seven alternatives stands with *syāt* which, as we mentioned earlier, has many interpretations. However, the interpretation "from a certain view point" seems to be preferred by most commentators. For the time being we may suppose this to be the correct meaning of *syāt* in the following alternative truth values :

A.

1 (*syāt*) the jar exists
2 (*syāt*) the jar does not exist
3 (*syāt*) the jar exists and (*syāt*) does not exist
4 (*syāt*) the jar is indescribable
5 (*syāt*) the jar both exists and is indescribable
6 (*syāt*) the jar both does not exist and is indescribable
7 (*syāt*) the jar exists, does not exist and is also indescribable

Kulkarni who seems to rely upon the above interpretation of *syāt* asks us to read each of these alternatives in conjuction with the corresponding explanations, i.e. E1 with A1 and so on.[3a]

E

1 With reference to itself
2 With reference to another
3 In succession with reference to itself and another
4 Simultaneously with reference to itself and another
5 With reference to itself and simultaneously to itself and another
6 With reference to another and simultaneously to itself and another
7 With reference to itself, with reference to another and simultaneously with reference to itself and another

Consider the first case which appears as *syād asti eva ghaṭaḥ*. The term *eva* is used as a linguistic technique for emphasis on limitation or exclusion. The existence of an entity is usually affirmed through its intrinsic (*sva*) properties, viz. substance (*dravya*), place (*kṣetra*), time (*kāla*), nature, (*bhāva, rūpa*), etc.

Thus "the jar exists as an earthern product unlike a chair made of wood". "The jar under consideration exists in, say, Kolkata, it does not exist as the similar jar in Jammu". With respect to this jar for every attribute we can have some entity "x" which does not possess this property. In other words if p is this jar having a property r, we can always have an existent q such that q does not possess r. This means that p is not q.

The second option (*syān nāsti eva ghaṭah*) can be interpreted in a similar way – "This jar does not exist *qua* human being. This jar does not exist in London" and so on.

In the third option the affirmation and negation appears successively. For example, "This pot exists (here on the table); it does not exist in the kitchen" clearly shows the interpretation of "successively".

A few commentators may claim that *syād asti nāsti ca ghaṭaḥ* implies existence and nonexistence simultaneously in the same sense. This interpretation is more in tune with *catuṣkoṭi* (third option) and is discussed later.

The fourth option involves the word *avaktavya* (*syād avaktavya eva ghaṭaḥ*). *Avaktavya* means inexpressible. It can be interpreted as "indeterminate", "undeterminable" or even "transcendental" In case of the last interpretation, the doctrine comes close to *catuṣkoṭi* and is discussed elsewhere. In case of the first two interpretations some analysis is necessary and will be found in conjunction with multi-valued logic later in this chapter. The fifth (*syād asti ca vaktavyaś ca ghaṭaḥ*), sixth (*syān nāsti cāvaktavyaś ca ghaṭaḥ*) and seventh (*syād asti nāsti cāvaktavyaś ca ghaṭaḥ*) involve simultaneity. Their interpretation is on similar lines. Note how Kulkarni avoids the transcendent in E(4) to E(7) by using "another". However, we are cautioned that without the use of *syāt* these statements become unconditional and paradoxes can arise from contradictory interpretations.

15.5 Multi-valued Logic

Usually we encounter bivalent propositions in which a proposition has only two truth values p and~p. However, in some cases we may have to deal with more options/alternatives than two. For example, you may be given three options by your employer in choosing the city where you can be located. In this case the options p_1, p_2, p_3 are mutually exclusive and p_1 would imply $\sim p_2$ and$\sim p_3$. But in some cases the alternatives need not be mutually exclusive. For example, if you win a lottery, the organizers may offer you two prize items out of three x, y, z, in which case you can have any one of the choices xy, yz, zx (x *and* y etc.). Of course, in both cases you may not exercise your right and your options will be four. What I am driving at is that as the number of alternatives is increased the symbolic expression of the problem becomes more and more difficult. For example, if we have an exhaustive system of n alternatives with different conditions or constraints attached to your choices then the problem becomes really formidable. In fact it ceases to be a problem of symbolic logic especially in such situations where the probabilities of occurrence of alternatives are different.

Instead of trying to use symbolic logic, the analyst should employ mathematical methods in operations research or similar quantitative techniques. Nevertheless, logicians have attempted the use of symbolic logic with partial success.

Let us take the case of the *saptabhaṅgī.* What is meant by *avaktavya*? Does it mean (a) indescribable in the sense of transcendental experience (b) undeterminable because of existing limitations in the scientific field?

Consider the usual ontological problem – does the human soul exist?

Some may say "yes"

Some may say "no"

Some may say "we can never know". We may take the third answer as indeterminate or transcendental. The statement "The soul exists" has multiple (truth) values : Yes, no and indeterminate.

The case (b) is slightly different. Suppose the largest prime number found till today has x digits. How many digits will the next higher prime have? Our past experience shows that sooner or later we are able to find the next greater prime. But we cannot predict when nor can we say how many digits it will have, because there is no formula for determining the next prime. We cannot even say that it will be the next higher prime.This problem is epistemic rather than logical. As Nicholas Rescher observes, "In Kleene's system a proposition is to bear the third truth value I, not for fact-related, ontological reasons, but for knowledge related epistemological ones; it is not to be excluded that the proposition may in fact be true or false, but is merely unknown or undeterminable what its specific truth-status may be".[4]

As we have already seen, a statement prefixed with *syāt* implies that there is a standpoint which makes the statement true. Most Jaina scholars treat *syāt* as "kathañcit" or "from certain viewpoint". Using this fact Gokhale has presented a model involving the existential quantifier.[5] A modified version of Gokhale's model is furnished in Appendix along with a method involving relational calculus.

Lukasiewicz in his trivalent logic has introduced a modal operator of possibility (M) and necessity(L)[6] "with a view to the future contingency interpretation of the third value I". It is discussed in Appendix.

Since there is no unanimity on the meaning of *syāt,* some critics contend that the model is not suitable for *syādvāda.*[7] We will not enter into this discussion since there can be many interpretations at various stages when something is uncertain.

15.6 *Nayavāda*

A doctrine closely related to *anekāntavāda* and *syādvāda* is *nayavāda.* Jainologists treat *nayavāda* and *syādvāda* as "varieties of *anekāntavāda*". *Nayavāda* lists seven standpoints or viewpoints mentioned below[8] [Of these 1-4 are the viewpoints of thoughts or things (*artha*) and 5 to 7 are the view points of "word" (*śabda*) each of these seven nayas reveals a part of the whole unlike *pramāṇa* which disclose the whole truth] :

1. *Naigama* (the common). This viewpoint does not distinguish between universal (*sāmānya*) and particular (*viśeṣa*) properties while referring to an entity. Of course, it does recognize that these characteristics exist, but treats them as absolute and self-sufficient.
2. *Saṃgraha* (the general) is a viewpoint which highlights the general (*sāmānya*) property ignoring the particular.
3. *Vyavahāra* (the practical) is the viewpoint of the common person who is not an expert or specialist.

4. *Ṛju-sūtra* reflects the view that "the modification (*paryāya*) exists". It refers to changing modifications rather than the abiding substance (*dravya*).
5. *Śabda* (the verbal) pinpoints differences among ostensible synonyms based on gender, number, etc. (e.g. *dārāh, patnī*).
6. *Saṃbhirūdha* (the subtle) is a standpoint which highlights nuances based on etymology among the words appearing ostensible "synonyms".
7. *Evambhūta* is a viewpoint which asserts that an entity can have a certain appellation only when it is performing a certain action and not otherwise. For example, an actor who plays the role of Rāvaṇa in a drama based on Sanskrit epic *Rāmāyaṇa* , He can be called "Rāvaṇa, the villain" only when he is playing the role.

15.7 *Eva* and *Syāt*

Eva and *syāt* are two terms which are found in *syādvāda* and often give rise to multiple interpretations. We have already mentioned *syāt* earlier. However, a deeper analysis of the usage of both these terms is needed. The views expressed in this section are borrowed from Mallisena's *Syādvādamañjarī* and Vādideva's and Vimaladāsa's interpretations.[9]

Let us re-write *Saptabhangī prmāṇa* :

1. *Syād asti eva ghaṭaḥ*
2. *Sÿan nāsti eva ghaṭaḥ*
3. *Syād asti nāsti ca ghaṭaḥ*
4. *Syād avaktavya eva ghaṭaḥ*
5. *Syād asti cāvaktavaś ca ghaṭaḥ*
6. *Syān ñasti cāvaktavyaś ca ghaṭah*
7. *Syād asti ñasti cāvaktavyaś ca ghaṭaḥ*

The term "eva" is used in *syādvāda* maxims as a qualifier in different ways.

1. It means "exclusion of unrelatedness". For example, in "This shell is simply white (*śaṅkhaḥ pāṇḍuraḥ eva*), "eva" implies that all shells are white. Its equivalent counterpositive is "if anything is not white, it cannot be a shell". This is similar to western "universal affirmative".

2. In the second case *eva* is used to exclude "anything other than substantive". For instance, "only Pārtha is the archer" (*Pārtha eva dhanurdharaḥ*). Uno uses complicated symbolization with which he himself is not satisfied.

   A simpler representation would be
   $f(x) \Leftrightarrow f(p)$
   where f(x) is "x is an archer", p means "Pārtha or Arjuna"

3. In the third case *eva* is used for "exclusion of absolute non-relatedness". For example in "The lotus is simply blue" or (*nilaṃ sarojaṃ bhavatyeva*) where *eva* refers to the negation of universal negative which is nothing but particular affirmative judgement.

15.8 *Saptabhaṅgī* : *pramāṇa* and *naya*

A two-fold division is sometimes made in respect of *saptabhaṅgī* sets :

(1) The *saptabhaṅgī-pramāṇa* whose propositions consist of the right knowledge (*pramāṇa*). This is regarded as complete statement (*sakaladeśa*).

(2) *Saptabhaṅgī-naya* in which the seven propositions are based on particular viewpoints. This kind is treated as a partial statement (*vikaladeśa*).

A complete statement simultaneously expresses infinite nature of an entity through the right knowledge. It conveys the entire reality, being the synthesis of all attributes.This reflects primacy of non-distinction (*abhedavṛtti*) over distinction, which, as it were, disappears in the union.

A partial statement emphasizes distinction, expressing attributes of an entity (such as jar) in succession with the help of a particular viewpoint (*naya*). This approach reflects *bhedavṛtti* where there is primacy of distinction over non-distinction.

The hallmark of the former is synthesis, simultaneity, non-distinction and right knowledge. The hallmark of the latter is analysis, successive enumeration, dinctinction and particular point of view. The following pairs would require exactly seven formulas to apply *syādavāda* (1) transience *(nāstitva)* and perpetuality (*nityatva*). (2) similarity (*sadṛsatva*) and diversity (*virupatva*), (3) universality (*sāmānya*) and particularity (*viśeṣa*) (4) expressibility (*vācyatva*) and inexpressibility (*avācyatva*).

For example, in (3) the seven fold formula would appear as

(1) *syāt sāmānyam*
(2) *syād viśeṣam*
(3) *syād ubhayam*
(4) *syād avaktavyam*
(5) *syād sāmānyāvaktavyam*
(6) *syād viśeṣāvaktavyam*
(7) *syāt sāmānya – viśeṣa avaktavyam*

Uno contends that the interpretation of pair-wise statements is according to the "rule of primary".[9a] For example, if particularity is primary the statement (1) above would be considered positive and (2) as negative. On the other hand if generality is in the dominance, (2) is positive and (1) negative. Quoting PNT, Uno argues that any attribute can thus be converted into a seven-fold system. [10]

According to Uno, "... the term *syāt* intends to denote equivocal (anekānta) aspect of reality from the universal point of view, and the term *asti*, etc. is employed with a view to informing the reality from a particular point of view".[11]

Verbs such as *asti* and *nāsti* by themselves indicate existence or non-existence unconditionally. In order to exclude alien natures, "eva" is employed. However, according to Uno *eva* itself may not be sufficient. In a proposition such as "a pot simply exists" (*asti eva kumbhaḥ*), *asti,* might be interpreted as unrestricted existence. It can be interpreted as say "a pot may exist as a pillar". To avoid ambiguity *syāt* is used along with *eva.* This looks strange to us, but ambiguous interpretations arise not only from the different metaphysical viewpoints but also from syntactic uncertainties.

Uno contends that the use of apparent contradictions in *syādvāda* are not confined to *asti* and *nāsti.* The rule of seven is applicable to other predications too. The determinants of the correct interpretation are time (*kāla*), nature (*ātmarūpa*), entity (*guṇin, artha,* locus of attribute), relation (*sambandha*), service (*upakāra*), locality of the entity (*guṇi-deśa*), contact (*saṃsarga),* and word (*śabda*).

A general rule is that *abheda-vṛtti* is possible only when a noumenal viewpoint (*dravyārthika naya*) is dominent and the phenomenal is viewpoint is subsidiary. On the contrary if the phenomenal view (*paryāyārthikanaya*) is important *bheda-vṛtti* is implied and attributes such as existence, etc. are considered distinct. According to Uno, "what is intended by *syādvāda* is to express neither existence nor nonexitence nor absolute identity of both from one and same point (*aṃśa*)".[11a] Existence is taken into consideration as having one condition (*svarūpa*) and nonexistence as having another condition (*para-rūpa*).

The usual criticism of this attitude by the opponents is that an entity can have contradictory characteristics. Jainas' rejonder is that such contradiction is only apparent and not real because they are ignorant of the doctrine of *syādvāda.*

15.9 Simultaneity and Succession

Uno has discussed at length the criteria to distinguish "with simultaneity" (*yaugapdyena*) from "in succession" (*krameṇa*) on several texts. We can only briefly present the gist.

The eight determinants mentioned above are employed in deciding whether an attribute like "existence" is considered distinct. One word cannot express an infinite series of attributes in the same breath, and the qualifier "in succession" is used. On the other hand when own forms of these countless characteristics are called non-distinct in reference to time, nature, etc. a single word such as existence (*asti*) implies that the entity has *ipso facto* all other characteristics. The expression "in simultaneity" is used as an adjunct.

The following illustrations should elucidate "non-distinctness"

E

(a) *Time :* You see a jar on the table. At the time of your cognition the existence of the jar implies that the remaining attributes are non-distinct from existence and the other infinite attributes exist *ipso facto.*

(b) *Locality* : Suppose an entity, say, a chair is located in this room. Its existence abides in that place. All other attributes abide in the same place and thus are non-distinct.

(c) *Contact* : Existence of an entity is in contact or inseparable from the entity. Hence the other attributes too are in contact with the entity and hence non-distinct.

(d) *Relation* : The relation between an entity and existence is "not different". Hence this relation prevails between other attributes (which are identical with the entity) too. They have the same relation with the entity, viz. nondistinct.

However, relation (*sambandha*) and contact (*saṃsarga*) are believed to have some difference. In the former, non-distinction is considered primary while in the latter it is regarded as secondary.

These examples are based on a proviso : noumenal viewpoint (*dravyārthikanaya*) is taken as primary and phenomenal viewpoint (*paryāyārthikanaya*) as secondary.

In the contrary case, the infinite attributes do not inhere in an entity, the non-distinction is unreal and superimposed on diversity (*abhedopacāra*).

While discussing Jaina concepts of *anekānta, syādvad, naya,* complete statement, etc. it is important to realize that there is no unique interpretation of a statement. A correct interpretation depends on the source (author) and context. The context in turn is a function of several provisos, conditions and exceptions.

Apparent Fallacies

Those who are ignorant of *syādvāda* often speak of the following fallacies:

1. "Contradiction" where opposite characteristics universality and particularity apear to dwell together.
2. "Nonexistence" where the loci of affirmation and negation appear to coexist.
3. "Infinite Regress" occurs when an entity is universal from one aspect and partiular from another aspect. These aspects can be correlative either because of one nature or double nature, viz. *astitva* and *nāstitva.* In the first case the fallacy of non-coexistence continues while in the second case two natures *astitva* and *nāstitva* are required. The process will continue *ad infinitum.*
4. "Confusion" arises when two contradictory aspects inhabit the same locus.
5. "Doubt" arises when the nature of an entity cannot be ascertained because of the status of the determinant is not clear.
6. "Transfusion" occurs when (a) existence is expressed wrongly by terms applicable to nonexistence and vice versa. (b) there is absence of determination. (c) determination of subjective reality is renounced.

Jainism believes in relativism or relativity. The doctrines such as *anekānta, syādvāda, saptabhaṅgī, nayavāda,* etc. reflect this philosophy. These doctrines contain mechanisms to differentiate several permissible interpretations. The general impression one gets from Jaina logic is that interpretations which are not ambiguous are prefered. Jaina logicians also seem to prefer interpretations pertaining to the empirical reality.

16

Catuṣkoṭi in Buddhism

16.1 *Catuṣkoṭi* as Extremes

The word *catuṣkoṭi* literally means four extremes. The Buddhist Middle Way teaches avoidance of extremes. Gautama exhorted his followers to abjure clinging to one particular view which provides only a partial knowledge of a thing. Those who cling to an extreme view do not recognize the possibility of alternate standpoints and seize one extreme as absolute. Nāgārjuna used *catuṣkoṭi* for various purposes, for spreading the Buddha's message, for reconciling the mundane with the transcendental, for defeating *Naiyāyikas* in many debates through *prasaṅga (reductio ad absurdum)* and so on.

These extremes can be illustrated in many quadrilemmas:[1]

1) (a) Existence (*asti, bhāva, sat*)
   (b) Nonexistence (*nāsti, abhāva, asat*)
   (c) Existence and nonexistence (*sadasat, bhāvābhāva*)
   (d) Neither existence nor nonexistence (*naivāsti, na ca nāsti*)
2) (a) Self (*sva*)
   (b) Other (*para*)
   (c) Both (*ubhaya*)
   (d) Neither-nor (*anubhaya*)
3) (a) One (*eka*)
   (b) Many (*nānā*)
   (c) Both (*ubhaya*)

(d) Neither nor (*anubhaya*)

4) (a) Identical (*tat*)
   (b) Different (*anyat*)
   (c) Both (*ubhaya*)
   (d) neither-nor (*anubhaya*)

5) (a) Self (*sva*)
   (b) Other (*para*)
   (c) Both (*ubhaya*)
   (d) Neither-nor (*ahetuka*), i.e. devoid of reason, i.e. by "chance"

16.2 The Meaning of Koṭis

First Koṭi : A exists

This reflects the viewpoint of the common person who accepts the existence of a thing as she perceives it without any analysis. This resembles naive realism to some extent. This *koṭi* is also accepted by the philosopher who analyzes the situation and concludes wrongly that whatever appears as the ultimate element in analysis is also the ultimate reality. If you perceive "A" it is A on account of its ultimate self (*svabhāva*). Such people cling to the affirmative "A exists" and are said to believe in *eternalism.*

Second Koṭi : A does not exist.

Here the person clings to the view that "A does not exist". For such a person even temporary cessations means permanent non-existence. This view is called *annihilationism.* In Buddhism this is also called *nihilism.* For nihilists the process of becoming loses relevance. The *Vaipulyaka,* one who clings to *śūnyatā* is also placed in the same category by Nāgārjuna.[2]

Third Koṭi : A exists and exists not

There are some scholars who cling to the position "A exists and exists not". This is ostensibly to bring about syncretism of the first two views "exists" and "does not exist".

Fourth Koṭi : A neither exists nor exists not

The fourth extreme -neither-nor reflects the position of total denial. Those who cling to this *koṭi* in fact have no right even to assert that a thing is not describable. If you cling to this *koṭi*, you forfeit even the right to make a statement of any knowledge, even relative knowledge. According to *Śāstra*, "it is fool's talk".[3]

Incidentally, *koṭi* also means ten million and *koṭi koṭi* in some Indic languages, implies "many", "numerous" or even "countless", e.g. *koṭi koṭi praṇāma* (*praṇāma*, for "obeisance or salutation") *Catuṣkoṭi* thus can be interpreted as "logical ground with four boundaries". K. Venkata Ramanan has rendered an excellent analysis of the third and fourth *koṭis* which appear ambiguous to the common person. He compares Buddhist ideas with Jainas' doctrine in respect of "is and is not"

According to him Jainas are epistemically relativists, but metaphysically pluralist. He points out a hole in Jainas' logic : "Their position is very unstable, to take relativism seriously is to deny ultimacy of difference and with the denial of ultimacy of difference plurality cannot stand. On the contrary, if they take pluralism seriously they cannot be relativists".[4] If Jaina scholars have reconciled this dichotomy, it shows their pragmatic approach which is possible because of the very ambiguity inherent in linguistic expressions "is and is not", "neither is nor is not", etc. We may call Jaina approach as the common man's way. This is precisely why their scholars tend to avoid transcendence and uncertainty as far as possible.

On the other hand, Buddhists despite being agnostic, prefer to discuss the transcendental dimension of the last two *koṭis*. This leads to many schools of interpretations. However, they also try to solve this problem at the subliminal level, so that the dilemma of alternative interpretations is avoided, but their logic often appears to enter the territory of mysticism.

16.3 *Koṭis* as Alternatives

The alternative statements such as "is", "is not", "is and is not", "neither is nor is not" need not always be extremes. Acording to K. Venkata Ramanan, "The alternative statements are different from the extremes precisely because the former are specific judgements made with the unmistakable awareness of other possibilities from other standpoints and their reflective judgements are pertinant to the mundane truth, the level of the relative".[5]

Kārikā mentions several teacings of the Buddha which involve contradictions. Thus "The Buddha has taught (of existence) of self as well as of non-existence of self; He has also taught of neither self nor no self".[6] (XVIII:6)

"Everything is true; nothing is true; everything is both true and not ture; everything is neither true nor not true. This is the teaching of the Buddha".[7] (XVIII.8)

K. Vankata Ramanan explains that if there were clinging, each one of the positions would become extreme and hence false. However, in absence of clinging there are no extremes, they are not wrong because they became mere alternatives or other possibilities : each of which is true and all are true.

According to him rejection of extremes does not mean rejection of the basic law of thought. The same animal cannot have and not have the horns on his head, and the ring finger is both long and short from different standpoints.

However, Buddhist scholars make it a point to emphasize that falsifications such as clinging to *koṭis* are relevant only for mundane events. The Middle Way does not reveal the ultimate truth. Being of conditioned origin it belongs to the phenomenal level. At this level what is important is the realization that alternatives are in the relative dimensions. However, at the level of transcendence or ultimate reality the contradiction "is and is not", "neither is nor is not" become irrelevant, not false.[8]

16.4 *Catuṣkoṭi* at two Levels

A logical deadlock often results from the lack of communication between two religions and also between two sects of the same religion. More often than not the cause relates to different meanings attached to the same words and expressions by various logical schools. Further, religious or transcendental premises cannot be proved and unless two debating parties subscribe to the same set of premises, confrontation is bound to ensure. We shall see later how scholars like Nāgārjuna tackled this logical impasse.

It is worth quoting Arnold Kunst in *The Concept of the Principle of Excluded Middle in Buddhism.*

> "It is permissible *in universo* to juxtapose against reality two arguments which appear contradictory to prove one thesis and it is permissible to pose one argument to prove two theses which appear mutually exclusive. It is not permissible to do so at the same time in one system, which as it were, assumes under these circumstances the weight of reality in the form of an adopted set of dogmas, doctrines or conclusions (*siddhānta*) whichever may be applicable".[8a]

Buddhist scholars, Indians as well as Chinese, sought to shift the problem to the subliminal stage where logical, linguistic and cultural differences do not create any obstacles. Śākyamuni's *catuṣkoṭi* affords a source to these scholars for this purpose. This four-fold truth value system offers four options (1) A (2) not-A (3) A and not-A (4) neither A nor not-A instead of the usual logical options A or not-A.

Language is a system consisting of symbols governed by semantic (pertaining to meaning) and syntactic (pertaining to the arrangement of symbols) rules. As Ichimura rightly observes, "Functionally naming an object by a symbol is referential, and linking another symbol to it is tendentious or purposive".[9]

We have already mentioned that a name A is always accompanied by its negative-A consciously or unconsciously. *catuṣkoṭi* helps those investigators explore two different levels of knowledge. First, at the conscious level, conventions to determine whether the propositional connection is valid or invalid on the basis of appropriate linkage of the universal. (e.g. "whatever is a product is impermanent") with its reference (e.g. a vocal word). Second, at the subliminal level where one's consciousness is decoupled from logic and language "no singular propositional linkage is ascertained, precisely because what is out there in convention as *A* is accompanied by its opposite *-A* resulting in the loss of referential existence".[10]

Thus there seem to be two levels of validity; one dependent on convention (*vyavahāra*) and the second is insight (*paramārtha*). These two terms are clearly explained in Nāgārjuna's *Mādhyamikaśāstra*:

> In teaching the doctrine (*dharma*) the Enlightened ones rely on the two truths, empirical (*vyavahāra or saṃvṛti-satya*) and transcendental (*paramārtha satya*). Those who do not differentiate these two truths do not understand the profound reality (*tattva*) in the doctrine of the Buddha. Without relying on the empirical truth the transcendental truth cannot be shown; without relying on the transcendental truth, the *nirvāṇa* cannot be realized.[11]

The insight that both these truths need be understood is called *dvaya-satya.* However, Buddhists do not consider these two realms of truth as totally independent – their relationship is best described dialectically as "simultaneously identical (immanent) and different (transcendent)" or "neither identical nor different".[11] Most Buddhists whether Indian, Chinese or Japanese seem to accept these two alternatives which characterize the unconventional *catuṣkoṭi.* These alternatives also appear to be implied in *pratītyasamputpāda, śūnyatā* and *tathatā* or "thusness". But ambiguity seems to be central to *catuṣkoṭi.* Consider what Nāgārjuna says in *Madhyamakakārikāśāstra*:

> Despite the fact that from the point of view of conventional truth (*vyavahāratas*) the realms of *saṃsāra* and *nirvāṇa* ought to be clearly distinguished. However, Nāgārjuna declares that (from the point of view of transcendental truth or *paramārthas*) no such distinction exists.[12]

The doctrine of dual truth has motivated some Buddhist scholars to attempt to bridge the gap between these two truths. In the well-known Buddhist expression, "the higher truth is immanent and transcendent simultaneously in the lower truth"[13], they posit that the dual structure is formed in the prelinguistic and post-linguistic mental processes. Both Indian and Chinese philosophers have contended that these two realms of reality coexist peacefully. Thus *tathābhūta, tathatā* and *paramārtha* are in concord with *loka-saṃvṛti* or *vyavahāra.* Fa-tsang (643-713) was a highly respected Huy-yen patriarch. He used the word *wu-ai* for perfect interaction between the phenomenal world (*hsiang*) and the transcendental world (*hsing* or *li*).

We have already pointed out that simultaneous existence of two worlds, transcendental and empirical creates many problems in logic. Most Buddhist logicians such as Dignāga and Dharmakīrti accept only two methods of cognition, viz. direct perception and inference.

(1) Direct perception (*pratyakṣa*) which we have seen, emanates from a chain of momentary beings. Here the perceived object (before it is clothed with constructive elements of the mind) is not only momentary but insubstantial without qualities which is believed to communicate with us only at the sensory level. What's more, this being belongs to the ultimate reality.

(2) Inference (*anumāna*) involves logico-lingual processes. This cognition belongs to the empirical world.

According to Nāgārjuna's thinking, the *pratyakṣa* which is nondualistic (*nirvikalpa*) activates the mind to create the semblance of two opposite correlates such as light and dark.[14] It seems, of the pair, the mind selects the dominating element for assertion, negating the other (e.g. asserting dark and negating light or vice versa). This process (*nāmakalpanā*) involves psycho-physical elements (*upādāya-skandha*) and indicates reciprocal functional relationship between a symbol say x and its negative -x.

16.5 Buddhist-Jaina Interaction

Those who study both Buddhist and Jaina logic have little doubt that each school influenced the other. It is interesting to understand their interaction which helps us have a greater insight into both these heretic schools of Indian logic.

It is usually agreed that the first four stages of Jaina *saptabhaṅgī* were developed by Mādhyamika Buddhists. The first two classes *sat* and *asat* are found in the Vedas, Upaniṣads and orthodox schools of philosophy owing allegiance to the Vedas.

That *sat* and *asat* could dwell together was asserted by Buddhist Mādhyamikas. Śaṅkarācārya, the renowned monist, was vehemently against the idea that two contradictory attributes could be present at the same time and same place. Mādhyamikas had to create two more categories to complete the system of *catuṣkoṭi – sat, asat, sat-asat,* neither-*sat*-nor-*asat.* Though Jainas adopted these four steps from Buddhists, to build their *saptabhaṅgī,* there was a fundamental difference. According to Venkatachalam, Jainas based their logic on their belief that existence and non-existence could be found at one locus at different times or conditions. Buddhists, on the other hand, maintained that existence and non-existence could be found simultaneously at the same locus.[15] This difference is of considerable importance to us. The common person can appreciate *saptabhaṅga* as conditional statements or different views keeping away the transcendental out of logic and epistemology. Barring a minority, most Jaina scholars prefer to retain the common man's interpretation. Even *avyakta* can be treated as a mere epistemological unknown as was pointed out earlier. When we come to the scientific topics, we will find that Jaina *syādvād* can be interpreted without entering the field of mysticism.

16.6 Genesis of Buddhist-Jaina Logic

Bhagchandra Jaiṇ in his paper "Rudiments of *Anekāntavāda* in Early Pali Literature" describes how the multi-view logic evolved in India. His views are based on early Pali literature.

He points out that Śākyamuni used the word *anekaṃsikā* to emphasize that all non-categorical statements need not be either true or false. This is similar to Jaina's *anekāntavāda,* but Jainas hold that all statements can have the potential of knowing the reality from one or more standpoints. *Anekānta* in general asserts truth of different standpoints.

Pali texts mention ten possible ways of claiming knowledge, which are found in the Buddha's sermons. One of them is *nayahetu* which is also mentioned in *Jātaka.* Jainas assert that Buddhists were influenced by the Jaina concept of *nayavāda.* The kindred concept of *syādvāda* has roots in Jainism which is treated as pre-Vedic religion. Originally there appear to be three-fold philosophy mentioned by Dighanakha :

1. I agree with all views
2. I agree with no views
3. I agree with some views and disagree with other views.[16]

These three alternatives resemble the first three options of *saptabhaṅgī.* Gautama found these options inadequate to answer some questions and he adopted the four-fold logic :

1. *Atthi* (it is)
2. *Natthi* (it is not)
3. *Atthi ca natthi ca* (It is and it is not)
4. *Na ca atthi na ca natthi* (It neither is, nor is not)

Miyamota observes that Jainas' *saptabhaṅgī* is equivalent to Buddha's four-fold logic such that the first three *bhaṅgas* are the first three steps while the next four *bhaṅgas* together are equivalent to the Buddha's fourth predication. But according to Bhagchandra Jain this is not tenable. He maintains that the first four bhangas are similar to the four-fold Buddhist scheme. The three subsequent *bhaṅgas* are Jainas' additioanal propositions derived from further studies. According to him all the seven propostitions could be true from relative standpoints while in Buddhist scheme only one proposition could be true. The propositions are not considered logical alternatives in Jainism in contrast to Buddhist views.[17]

We may conclude this brief genesis by mentioning five developmental stages of *anekāntavāda* as conceived by Bhagchandra Jain[18]:

1. *Ekaṃsavāda-Anekāntavada* : Early Jainas classified statements as (a) *ekaṃsikā dhamma* (b) *anekaṃsikā dhamma.*
2. *Sat-asat-ubhayavāda*
3. *Avaktavya* which we have already analyzed in detail (chapter 15).
4. *Saṭabhaṅgī* detailed in chapter 15.
5. Two-fold *naya* and seven-fold *naya*, which we have considered earlier.[19]

17

Logical Impasse

17.1 *Pudgala* and Nāgārjuna's Solutions

We pointed out in chapter 7 that the Buddhist attitude towards the transcendent was agnostic. Nevertheless the transcendent is introduced sometimes either as an axiom (e.g. ultimate reality) or goal (attaining, say, *nirvāṇa*). Being a religion based on ethical foundation, it cannot escape transcendental concepts.[1] But as an empirical system it cannot totally ignore concepts born in what a common person calls reality. When the transcendent and reality come together there is bound to be a deadlock in logic.

The concept of *anātman* implies that, we cannot conceive of an entity or an individual whose biography we can clearly narrate. This is a serious handicap for any Buddhist scholar who wants to express anything about an entity which an ordinary person calls a specific individual, say, Bhāskara I or Varāhamihira. What's more, since even a Bhāskara or Varāhamihira is ever changing we cannot even use a common name "person" for the "doer" or "actor". *Pudgala* which is a semi-person was possibly created for this purpose. The concept of *pudgala* (*puggala*) as an empirical self, though conditional, was also needed to bridge the gap between the mundane and the transcendental. *Pudgalavādins* found in *Kathāvatthu* a passage :

"There is the person who works for his own good. And material quality is known in the sense of a real and ultimate fact".[2]

Kathāvatthu refers to "pudgala" quite often as the word used by the Buddha himself for a hypothetical conditioned self.

The orthodox *Thervādins* continued to maintain that neither *ātma* nor semi-empiral *pudgala* existed. *Pudgalavādins,* on the other hand, contended that *pudgala* was a semi-trans-empirical agent coexisting with transcendental entities such as *rūpa, dhammas,* etc. *Kathāvatthu* discusses a full-blown controversy between *Thervādins* and *Pudgalavādins* involving two classes of entities :

1. The empirical person who carries with him psycho-physical elements such as *rūpa-dhamma.*
2. Trans-empirical *dhammas* (*rūpa, vedanā,* etc.) which are believed to be known in the sense of genuinly real thing.

These classes are not well-defined and appear to overlap.

17.2 *Thervādins* vs *Puggalavādins*

Thervādins tried to create two classes which they erroneously thought were mutually exclusive :

1. x (subject) is known as a genuinely real thing.
2. x is known in the same way as a genuinely real thing is known.

Let us call these propositions p(x) and q(x). *Thervādins* (T) questioned *Puggalavādins* (P) as follows :

T : Is *puggala* (y) known as a genuinely real thing?

P : Yes (= p(y))

T : Is puggala known in the same way as a genuinely real thing (e.g. dhamma) is known?

P : No (= -q(y))

T : You are wrong. If you affirm the first position as p(y), you should also affirm the second proposition "q(y) ". Your position has become p(y) .-q(y) since you negated the second position . If you negate q(y) you should negate p(y) too in which case you would get -q(y) .-p(y).[3] This contradicts your answer "p(y).-q(y) ".

Thus *Thervādins* appeared to win the first round of disputation. Not to be outdone, *Pudgalavādins* used a similar strategy to turn the tables :

P : Is *puggala* not known as genuinely real thing?

T : No, it is not so known (-p(y)).

P : Is *puggala* not known in the same way as a real thing is known?

Thervadins were confused because unreality of *puggala* (empirical self) is known through the same trans-empirical insight in which rūpa-dhamma, etc. are identified as real.

T : Yes it is not not so known in the same way (i.e. q(y), because of double negation).

P : If you negate our thesis, our first proposition p(y) then you should also negate the second (so that -p(y).-q(y)).[4] But you negated the first and affirmed the second (so that -p(y).q(y). If on the other hand, you wish to affirm the second proposition, you should also affirm the first (giving q(y).p(y) which contradicts -p(y).q(y). You have lost your case.

It is not difficult to trace the reason why the logic has failed in the above case. In any debate between two parties it is essential that every term and expression in an argument is understood by both the parties in the same sense. In case of the two disputing parties their premises should be the same and logical tests should be identical. If this does not occur there is a communication gap leading to blind alleys.

17.3 *Mādhyamika's* Dialectic

Mādhyamika's solution to such problems is based on creating similar and dissimilar instances and using the technique of *anvaya* and *vyatireka* without ambiguity.

In the above case, *Puggalavādins* treated *puggala* as belonging to the same class as trans-empirical dhamma for p, but for q they treated puggala belonging to the empirical class giving p.-q.

Thervādins made a similar mistake. They denied p but affirmed q, i.e., treated *dhamma* and *pudgala* as vipakṣa for p but *sapakṣa* for q. This made them posit -p.q.

This is not the end of the story. There was the third and the fourth round, viz. *Puggalvādins'* refutation and *Puggalavādins'* application, and finally *Puggalavādins'* conclusion. For details you may refer to Ichimura's complete "Table of Mutual Invalidation".[5]

Actually Nāgārjuna provided a solution to *pudgala* controversy in Śāstra, chapter 10 (Examination of Fire and Fuel) in which he used metaphors "fire" for *pudgala* and "fuel" for psycho-physical elements of *skandhas.* Combustion occurs when fire and fuel are in contact. In the same way *pudgala* is activated when it is carried with *skandhas.* His argument runs as follows : [6]

1. If fire is identical with fuel it means the agent (fire) is identical with the object being burnt. If fire is different from fuel, there should be fire without fuel. In the latter case fire would continue to burn for ever without any fuel or without the necessity of burning fuel again. It would be one without any function.

If the fuel which is being burnt is identical with fire, when the fuel is being burnt alone, with what agent could it be burnt further?

If fuel is different, fire cannot reach it and the unreached cannot be burnt. Moreover, whatever abides unburnt cannot be extinguished, being inextinguishable, it must remain like one which is self-existent (*svaliṅgavān*). (V5)

Nāgārjuna's dialectic involves weighing pros and cons, positive and negative sides of a proposition. The following verses characterize his technique.

If fire depends on fuel and vice versa, which one of these should come into existence first; depending on which does fire burn fuel? (V8)

Fire does not arise by depending on fuel, nor does it arise without depending on fuel, nor is fuel burned depending on fire, nor does it burn without depending on fire. (V12)

Fire does not arise from anything other than itself, nor is fire found anywhere in the fuel. Of this fuel every alternate feature has already been said just as it was examined in the passage of, present past and future of motion. (Here chapter II "Examination of past and future motions" V.13 is recalled)

Finally fuel is not fire nor is fire found elsewhere other than fuel. Fire does not possess fuel, nor is fuel found in fires, nor is fire found in fuel. (V.14)

Let us see what Nāgārjuna has achieved. This is not just *prasaṅga vākya (reductio ad absurdum)* simpliciter. Through metaphor of fire (*pudgala*) and fuel (*skandhas*), he has juxaposed two contradictory propositions. Earlier the logical method of *anvaya* and *vyatireka* created a deadlock because of the ambiguity in the very concept of *pudgala.* Here Nāgārjuna adopted a dialectic method. The audience is presented with two contradictory statements which are equally true (or equally false). The upshot of his dialectic is that fire and fuel appear simultaneously identical and different. This introduces a dual-natured variable.

Ichimura emphasizes that Nāgārjuna's dialectic is anchored in logic of similar-dissimilar classes. According to him "inducing a contradiction in the logico-linguistic sphere of the mind to bring about total identification within the referential sphere of the mind, is effectively the same thing as shifting the matter toward the trans-empirical sphere". [7]

17.4 Nāgārjuna's Refutation of *Nyāya*

The following illustration shows how Nāgārjuna used his dialectic to refute Naiyāyikas' logic. The metaphor of light and darkness is often used to refer to the contrasting couples such as good-bad in most philosophies. However, according to Nāgārjuna the dichotomy of the world in the pairs of opposites can best be understood by analyzing both sides rather than having a one-sided view. *Naiyāyikas* adhered to the system of *pramāṇa* or "instrument". The cognition of an object take place by the cognitive instrument. The candleflame is identified with the faculty of cognition and darkness stands for the object in this metaphor. The cognitive faculty and the object are believed to "meet"; somehow.

The system of *pramāṇa* is based on a grammatico-linguistic principle, viz syntactical categories (*kāraka*) and significative power (*samākhyānimitta*) of linguistic symbols. In *Nyāyasūtra* Nāgārjuna's thoughts are concisely parahrased :

> Perception cannot be established in past or future because it arises only from the contact of sense-faculty and its object which is confined to the present moment. But if perception and its object are simultaneous, since there is a fixation between cognition and its object there is no successive occurrence of cognition.[8]

Vātsyāyana's argument against *Mādhyamikas* is that the role of the *pramāṇa* is not confined to the present moment so long as it is fixed to the syntactical category (*kāraka*). A musical instrument is a *pramāṇa* for producing sound, but the latter can be seen as a *pramāṇa* for identifying the instrument. Depending on the context, *pramāṇa* and *prameya* are interchangeable. Vātsyāyana further contends that both *pramāṇa* and *prameya* are equally involved in the realiztion of action (*kriyāsādhana*), though the former is regarded as a means of cognition (*upalabdhisādhana*) whereas the latter is regarded as object (*upalabdhiviśeṣa*).

The contentious issue here is "whether *pramāṇa* and *prameya* are fixed in a given syntactical context and whether they reciprocate their functional identities within one and the same context".[9]

In *Vigrahavyāvartani*, Nāgārjuna poses a difficult question – "Is *pramāṇa*, say, perception is self understood? If not, there should be a need of another set of *pramāṇas* to understand the initial set of cognitions and *ad infinitum*",[10] Naiyāyikas invented a plausible explanation using the metaphor of candle-light : the light illumines itself as well as others. This is a self-reflexive apprehension.

Nāgārjuna's argument is based on similar classes (*sapakṣa*) and dissimilar classes (*vipakṣa*) used in the positive instantiation (*anvaya*) and its contraposition (*vyatireka*) though there is no explicit reference to this methodology. Inchimura presents the arguments based on Nāgārjuna's *Vigrahavyāvartani*:[11]

(1) p is the proposition "light illuminates itself" (2) q is the proposition "light illuminates others" (3) x represents an entity *sapaksa* with "light" (4) y is a variable entity belonging to the *vipakṣa* (dark) light and dark are believed by Naiyāyikas to meet at a point establishing a contact. Nāgārjuna's argument based on the concomitance of these two propositional functions have a reference to the same spatiotemporal region.

Karika 36 – *Anvaya* and *Vyatireka* co-present
Where total contradiction results $(x)\ [p(x).q(x)].\ (y)[-q(y).-p(y)]$
Light illuminates itself and others $(x)\ [p(x).q(x)]$
Dark obstructs similarly $(y)\ [-q(y).-p(y)]$
(Dark and light are taken as opposite to each other)
Karika 37 – (*Anvaya* only, *vyatireka* negated)
Where x illuminates itself and others $(x)\ [p(x).\ q(x)]$
Dark is not operative $-[(y)\{-q(y).-p(y)\}]$
Hence how can light illuminate anything? $(xy)\{p(xy).q(xy)\}$
Karika 38 – (*Anvaya* and *vyatireka* present)
Does light illuminate dark at the moment of arising?
$(x)\ [p(x).q(x)]$
No Light does not reach it from the beginning
$(y)\ [-q(y).-p(y)]$
Conclusion – *There is total contradiction*
$(x)\ \{p(x).q(x)\}.(y)\ \{-q(y).-p(y)\}$

Karika 39 – *Anvaya* only, *vyatireka* negated
If light illuminates dark without reaching it (x) [p(x).q(x)]
Dark cannot be in operation -[(y){-q(y).-p(y)}]
This light is supposed illuminate all the world (xy) {p(xy).q(xy)}
Ichimura supplies two more arguments which relate to *Karika* 37 and 39 – It would be interesting to present them :

K 37C *Vyatireka* only (*anvaya* negated)
Whenever dark y obstructs from both (y) [-q(y).-p(y)}
No light is capable of illuminating -[(x){p(x).q(x)}]
How can light illuminate anything? (yx){-q(yx).-p(yx)}
K39 C *Vyatireka* only, *Anvaya* negated (y) {-q(y). -p(y)}
If dark destroys light without reaching it
No light is supposed to be capable of illuminating
-[(x){p(x).q(x)}]
This dark is supposed to obstruct light in all world
(yx) [-q(yx).-p(yx)]

It is interesting to see how Nagarjuna draws a conclusion from the above arguments in his autocommentary[11a] above. *Pramāṇa* and *prameya* cannot exist by themselves, since they interact (*sūtra* 2). When there is *prameya,* a *pramāṇa* becomes a (real) *prameya.* (Thus) the *pramāṇa* is established by (the function of) the *prameya.* Thus by being mutually dependent, each one obtains its own existence as *prameya* or *pramāṇa.* Therefore (one and same) *pramāṇa* becomes both and so does *prameya.* Thus *pramāṇa* and *prameya* are established upon reciprocal dependence (*apekṣasiddhi*) and are brouht into existence through mutual dependence (*anyonyotpādaka*). Therefore *pramāṇa* cannot be established independently.[12]

17.5 Nāgārjuna and *Mādhyamika*

Nāgārjuna is regarded as the greatest *Mahāyāna* thinker and the founder of *Mādhyamika* school. He also authored many books, mentioned in chapter 8. However there are many controversies relating to his identity, writings and other dates.[12] Some scholars even believe that there were more Nāgārjunas than one.

For us his treatises *Suhṛllekha* and *Ratnāvalī* are important. The first contains a few rules about the king's moral religious behavior. The king is advised to judge situations as well as people by using the logic of *catuṣkoṭi,* viz. x is A, x is not-A, x is A and not -A, x is neither A nor not -A.

This has a four-fold truth value and is more flexible than the usual two value-system – x is A, or x is not A. Though it violates the usual laws of logic, it can be used when a judgment involves matters that are ambiguous, transcendental, unintelligible or oscure and even those empirical things whose knowledge is not easily accessible.

According to one legend Nāgārjuna did not fully understand the Mahāyāna doctrine taught by an old monk, and hence he went to the Nāga king's palace at the bottom of the ocean. He studied Mahāyāna texts at the king's library for ninety days. Then came the insight which is transcendent and two-fold :

Dharmas neither arise nor perish. They are neither non-arising nor non-perishing. This insight of *śūnyatā* according to Ichimura is two-fold :

> (1) The insight which repudiates arising non-perishing regarding all phenomenal elements and simultaneously (2) that further liberates the logico-linguistic process of holding on the thoughts of non-arising and non-perishing.[13]

In other words this insight into *śūnyatā* leads to a *catuṣkoṭi* type logic – you see all phenomena not only as neither arising nor perishing but also neither non-arising nor non-perishing. Those who realize this actually understand them as "pure and immaculate" like *nirvāṇa.* This indicates that they have reached the first stage of Bhodisattva characterized by non-falling back.

Ichimura considers various points in relation to Nāgārjuna's dialectical method in the above illustration. Briefly,

(1) The affirmative (xy) {p(xy).q(xy)} and negative (yx) {-q(yx).-p(yx)} are both derived from the respective contrapositions.

(2) While x and y are mutually exclusive (similar and dissimilar classes) they are copresent in both cases. The only conclusion we can draw from this contradiction is that x and y are identical as well as different simultaneously. This looks absurd. (see 3 below)
(3) According to Nāgārjuna, *pramāṇa* and *prameya* cannot exist by themselves since they interact. This is a case of *apekṣasiddhi* or reciprocal dependence, and their existence results from mutual dependence (*anyonyotpādaka*).
(4) Nāgārjuna's method was facilitated through the insight that any given moment in consciousness is dualistic having *anvaya* and *vyatiraka* as momentary components.
(5) Nāgārjuna realized that our linguistic statement "light illumines darkness" has no independent referential object.

There is no doubt that the Nyāya argument had an inherent self contradiction and the phenomenon of "light illumines darkness" can be appreciated if the variables are considered functionally dependent.

However, Nāgārjuna's solution though ingenious has a stamp of pre-scientific thinking and displays his desire to adhere to the doctrine of momentariness which is a transcendental premise. Without prejudice to the belief in the epistemic truth of instantaneous beings, it is possible to explain both the problems, one relating to the sound and the other concerning light-dark interaction.

The first controversy can be easily tackled if we explain to both Naiyāyikas and Mimāṃsakas the communication gap : the meaning of "sound" and the corresponding premises linking sound with permanence / impermanence. The second controversy arises from the lack of scientific knowledge regarding the nature of light and dark. Different shades of light or darkness merely indicate, the intensity of the "visible" light or a certain range of electromagnetic radiation. There is a single variable, say, p which shows the intensity of light at any given point which is a function of location (r) or (x, y, z) Its value p(r) can be determined if we know the initial values of p(r) before the light source of the known power is introduced. From the viewpoint of science it is necessary to realize that only one variable is involved : the concept of light-dark should be replaced by the intensity of light at a point. The intensity varies inversely as the square of the distance from the source.

Nevertheless, given the level of physics that existed when Nāgārjuna lived, his conclusion relating to interdependence is a remarkable advance in logic and epistemology. What's more in his dialectic he seems to anticipate the logical method of *anvaya* and *vyatireka* which came into existence after Dignāga.

18

Logic and Dialectic Outside India

18.1 Confucius and Motzŭ

Confucius (ca 450 BCE) the renowned philosopher was a teacher of young aristocrats. He is regarded as a moralist who tried to replace traditional religious practices by a socio-political system based on moral values. He also taught that abstract systems are not useful unless the actions of individuals are interpreted taking into consideration the circumstances attending their behaviour. Though this thinking involves the elements of pragmatism, the base of his philosophy was morality. In his way (tao) he stressed the importance of benevolence (jen) and reciprocity) (shu).

Motzŭ (ca 480-390) is usually looked upon as Confucius' rival. He adhered to utilitarian philosophy. According to him :

> Any principle which can elevate conduct should be perpetuated. That which cannot elevate conduct should not be perpetuated. To perpctuate anything that cannot elevate conduct is nothing but waste of speech.[1] However unlike Confucius who advocated "graded love" depending on the remoteness of relationship, Mohists believed in "universal love".

In the domain of logic Confucius found that the significance of names or predicables could be used to classify things and actions. However, such a criterion sometimes leads to some "predicated" becoming empty.[2] According to Ichimura, Motzŭ developed a system of logic, perhaps the only indigenous system in the history of Chinese logic. He quotes Hu Shih who implicitly defines inferential logic.

> The reasoner ought to note and observe the happenings (literally, "becoming so") of all things, seek the order or relation between the various judgements, define the subject with the predicate to express his meaning in a proposition by giving the reason (i.e. by the statement to begin "because" (*ku*) in a premise and support the reason-conclusion relation *by selecting instances on the principles of agreement (t'ung) and difference (i)*.[3]

It is easy to see that *t'ung* and *i* are similar to *anvaya* and *vyatireka.* Thus the Mohist inference fairly agrees with Indian logic especially post-Dignāga Buddhist method of presenting inferential logic in two steps.

18.2 Sêng Chao

Chinese logic resembles its Indian counterpart to a great extent. It may be recalled that Indian syllogism containing *anvaya* and *vyatireka* combines inductive and deductive procedure. While Mohists did not resort to dual instantiation, their method contained *Hsiao* statement expressing a proven inductive relation based on the universal agreement and difference.

By the sixth century the Chinese had fully accepted *Mahāyāna* as a doctrine superior to *Hīnayāna. Mahāyāna* insight of *dharma-śūnyatā* (*king hing*) is considered higher than *Hīnayāna's dharmasvabhāva.* They also embraced the concept of *Bodhisattva-yāna.* This path prescribed six forms of virtues mentioned in *Prajñāpāramitā-sūtras* to which four more were added later. These Ten *Pāramitās* were meant for "one who seeks to realize ultimate insight" (*bodhi-sattva, p'u-sa*).[4] A unique feature of these *Pāramitās* is that they do not prescribe detailed actions to be taken by a Bodhisattva – he uses his insight of *śūnyatā* for this purpose, in specific cases. This special ability helps a Bodhisattva help others and it operates at both levels, empirical and transcendental.

Sêng-Chao (384-413) was a Taoist who converted to Buddhism. He approached the dialectic by a route that differed from Nāgārjuna's *reductio ad absurdum* (*prasaṅga-vākya*). His method involves a paradoxical conclusion. In fact this method is adopted by many philosophers who reach blind alleys in solving riddles especially of transcendental nature. We will see later that modern scientists facing the quantum conundrums have turned to eastern philosophy which temptingly offers a solution in contradictions.

According to Ichimura our use of language is responsible for some misconceptions. We are so attuned to this linguistic influence that we reflexively feel that things exist according to what we learn through language.[5] Seng-chao used the insight of *śūnyatā* to explore the subliminal mind He presented a number of paradoxes which had contradictory arguments but related to a single reference.

Two of the paradoxes may be quoted :

1. "If we want to express the real (*chên*) we go against convention (*su*). If we follow convention, we fail to express the real... When people say that things are abiding (*chu*) I say that they are 'gone' (*c'hü*) When they say that things are 'gone', I say they are 'abiding'. Although 'gone' and 'abiding' are different in expression, what they mean points to a single reference".[6]
2. "... Accordingly the large *Prajñāpāramitā-sūtra* (*ta-p' in-pan-jo*) says : Dharmas are called metaphorically as 'unreal' (*chia-ho-pu-chê n*) just as a magically created man is. For we cannot say that there is no magically created man, but only that such is not a real man".[7]

Sêng, influenced by Nāgārjuna and Mahāyāna philosophers in China realized that insights offered by (1) Dependent Origination (*pratītyasamputpāda or y' uan-ch' i*) (2) *śūnyatā* (*kung-hsin*) (3) *prajñapti* (chia-she) or linguistic practicality and (4) *madhyama (chung-tao)* had a large identical or complementary contents. The *T' ien-t' ai* school founded by Chih-i flourished about a century and a half after Sêng-Chao. Chih-i's system was based on Nāgārjuna's concepts of *śūnyatā, prajñapti* and *madhyamā.* Briefly, "all phenomena are initially identified directly with Dependent Origination (*yüan-ch'i*). Secondly, they are directly identified with emptiness (chi-k'ung); third, they are directly identified with linguistic convention; fourth, they are directly identified with Middle or the transcendent (*chi-chung*)".

This is a system where starting with the human defilement, the students progressively acquire higher insight till they reach the last stage where they see things "as they are" (*tattvasya lakṣaṇam*) – totally free, but in harmony.[8] This is the realization of Middle Path according to Chih-i.

Why did Sêng-Chao adopt the method of paradox instead of using Nāgārjuna's technique of *reductio ad absurdum?* Ichimura ascribes the reason partly to the structural differences between Sanskrit and Chinese. The latter is monosyllabic and ideographic while Sanskrit uses arbitrary symbols.[9] Moreover, Chinese language unlike Sanskrit is non-inflectional. He also feels that *T'ien t'ai* philosophy builds a solid bridge between the phenomenal (*shih*) and transcendent (*li*) in everyday life. Indian Buddhists did not completely identify empirical phenomena with transcendental, except perhaps in pure theory. However, I feel that resorting to paradoxical method when there is logical or epistemic deadlock is adopted in almost all branches of learning including in hard sciences. This topic will be discussed in Part III.

A few illustrations in paradoxical approach would indicate how Sêng-chao and his followers tried to reconcile the phenomenal and transcendental worlds.

> The *Prajñā is* subtle and formless and cannot be said as existent. Yet because it is functionally limitless it cannot be said non-existent... Although knowing and not-knowing are different in expression, they are not different in terms of the *Prajñā* insight.[10]

Sêng-chao cites the following conversation between Indra and Subhūti :

> Then, the lord of gods questioned, "In what reference should I seek the *Prajñā* insight?" Subhūti replied, "You should not seek it in reference to *rūpa.*" nor should you seek anything separate from *rūpa.* Subhuti again said, "Seeing, the causality of Dependent Origination means seeing the *Dharma*; seeing the *Dharma* means seeing the Buddha".[11]

"Things (*dharmas*) are neither different from an individual self (*pudgala*), nor is it the self different from things, and that things and the self inexpressively meet together".[12]

Finally, it is necessary to assert that *catuṣkoṭi* though not mentioned explicitly, is assumed in many paradoxes as, e.g. in Sêng-chao's famous definition – "*Prajñā* is neither existent nor non-existent" or "*Prajñā* is neither real nor unreal".[13]

18.3 Logic in Illogic : Zen

Contradictions, oxymorons and irreconcilables characterize the mystical aspects of most eastern religions. In Japanese Buddhism or *Zen* (from *Ch'an*) we find that these features reach the climax and illogic almost replaces logic.

Zennists trace their Buddhist link to the Buddha's Flower Sermon. On the mountain Gautama merely stood with a golden lotus. None of his disciples understood what the Master was trying to say except Mahākasyapa who smiled. Only he comprehended the Buddha. The Buddha made him the successor.

Zen masters do not deliver sermons, do not engage in abstruse discourses, and do not propound any theories. They behave in a bizarre manner. Their contradictory and shocking behavior is believed to convey the essence of Buddhism. A few illustrations will elucidate the point :

> A master Gutai was asked what Zen meant. He merely lifted his finger. Another guru kicked a ball and a third teacher slapped the student who asked the question.[14]
>
> A group of Zen masters gathered. In the conversation that followed, the general consensus was that there is no Buddhism, no enlightenment and *nirvāṇa* is destitute of any meaning. In fact they were playing a game, trying to outdo as well as trap others.
>
> A Zen master "may ask his disciples to rip their scriptures to shreds and avoid words like Buddha or *nirvāṇa* as if they were smut".[15]

Just as Gautama used a unique method to communicate with Mahākasyapa at the Flower Sermon, Zen masters use unconventional methods using blasphemy and even violence. This looks like a shock therapy, but a patient disciple is believed to be amply rewarded.

The repertoire of Zen *roshis* (teachers) contains accessories; *zazen, koan* and *sanzen. Zazen* (seating meditation) is practiced by monks in lotus position in what appears as endless silence to the outsider.

Koan means a problem outwardly meaningless or self-contradictory. For example, a master may ask "What was the appearance of your face before your ancestors were born"?[16] Students gradually learn from these apparently illogical questions, not from books, but through meditation. They are "awakened". When she is wrestling with a *koan*, the student meets the master twice a day, alone. This is called "consultation concerning meditation" (*sanzen*). The student mentions the question and the answer she has found. One of the two results follows (i) the answer is accepted, a rare event (ii) the answer is rejected, which is believed to be a "greater service" because the student has an opportunity to correct herself. The master monitors the student's progress over a prolonged period, indirectly helping her to complete her training.

This unconventional method of coaching can be interpreted in many ways. One may think that Zen masters try to convey an experience that cannot be verbalized. One may suggest that the master has nothing to tell or has no solutions and he is merely subjecting the student to contradictions as an escape route. However, according to Smith :

> First, Zen logic and description make sense only from an experiential perspective radically different from the ordinary. Second, Zen masters are determined that their students attain experience itself; not allow talk to take its place.[17]

18.4 Tibet and Mongolia

According to Stcherbatsky original contribution by Tibet and Mongolia to Buddhist logic is minimal. Nevertheless Tibetan literature is important because many Indian logical treatises are extinct in India, but they have been preserved in Tibet through their translated versions.

While the works of Vasubandhu are not found, the main works of Dignāga, Dharmakīrti and Dharmottara have been preserved. The most outstanding logicians and translators are Chaba-chos-kyi-senge (1109-1169 CE) and Tsoṅ-kha-pa (1357-1419).

For our purpose Tsoṅ-kha-pa's logic course "Dispelling the darkness of mind by aiming to understand seven books (of Dharmakīrti)" is important. Wayman calls it the *Guided Tour* through the seven books of Dharmakīrti[18] and we shall refer to it as such. Its elucidation of the concepts *oneness* and *multiplicity* are germane to the quantum dilemma. In what follows I have heavily borrowed from Wayman.[19]

Constructive Thought

Constructive thought (*kalpanā*) is present in cognition when the sense object (*viṣaya*) appears with the cognizer feeling that there is "generality character". Nonconstructive thought (*akalpanā*) on the other hand, accompanies cognition with a feeling that "this is an individual character" (*svalakṣaṇa*) or a nonactual support.

Constructive thought with application is of two types. The first consists of cognition (at the time of a signal) where there is a combination of name and conventional description, e.g. imagination "The tree has leaves and branches". The involving application to a feature involves combination of specialized support (factual base) and specialized feature (*dharma*). For instance imagination "That person has a stick".

Constructive thought considered by appearing sense object (snan yul) has three kinds : (1) that which is restricted to the generality speech. For instance, "It's a pot" is the stream of consciousness of one who is *not* familiar with signal (sigo) that is given. (2) that which is restricted to the generality feature (*dharma*), i.e. a pot's feature, also in case of one who is not familiar with the given sign.

Constructive thought can be classified by the occasion (*prayojana,* dgos). (1) that with a signal as a basis, e.g. cognition which understands the generality of a pot (2) that which superimposes another entity, e.g. cognition of "water in a mirage" (3) that which is out of sight (*parokṣa*).

Parokṣa too has been classified as (1) cognition based on the well-known necessary conditions (*upādāna*) used in inference (2) *ānumānika* or the derivative of inference (3) *smārta* derived from memory or perception of the past (4) *ābhilaṣika* or derived belief that follows speech.

Nonconstructive thought has two kinds (a) delusion without constructive thought which is either delusion of sense cognition (e.g. appearance of double moon) or delusion of mental cognition, e.g. a vivid dream. (b) nondelusive cognition, viz. all direct perceptions (*pratyakṣa*).

Delusions are also divided into many types, but we need not consider the details.[20]

Oneness and Multiplicity

Tsoṅg-kha-pa interpretes Dharmakīrti's conception of "one" and "multiplicity" as dependent on constructive thought. Oneness is a *dharma* which does not arise in *kalpanā* as multiple. Multiplicity is a *dharma* which arises in *kalpanā* as multiple.

Oneness has two kinds. The first is substantially "one" (rdzas gcig), is something appearing in direct perception without difference, e.g. created and imperament. The second type is "exclusive one" (*ldog pa gcig*) is like a pot, a pot.

Difference means the difference between the name of the entity and *dharma* which proves the basis. Its two kinds are :

(1) Substantially different (rdzas tha dad) signifies that there is the appearance of difference in direct perception, e.g. a pillar and a pot.
(2) Exclusively different (Idog pa tha dad), e.g. created and impermanent.

The role of construction should not be underestimated : the point instant and constructed imagination are linked by "conformity" or "correspondence" or "similarity". Stcherbatsky calls it a "similarity between things absolutely dissimilar"[21]

I have mentioned elsewhere that the construction-judgment aspect which leads to cognition of the image in the empirical world can be treated as a secondary source of knowledge which is partly dependent on the individual's heredity and upbringing.

Concatenation of Syllogisms

Tibetan logicians and debaters became quite adept in presenting arguments in a chain. In this art the reason in the first syllogism becomes the major term in the second and so on.

For example, if there is A then there is B, because C exists. But C *does* exist because there is D which in turn exists because there is E and so forth. In a debate the opponent, of course, is free to contest every constituent syllogism at any stage Chaba-choikyi-senge (1109-1169 CE) a renowned lama devised a brief method of such a chain called "sequence and reason".[22]

It may be mentioned that when Buddhism declined in most parts of India, it survived in three places :

1. Nudea in Bengal, along with Nyāya-Vaiśeṣika.
2. China and Japan where it was founded upon Śaṅkarasvāmin's *Nyāyapraveśa.*
3. Tibet and Mongolia where the monasteries continued their studies based on Dharmakirti's *Pramāṇa-vārtika.* Needless to say for the historian of Buddhism and Buddhist logic, Tibetan literature continues to be the richest source.

19

Knowledge, Wisdom and Love

19.1 Introduction

Since Buddhist logic subsumes epistemology, a question arises as to how Buddhists acquire knowledge. If there are only two sources, direct perception and inference, Buddhist epistemology should have been restricted to a low level. This is certainly not so because what Buddhist call "direct perception" is only the beginning of the process which culminates in what *we* call perception at the empirical level. There is an intervening chain of understanding, judgement, construction, conception and so forth. Inference involves the process of relating the mark to the object which is inferred. In this process our mind uses the entire knowledge it has acquired; every experience increases the stock of knowledge, which is then used in perception. Although inference is considered more remote than direct perception it involves the connection of two concepts; the first relating to the mark (*lakṣaṇa*) and the second pertaining to the object inferred. The mental journey in case of inference is much longer and the process of cognition occurs twice; first in relation to the mark and second, in relation to the inferred object.

This inner capacity of the mind is extremely important because those who are engaged in the eight-step path towards *nirvāṇa* are at different stages and at each stage their mind becomes richer. It is perhaps because of the preoccupation with this time-consuming exercise that hard science seems to have been neglected by Buddhists. But modern scientists have begun to show great interest in this training of the mind which may shed considerable light on the mind-body relation on the one hand and mind-brain connection on the other.

The second question that arises is how knowledge is related to compassion and love which constitute a *sine qua non* of Mahāyāna Buddhism. In chapters 14 and 15 we tried to relate *śūnyatā* to logic and dialectic. In this chapter we will address two questions mentioned above. This will enable us to coordinate various factors that will ultimately lead to finding a rightful place for Buddhist logic and Buddhism in the integral approach to human condition discussed in chapter 31.

Mādhyamika which avoids extremes and uses the "middle way" can provide us insight into the process of enriching the mind.

19.2 Ignorance and Knowledge

To a question put to the Buddha by a *theri*, about the relationship between *saṃskāras* (formative forces) and *kleśa*, the wise replied that it is the ignorance which leads to *kleśa* which in turn lead to deeds and the inevitable rebirth. In reality there is no "entity" which is the cause of suffering.

Ignorance at the mundane level can be eradicated when the wise show the way to explain the nature of illusions. The process of eradicating ignorance goes hand in hand with the acquisition of true knowledge. According to *śāstra* in the ultimate reality there is no difference between knowledge and ignorance just as there is no contradiction between the empirical and the unconditional reality, *nirvāṇa.*[1] *Prajñā* is the ultimate principle of knowledge. But this word has another meaning, viz. unconditioned reality. Another word *prajñāpāramitā* is often used to indicate the ultimate reality. According to *śāstra* this eternal nature, (*dharma-sthāna*) is not "created" even by the Buddha.[2]

Prajñā as the ultimate doctrine of knowledge has two types – eternal and functional. According to *śāstra* it is the latter which expels ignorance and leads you to the eternal *prajñā* where there is no difference between ignorance and knowledge. *Śāstra* also mentions three types of mundane knowledge – (1) literature, art, religious rituals, etc. (2) knowledge that makes us free from birth in the inferior regions, (3) knowledge of transcendental nature which frees us from clinging to the notion of "I" and "mine" and also removes defilement. This is also the knowledge of *śrāvakas,* and *pratyeka-buddhas* into whom streams (*āśravas*) of defilement flow no more.[3]

Above all these kinds, is *prajñāpāramitā.* It is the knowledge for the benefit of the entire humanity. Moreover, it encompasses not only cognitive sphere, it also covers emotion and compassion. It should be noted that the notion of this supreme knowledge shows how love and compassion are integrated with the intellect.

The hierarchy of knowledge leads to another hierarchy of comprehension or vision, metaphorically called "eyes".

At the lowest level are the eyes of flesh (*māṃsacakṣus*). Above these are the eyes of gods (*divyacakṣus*). At both levels the determinate is mistaken for the absolute, though the latter "eyes" enable you to perceive "arising and passing away" of momentary beings in various spheres of existence. The next higher level is the eye of wisdom (*prajñācakṣu*) which is free from errors and focussed on *nirvāṇa.* Above this lies the eye that comprehends different natures of individuals and shows how they can be helped. According to *śāstra* it is called *dharmacakṣu* because the wayfarer acquiring it is now fit to enter *dharma* or unconditioned reality. The last stage is the eye of the Buddha (*Buddhacakṣu*) This supreme eye comprehends all types of "sights" and indicates the completeness of the process of perfection.

19.3 Paradoxical Teaching

According to *sūtra, dharma* is taught in several ways, depending on the context and the capacity of the student. It may be taught in terms of *existence* or *non-existence,* permanence, or impermanence, self or "no self". Contradictions which appear in such teaching without reference to the circumstances are only illusory.

For example, the Buddha's teachings that the self exists and that it does not exist, both are true.[4] The first predicate is for householders while the second is for the ascetic who is seeking *nirvāṇa.*

Śāstra contends that these different teachings are all true, yet none of them is absolutely true. *Śāstra* helps us in having in insight into relativity. It makes it clear that of the contradictory parts, one belongs to relative reality and the other to ultimate reality. This should prompt us to interpret *catuṣkoṭi* – like logic appearing in quantum paradoxes. This dichotomy referring to the realities is often called *two truths.*

These two truths are also expressed in four *siddhāntas. Śāstra* maintains that "all these are true and there is no mutual contradiction among them".[5] These are actually four standpoints and may be called mundane, individual, remedial, and ultimate but the main difference is between the mundane and ultimate.

The essential characteristics of the mundane truth is *conditionedness (pratītyasamutpāda).* For example, being of the individual is a mundane truth dependend on five *skandhas.* If we maintain that only *skandhas* exist, we are guilty of an error at the mundane level. *Śāstra* observes that because of different specific tendencies of individuals, it is necessary to choose the right standpoint for a particular individual. A truth is also taught as if it were a remedy. In Buddha's *dharma* every disease of the mind has a remedy. For example, observing and cogitating over physical impurity is a remedy for lewdness and passion, while it is not a suitable medicine for anger. Cultivation of compassion is the remedy for anger. Similarly the antidote for stupidity is contemplation on the causes and conditions of the things.[6]

The ultimate truth is unconditioned unlike the mundane or relative truth. This fourth truth (*siddhānta*) alone is comprehensive by which we mean it cannot be annulled while in the first three cases cancellation is possible.

While explaining the meaning of Mahāyāna, *śāstra* says that "the sphere of the speakable is the domain of the determinate; the sphere where the words do not reach is the highest *dharma*".[7]

19.4 Attainment of Dharma

Madhyamakas mention three doors to *dharma*; analysis (*abhidharma*), criticism (*śūnyatā*) and moral code (*piṭaka or vinaya*). *Abhidharma* investigates the unique nature of a particular entity. However, since the concept of unique nature is only relative, it is *śūnyatā* which tells you that the conditioned is responsible for such apparent uniqueness; *vinaya* is the practical side of path finding.

For us the most important "entrance" is criticism which shows that the elements found in analysis have no absoluteness, because such absoluteness would prevent them from "becoming" and violate the basic principle of ever-changing world. The method of this criticism is *reductio ad absurdum.* It is pertinent to recall that in Nāgārjunian dialectic this method is frequently employed. Unfortunately *śūnyatā,* because it leads to a negative conclusion in an argument is often mistaken for negativism.

At one place *śāstra* says that it is not the business of *vinaya* to investigate the ultimate nature of reality.[8] These "doors" appear to convey inconsistent messages but those who have cultivated *prajñāpāramitā* realize that it is only an illusion because their description involves different levels of reality. In ultimate reality these levels disappear; the differentiating designations *śūnyatā, tathatā, dharmadhātu, bhūtakoṭi,* etc. all vanish.

19.5 Buddha's Silence

We mentioned in chapter 7 that Buddha remained silent over some transcendental interpretations. This silence over the questions, fourteen in all, have led to, many interpretations.

Mādhyamika's interpretation is quite interesting. According to *śāstra,* the Buddha did not answer these because the points of these questions, viz. absolute existence and absolute non-existence of the world and the soul are untrue, false.[9] This appears a laconic explanation but its exposition is also found in other places in *śāstra.*

Most people have a habit of clinging to a concept or object. This prevents them from seeing the nature of reality. Hence even if the Buddha had tried to enlighten the questioners, his answer would have been misinterpreted according to the individual's tendency. They would cling to "is", "is not", "permanence", "immanence", and even *śūnyatā.* It appears the Master preferred silence lest his answer should raise other useless questions because of the listener's misinterpretation arising from clinging. *Śāstra* makes it clear that the Buddha does not change the order of things. He answers, when he chooses to answer, only the truth. The following quotation shows that the Buddha only enlightens, he does not interfere in the course of nature :

> The sun, for example, does not make anything tall or short nor does he level (all things) down to the ground. It illumines all things equally. This is the case even with the Buddha. He does not make the non-existent existent nor the existent non-existent. He always speaks the truth; and by the light of his wisdom he illumines all things.[10]

19.6 Wisdom and Compassion

It is rare to find that wisdom and compassion are considered epistemically equipotent. But this is what Buddhism, especially *Mahāyāna* school teaches. It calls *prajñā* the principle of comprehension. According to K. Venkata Ramanan, "There is no absolute division between intellect on the one hand and the feeling on the other".[11] These two elements are actually called the phases of comprehension.

Śāstra's comparison between the "small way" (*Hīnayāna*) and "great way" (*Mahāyāna*) is interesting. The former is called the way of the *śrāvakas* or "hearers", when *śrāvakas* follow this path they can terminate *avidyā* and control passion, but being conditioned by fear of birth and death, they do not seek buddhahood. They are also incapable of understanding the relativity (*śūnyatā*) of *dharma.*

According to *śāstra,* Mahāyāna is a non-exclusive path. It originates in empirical reality but its goal is *prajñā* the knowledge of all forms. The great way is also called the way of perfection (*pāramitā*) having the sense of the undivided.

Śāstra speaks of six types of *pāramitās,* collectively called *prajñāpāramitā* in connection with merit and wisdom.[12] Of six *pāramitās prajñā* is the most important without which the other five would not be effective. The latter are charity (*dāna*), moral conduct (*śīla*), endurance (*kṣānti*), effort (*vīrya*), concentration and meditation (*dhyāna*). It is impossible to discuss here thirty-seven factors and six kinds of perfections mentioned in *śāstra. Prajñā,* no doubt, constitutes the guiding light to the wayfarer. According to *śāstra* the thirty-seven factors constitute the way that leads to *nirvāṇa.* Faring on this way, one reaches the city of *nirvāṇa.* The city has three gates, viz. *śūnyatā, animittatā* and *apraṇihitatā.*[13] We have already discussed *śūnya* which is the comprehension of non-substantiality of objects in the mundane reality. *Animittatā* asks the wayfarer not to cling to the things of determinate nature. *Apraṇihitatā* teaches the wayfarer to desist from resolving (*praṇidhāna*) to do actions stemming from passion.

Dhyāna and *samādhi* are not only rigorous tests of endurance; they constitute epistemic dimensions of what appears basically as a spiritual attainment. The wayfarers experiment with their minds through the exercise of the elements of boundless heart.[13a] Note how both the heart and mind come together. *Śāstra* also describes eight exercises of getting mastery, nine sequential exercises of concentration and ten exercises of all-pervasiveness. It observes that these exercises are similar to testing a horse before riding.[14]

It would be worthwhile to quote K. Venkata Ramanan who summarizes the wayfarer's goal :

> In the Mahayana, the *sâstra* observes, all these three doors which are essentially of the nature of wisdom, insight, have for their ultimate object the universal reality. By means of these one beholds that the world is itself *nirvāṇa*"[15]

19.7 Bodhisattva's Status

Bodhisattva's position in Mahāyāna seems to indicate that at a certain point in the history of Buddhism the self-development was considered not only an achievement but also an opportunity to contribute one's wisdom, love and compassion for the welfare of society. Bodhisattva's status is unique in that he sacrifices Buddhahood and devotes his career for helping other wayfarers.

According to *sāstra, bodhi* means the way of all the Buddhas, *sattva* means the individual; it also means the great mind. This individual (who is called *bodhisattva*) seeks to realize exhaustively all the merits of the Buddha. This thought of his is unbreakable, indestructible, firm like the diamond-mountain. This is the meaning of great mind.[16] (86a)

About the status (*nyāma*) of the *bodhisattva, sāstra* says that he develops the ability to meet any contingency thanks to his insight and boundless compassion. The capacity is called *anutpattika-dharma-kṣānti* (his capacity to endure and sustain the truth of unborn *dharma*) When he achieves this capacity, he comprehends the entire world as *śūnya.* He achieves a stage called *pratyutpanna samādhi,* in which he feels the presence of Buddha constantly. In fact, it is believed that Buddhas are watching his progress and they remind him of his vow, when he shows a let-up in his progress. At a certain point he becomes an *irreversible bodhisattva* when he has cultivated enough strength and when he realizes that the understanding of *śūnyatā* and infinite compassion are two sides of the same coin. He is now in the state of *anutpattika-dharmakṣānti.* The bodhisattva has progressed to such an extent that Buddhahood is only a small distance away. He now has to make a choice :

1. He may proceed to become a Buddha.
2. He may prefer to remain a Bodhisattva for ever "helping other people to cross the ocean of birth and death".[17]

19.8 Exploring the Mind

The path to *Nirvāṇa* contains exploration of the inner space or the mind. We have mentioned *dhyāna* and *samādhi,* the last steps in the eight-fold system. In fact, there are many methods which are used to train the mind. In English they may be called meditation, concentration, imagination, visualization and so forth. Various schools use different methods of training the mind. Among those scholars some seem to have paid considerable attention to Tibetan methods for their mind-brain research. In what follows I have mainly borrowed from the works of Varela and Depraz.[18]

Traditionally Tibetan Buddhists follow three visualization methods prescribed by Theravāda, Mahāyāna, and Vajrayāna.

Theravāda emphasizes cultivation of mindfulness and nondistraction to banish ignorance. Asaṅga defines mindfulness as "the non-forgetfulness of the mind with respect to a familiar object having the function of non distraction". [19]

Many methods are used to bring about "stability of attention". The generic name for this meditation is *śamatha.* In Tibetan it is called *zhi gnas.* It roughly means quiescence.

In Mahāyāna, consistent with its doctrine this renewed awareness is extended to the concerns for others.

Vajrayāna which is a tantric school has a preliminary practice called (*ngondro*) which is intended to purify one's mind. It also uses methods to effect transformation of one's psychophysical reality. According to Varela and Depraz, "Vajrayāna deals with a symbolic reconstruction of one's self". This tantric school heavily borrows from ancient Indian methods of *sādhanā* in which traditionally, tantriks use certain adjuncts such as gestures (*mudrās*), *mantras, yantras* (geometrical figures), *maṇḍalas* (circles), etc. In Vajrayāna, the practitioners use an imagined gestalt with a central figure (*yidam*). Varela and Depraz observe that one becomes a totality that is embodied in *yidam's* character. In Indian tantra, the worshippers identify themselves with a deity and there is a triad of mantra-yantra-deity whose components are believed to be interconvertible.

19.9 Tonglen

Tonglen, one of the methods of mind training has aroused much interest among western scientists interested in exploring the mind-brain connection. *Tong* stands for "letting go" and *len* means "taking in". "Giving and taking should be practiced alternately that alteration should be put on the medium of breath".[20]

Tonglen, like *śamatha* and *yidam visualization* is practiced several times. It is believed that its repeated practice over a long time in conjunction with other methods leads to the weakning of the reflex "me first". It is gradually replaced by the precedence of "others" or "humanity" consistent with Mahāyāna doctrine and *bodhisattva's* main goal, Varela and Depraz explain why *tonglen* is effective :

> It is essential to remark that *tonglen* is eminently a practice based on the existing intersubjective nature of one's experience. The exchange is possible only because humans are already immersed in a network of empathic relations.[21]

Limited space prevents us from describing *tonglen* in detail, but we shall revert to this topic in Part III when we consider mind-brain correlation.[22]

20

The Three Laws

20.1 Western Logic

The three laws relating to identity, excluded middle and contradiction are not totally independent. In case of Buddhist logic they are so enmeshed with one another that they should be studied together. However, it would be worthwile to say a few words about the law of excluded middle as found in western logic.

Excluded Middle

We saw in chapter 2 that the quantum riddle raises a question as to whether the law of excluded middle is subject to any limitations. This Aristotelian law is called *exclusi tertii principium.*

It can be expressed as :

1. A is B or not-B
2. A proposition is true or false (not true)

Thus Rama is a human being or not a human being. There is no third alternative – *tertium non datur,* i.e. "a third is not given".

It appeals to our mind as a sound principle which even the average person understands. It is of course, assumed that the law is applicable to meaningful statements. For example, the statement "Poverty is white and long" is meaningless, though grammatically correct, but we cannot say that it is true or false.

However, this law is not accepted by some thinkers such as Brower. The reason is the very word "true" has more meanings than one. According to Brower "truth" can be defined only in terms of verifiability. This makes the concept of truth epistemological. If the truth of a proposition cannot be verified then the proposition becomes meaningless. This line of thinking leads to a three-fold division of propositions :

1. Propositions which are verifiable.
2. Propositions whose contradictiories are verifiable.
3. Propositions which are neither verifiable nor are their contradictories verifiable.

According to Brower then the residual propositions in (3) are meaningless. Hence the law of excluded middle does not hold good in such cases. But what is meant by "verifiable"? It means something that *can* (in theory) be verified and not necessarily that which has already been verified.

If the law of excluded middle is not accepted, a strange consequence follows. If p is a proposition that is neither true nor false, then it is false that p is false which means that the principle of double negation, viz. not not p = p does not hold good.

Suppose there is a place X where it rains during the period July-September. Consider this question – did it rain at X on 1st August 1908? We know from the history of X that its climate has not changed much. We also have many records showing that X received rainfall on the first of August (in the years other than 1908) but not a single known contrary instance. The proposition "it rained at X on 01-08-1908" cannot be verified since we cannot go back in time. But we accept inductive generalization and maintain that it probably rained at X on that date. Though epistemologically there is no direct evidence of the rainfall, its truth appears probable. *A fortiori* statement "it rained at X on 1st August 1908" is certainly meaningful. In the worst case, we might have erred in our judgement, i.e. it may not have rained on that day. The law of excluded middle still holds good. If induction tells us that X either receives or does not receive rainfall every day it would be churlish to assert that X has neither received nor not received precipitation on a certain day.

In order to preserve the law of double negation $\sim \sim p = p$, western philosohers prefer to retain the law of excluded middle.

20.2 Contradiction

The process of identification of the empirical reality as a construction by the human mind was explained earlier. This process itself contains the germs of contradiction. The mind apprehends the boundary which separates the identified knowledge *A* and the rest of the universe, viz. not A. For example when we perceive a green patch, there is a dichotamy, "This is green" and "that is non-green". The second part is a very vast region comprising the universe of discourse excluding "green".

In Buddhist logic "the law of contradiction is nothing but the expression of the fact that all cognition is dichotomizing, and relative. We can actively cognize or determine a thing only by opposing it to what it is not".[1]

According to Śāntirakṣita, "There is on the one part not the slightest bit of what there is on the other".[2] Hence this is nothing but the law of excluded middle which he calls *tṛtiya-prakāra-abhāva.*

This split into *A* and not-A can have other characteristics in addition to what we call logical contradiction. In certain cases such as light and darkness, the dichotomy leads to two dynamic or warring parts. For example, light and darkness try to expel each other. This is unlike the two opposites blue and non-blue which can co-exist peacefully. However, this difference between static and dynamic exclusion is not relevant to the basic assumption of Buddhist logic according to which what appears in empirical reality as opposing entities reflect functional dependence. The ultimate reality consists of instantaneous moments and the last moment contains totality of all causes. Hence the law of causation is always operative whether the nature of the dichotomy is static or dynamic. However some scholars feel that these two "types" lead to different consequences as regards the law of excluded middle. This law is true in case of static dichotomy while it may not be true in case of the dynamic variety. For example, when light and dark interreact there can be "total light" and "total darkness" at the extremities and other twilight like states between them. This means at least three real (transcendental) moments are required to produce the phenomenon. This problem has led to many controversies which we need not discuss. Two points need to be recalled :

> (1) Between any two transcendental moments there cannot be any contradiction, what exists is the causal law. (2) At the phenomenal level, if we have a series of appearances a, b, c, d, ... between total light and total darkness, a, b, ... are all *different* things and law of excluded middle becomes meaningless.

We have already explained earlier that in modern theory there is only one variable (frequency) and not two, viz. light and darkness.

Some logicians recognize another law called the Law of Otherness. If we see a patch of blue, the principle of dichotomy divides the universe of discourse in blue and non-blue. But the negative part covers an illimitable things and qualities. For instance "white" belongs to it but is only a part of it. It can never be blue nor is it the whole of non-blue. It is "other than" blue. Hence this law of otherness depends on the law of contradiction.

An intersting case arises when you consider a certain shade "X" of blue and compare other shades of blue in succession so that the difference between X and the other than X continues to decrease. At a certain point you reach a limt where you cannot distinguish between X and the chosen variety of blue. Thus Identity is nothing but the limit of the difference between X and other shades of blue. This is the identity of discernibles.

Contradiction is one of the most important laws in Buddhist logic. In fact, other laws such as the law of contradictory predication, law of efficient oppositon, logical antiphasis, law of otherness, law of identity, law of excluded middle are either its varients or laws dependent on it. Compare this with Aristotle :

> The same can appertain and not appertain to the *same* at different times in different respects or can possess two contradictory qualities at diffrent times; the thing may be cold at one moment, and hot in the another.[3]

Other Indian schools subscribe to some of the above laws, but do not consider them as important as Buddhist. For example, *Naiyāyikas* declare about the law of contradiction : "That is the meaning of contradiction that two things cannot coexist together at the same place and same time".[4]

Jainas' views on contradiction are perhaps the most interesting. They do not believe in the law of contradiction unlike Buddhists ("every things is noneternal because matter is noneternal") and *Sāṅkhyas* ("everything is noneternal because matter is a fiction"). Jainas maintained that everything is eternal and not-eternal. This appears similar to one of the options of *catuṣkoṭi* of Nāgārjuna mentioned earlier. However, we have already seen in chapters 15 and 16, Jainas usually interprete contradictory prdicates as different points of view. Their theory implies that the truth of a proposition is somewhere between assertion p and denial ~p; both p and~p are false.

According to Dharmakīrti contradiction is complete mutual exclusion. This leads to the law of double negation or mutual negation which can be approached either from p or ~p.

Thus $\sim(\sim(p)) = p$
and $\sim(\sim(\sim p)) = \sim p$

20.3 Law of Identity

We have already considered the various interpretations of this law. Some more interpretations may now be considered.

It is interpreted as "the law of identical sense". But Buddhist scholars usually reject this equivalence, because according to Dharmottara, different statements giving the same sense cannot be a logical topic.[5]

In chapter 3 we mentioned the biographer's concept of identity. This is sometimes called the Law of Constancy closely resembling the common man's concept of identity. A person or a monument may have a biography of ninety years. Despite the changes that occur in them the biographer would use the same appellation say "Nehru" or "Qutub Minar" as the case may be. This concept of identity in empirical reality necessarily implies continuity or duration of time. Buddhist scholars do not seem to have a standard for such duration since they perceive an ever-changing world. Roughly, it may be called the Law of Identical Construction because an image projected by a moment of ultimate reality is "constructed" by the mind. They are not sure how this pragmatic use of identity should be defined. This is clear from what Stcherbatsky says :

> The Forms, the nature of the general essences superimposed upon reality are immutable and eternal. There is no power in the world which could change an Ens and convert it into a non-Ens. The almighty god Indra himself cannot alter the essence of things.[6]

What Buddhist treat as the law of identity pertains to one part of judgement viz., analytical judgement. The following example will elucidate the concept. In the proposition "This is the white snow", the subject lies in "this". Two concepts "snow" and "white" are the concepts which are connected by the identity of objective reference. This is the Buddhist law of identity which was mentioned earlier especially in connection with Nāgārjuna's refutation of *Naiyāyikas.*

In chapter 10 we considered another law which is closely related to the law of identiy, viz. the the law of conformity which need not be explained again.

Sāṅkhyans have their own law of identity, the identity of cause and effect (*satkāryavāda*) which Buddhists fought tooth and nail. The law of contradiction implies that no thing has a life greater than an instantaneous moment. Hence the cause and effect projected from different moments cannot be equal.

It seems that these three (western) laws and especially the law of identity has various interpretations. In the quantum world, "violations of logical laws" means the violation of modern western law. This fact should be kept in mind when we analyze micro phenomena.

Since there is so much confusion about these three laws, two eminent scholars' opinions would need to be quoted.

According to Sigwart these terms, viz. identity, oppositon and contradiction "have become unserviceable in philosophy since quite a Babylonian confusion of language reigns in their application".[7]

An interpretation of the law of identity by W. Hamilton deserves to be mentioned. According to him " A is A" connotes an assertion of identity between the whole concept and its part in comprehension. In Buddhist logic, the identity between *śiṃśapā* and "tree" mentioned earlier provides an example. Hamilton calls it the principle of *logical affirmation.* J.S. Mill rightly differs from this view and remarks that Hamilton's interpretation can be correct only in case of analytical judgements. You will recall that this type of "identity" is nothing but (i) the statement $q \in T$ where q is one particular *śiṃśapā* and T is the set of all trees or (ii) $S \subset T$ where S is the set of all *śiṃśapā* trees.

Part III

Quantum Dilemma

21

Buddhism and Science

21.1 The Concept of Science

Before we consider the relevance of Buddhist logic in the conundrums of quantum theory and relativity theory, we should be able to answer the following questions :

1. What is science?
2. Does Buddhism provide conducive environment for the growth of science?
3. Should spiritualism in its broadest sense be considered a dimension of science?

In this chapter we shall consider the first two questions. The third question, which has acquired considerable importance as a facet of liberalization in the post-RQ scientific thinking, will be addressed later.

Etymologically the word science comes from Latin *scientia* which means knowledge. In its broadest sense science connotes a body of knowledge about nature gained through observation, experimentation and deduction. In English "science" usually means "natural sciences" which subsume physics, chemistry and biology, and which are sometimes called exact sciences. It should also include mathematics and logic. The restricted use of the word science can be ascribed to Rene Descartes (1596–1650), philosopher and mathematician who believed that all science is certain, evident knowledge. He rejected all knowledge that was merely probable. He seemed to harbor the misconception that all scientific phenomena should be mathematically expressed to be credible. Unfortunately we know today that except deductive logic and pure mathematics all sciences are probable. The analytic-synthetic dichotomy mentioned in chapter 4 was represented in science before Newton by Descartes and Francis Bacon (1561–1626), followers of deduction and induction respectively. It was Newton (1642–1727) who synthesized both these methods in his *Principia*.

In French the word "science" and in German its equivalent *Wissenschaft* is used in a much broader sense to connote social sciences and even humanities. The trend among the writers in English seems to be towards a broader connotation, once restricted to natural sciences. Psychology, politics and sociology are now often categorized as science.

In Sanskrit and many Indian languages the word *śāstra* can mean knowledge, science, precept, theory or even command. There are other two words *jñāna* (knowledge) and *vijñāna* (knowledge, science) often used in Indian languages.

Interestingly, linguistics was regarded as science in ancient India. The West seems to have followed suit only recently. In India there was also a science of ritual. The western science has yet to bestow that status on the systematic study of ritual.

21.2 Features of Science

Since science can have as narrow a connotation as natural science and as broad a meaning as any systematic study of any branch of knowledge it is difficult to draw a line. In consonance with the present trend we shall consider science broad enough to include social sciences and linguistics but narrow enough to exclude history and literature. Instead of defining science it would be better to discuss its characteristics.

We can identify six features of science – social knowledge, empirical adequacy, abstraction, consistency, provisional nature, and generalization.[1]

Social Knowledge

By social knowledge we mean the knowledge to which the public in general or certain social subgroups have access. The behavior of humans and animals can be studied by all of us. All of us can, if we have sufficient interest and ability, study history, geography, literature, mathematics and logic. The knowledge gained by us in these areas may be called social or public knowledge.

A characteristic of social knowledge is that it can be communicated to those who are interested in it. We may not be engaged in nuclear physics research but we can obtain the knowledge from experts and understand it to the best of our ability. What's more we, too, can participate in its acquisition if we have the ability.

There are certain types of personal or unique experiences which cannot be translated into public knowledge. If you are a yogi you may reach the stage of *samādhi* or a superconcious state which gives you indescribable bliss. If you are practicing one of the several methods of tantra, you may feel that you have been able to arouse the *kuṇḍalinī* and direct it to the *sahasrāra* which gives you ecstatic pleasure. that you cannot describe. You can only vaguely say that "I have been drinking the nectar... I felt as if I merged with the superconscious Śiva-Śakti". Or you may have periodical trances during which you feel you had communion with God.

These are your personal experiences which cannot be shared by the public; at best you may try to convey them in approximate language with a proviso that they are in fact indescribable. Even if others have similar experiences these cannot be compared because they are strictly private.

We should exclude these experiences from the purview of social knowledge. Science is, however, only one subgroup of social knowledge.

Empirical Adequacy

Any scientific theory has to be tested empirically. An observed phenomenon is described by scientific theories or models which should fairly agree with experimental results.

A model may consist of an exhaustive list of rules with exceptions. This is the mode one follows in linguistics and to some extent in sociology and economics. Statistical methods are used in such areas as sociology and demography. In natural sciences mathematical models can be designed. In physics, mathematics is extensively used as a tool.

In some areas it is not possible to use quantitative methods and one may have to be content with the statements showing cause-effect relationships. Mathematical methods lend greater precision to theories and we feel that in such areas as physics, the world can be described with great accuracy.

Empirical adequacy does not merely mean agreement of a model with the experiments which have already been conducted. For, given the already obtained results, a trivial model can always be designed which will best fit the data. A theory must be able to predict the results of future observations. It is only in mathematics and deductive logic that prediction can achieve cent percent accuracy. Even in physics there is a margin of error attributable to the limitations of instruments and human perception. In social sciences considerable deviation can be accepted because these studies involve human behavior which cannot be encapsulated in mathematical formulas. The statistical models used in social sciences merely indicate the possible pattern of behaviour in terms of a range. They cannot be applied easily to an individual. For example, if it is found that the incidence of cancer has a strong correlation with smoking and drinking, we cannot say that John who is a chain smoker and a heavy drinker will have cancer. One should not even be excessively surprised if one finds him hale and hearty at the age of ninety-five.

Abstraction

Abstraction was considered at length in earlier chapters. In science it appears in different forms and serves many purposes.

In science we do not find reference to proper nouns, it is the class names that appear frequently. Unlike in literature, there are no Hamlets, Ophelia, Rāma, Kṛṣṇa or Julius Caeser. Science studies men, animals, gold, iron, speed, color and so forth. You will never find a physicist naming individual atoms Tweedledom, Tweedledee, Tom, Dick and Harry.

Science is impersonal, which implies to some extent the process of abstraction, and also the fact that science is public knowledge. You will not find in scientific formulas any reference to the scientist who devised the theories or conducted the experiments. You will not find in the formulas any mention of the time and place of the experiments unless they constitute essential elements of the formulas.

In certain sciences especially in physics abstraction goes farther than mere classification. A theory may introduce certain abstract parameters whose existential status may not be fully comprehended. Electrons, protons, electromagnetic and gravitational fields and a host of the parameters used in physics cannot be seen. A scientist tries to correlate different phenomiena and in that process may introduce such entities as "electrons" whose properties can be studied but which cannot be seen or whose status (whether it is a particle or a wave) may be uncertain.

Even in geometry we have such concepts as "point" and "line" whose existential status is dubious. But such entities help us in building the vast superstructure of science.

In Freudian psychology the human mind is described in terms of the *id* (instinct), *ego* (self) and *superego* (conscience) which are abstractions. Freud freely borrows concepts from dynamics to describe psychological phenomena especially those relating to the unconscious. So long as such entities and concepts form a consistent system and help us understand human behavior, their indeterminate existential status per se should not detract psychoanalysis from being a science.

Consistency

Any theory which seeks to explain the world should be a consistent system. This consistency refers to the internal logical consistency of the components in the model : it does not refer to the agreement of the experimental results with theory, an aspect that is covered under "empirical adequacy".

If your theory consists of several mathematical/logical assumptions, they should not contradict one another. For example, we have seen that God does not exist in Buddhist epistemology. It would be erroneous to introduce God's intervention as a special case to explain a miracle performed by a Buddhist saint, however, venerable.

Such internal contradictions can be removed by redefining our concepts.

Provisional Nature

A scientific theory is always provisional. This is emphasized not only by scientists but also enlightened epistemologists like Rand. As the human ability for scientific observation improves, the scientist may find deviations which could not be detected by previous crude instruments. These deviations are usually of a smaller degree in the sense that you do not have to totally reject the older theory. A refined theory has to be developed in such a way that the older theory can still accommodate the results within a certain limit.

The Newtonian mechanics is now replaced by Einstein's theory of relativity. Nevertheless the older mechanics can still be used when relative velocities are not very high or close to the velocity of light.

A wise scientist always accepts the fact that his theory is valid in the present state of human knowledge. Since there are gradual changes in theories to accommodate new discoveries, science marches ahead usually without any U turns. This is precisely why despite being called "revolutionary", both quantum and relativity theories have not made the old theories redundant, these are still relevant within certain limits. This characteristic of science is sometimes captured in the maxim – science is progressive.

Generalization

In science there is what Einstein calls "stratification of the scientific system".[2] As science progresses, special laws lead to general laws. For example, the orbits of the planets can be comprehended with the help of Keplar's laws, and the behaviour of the falling objects can be understood by Galileo's experiments. However, Newton's gravitational theory incorporated both these theories and raised physics to a higher level.

The process of unification or integration of different theories has been going on for hundreds of years though it has been in the limelight only recently. The process implies diminishing of the number of primary concepts and their interrelaions. In a sense, this is consistent with the principle called "Occam razor".

In modern physics, quantum theory explains the world at the micro (subatomic) level, while relativity theory admirably describes the world at the macro or astronomical level especially when the velocities approximate the velocity of light.[2a] Unfortunately, these two theories appear inconsistent in some areas. Scientists have been struggling to have a unified theory which could subsume both the theories, but their progress seems to be tardy. Some thinkers even dream of a "theory of everything".[3] Whether such a theory is possible at all only the future generations will know.

Falsificationism

We have already discussed the general characteristics of science, and how scientific theories are formed. There is a problem which is not connected with a particular scientific theory and its verification but which relates to a criterion for classifying a knowledge as science. The general features can only provide us with a rough guide, but usually a need for a sharper criterion to decide whether a body of knowledge is science is felt by epistemologists as well as scientists.

An interesting theory called falsificationism was advanced by Karl Popper (1902-1994), Austrian philosopher, logician and sociologist. Popper maintained that scientific generalization cannot be conclusively verified; but it can be falsified by a counter-instance. His theory is based on the fact that a scientific theory rests on induction and is always probabilistic.

Popper's falsificationism principle affords a powerful tool to decide whether a statement or a group of internally consistent statements is scientific or nonscientific. If a statement in principle can be falsified it is a statement relating to the province of science. If it is not falsifiable then it is nonscientific. We shall call such putative knowledge "nonscience". It should be remembered that adjectives "scientific" and "nonscientific" will be used accordingly and a particular hypothesis classified as scientific will be true only when validated.

The following illustrations will elucidate the scope of these words :

E1

(a) A person claims that he can walk on the surface of water. This is a scientific statement inasmuch as it can be falsified.[4]
(b) A person claims that he is an *avatāra* (incarnation) of Vishnu, a god widely worshipped by Hindus.

This is not a scientific statement, since it cannot be falsified. Popper's test from a certain angle appears to be liberal if we use it properly. Once a statement is classified as nonscientific we need not assert its truth or falsity. We have an agnostic attitude and refuse to comment on the merits of the statement since it is not in the province of science, but is a matter of faith.

(c) In English orthography the consonant *q* is followed by the vowel *u* with a few exceptions.

This may be called a scientific statement pertaining to linguistics. It is falsifiable. If you inspect the words beginning with q in a dictionary you will find that the statement is also true. The only exception to the general rule will be found in such words as qintar, qant, and qwerty which are so few that they deserve to be called exceptions.

21.3 Scientific Environment

Buddhism is usually considered agnostic. It has no divine God; it does not believe in the soul.

Its attitude towards afterlife, eternity, infinite space etc. is that these pertain to the transcendent. It was mentioned in chapter 7 that the Buddha himself preferred to remain silent about metaphysical matters. In fact the questions, fourteen in all, which the Master refused to answer are called *avyakta-vastu.*

Agnosticism is conducive for rational thinking and it is reasonable to assume that a scientist can work without the fear of the guardians of a dogma. It was mentioned earlier that Śākyamuni advised his disciples not to accept blindly what he told them, and insisted that they should themselves find the truth of his teachings.

This liberal non-dictatorial approach is respected even today by the monastic authorities. The present XIVth Dalai Lama observes :

> If one's faith is based simply upon authority – because the assertion one believes was stated by an authoritative person or scripture – such faith is not very stable or reliable. In contrast there is another type of faith that arises in dependence upon careful and sustained investigation. Such faith is based on knowledge. Qualities such as faith and compassion that are to be nurtured as one follows one's spiritual path are to be cultivated on the basis of reasoning and knowledge.[5]

Of course, the Buddhist spiritual leader is aiming at syncretism of science and spirituality. His views on modern science are worth mentioning, "I believe that it would be very fruitful to investigate the relationship between the mind and brain in relation to those various degrees of subtlety of consciousness".[6]

This is not to suggest that Buddhists always embraced science willingly. For instance Cabezan asserts that before Chinese took over Tibet in 1959. Tibetan monastic elite displayed scepticism towards western science. However, here the reason could be attributed to xenophobia which people belonging to one culture harbour against anything coming from a different culture. To Buddhists "whites" were total aliens and their distrust for these colonists can be appreciated .

The greatest contribution to science during the last 400 years has been made by the west. It is a paradox that Christianity, the religion of most Europeans has always been at loggerheads with science. Christianity is a dogma; it believes in revelation chronicled in the Bible. It believes in one God. Any view which is in conflict with the scripture is blasphemy. We need not repeat here what historians have recorded; how scientists were persecuted, how some of the nonbelievers were burnt at stake for perceiving reality empirically and rationally.

This is not the place to discuss the causes of this paradox : those who contributed most to science always had to fight a powerful adversary, while those (for example, Buddhist) who were not fettered by religious dogma, did not show much progress at least in "exact" sciences.

It should not be thought the dogma is powerful only in religion. It can be equally strong in other environments : dictatorship (Hitler's Germany), communism (erstwhile USSR) provide good examples. Whether science will progress or not in such environments depends upon the attitude of those who wield power.

21.4 Empiricism and Methodology

According to Gerald Du. Pré, "Buddhism is a scientific religion because it is based upon direct experience. It is empirical".[7] This seems to be the view of most writers.

Empiricim is the principle "which holds that sense experience is the only source of knowledge and affirms that all knowledge is founded on experience and through experience".[8]

Buddhist epistemology appears to follow empiricism. Buddhist scholars believe in total experience. Moreover, it recognizes two source of acquiring knowledge, direct perception and inference. How does this compare with what we call scientific investigation?

Pratykṣa is only a flash or a sensation. To perceive an empirical knowledge requires construction, judgement and so on which totally belong to the mental apparatus. Thus the final results need to be interpreted which again is done by the mind. There is no doubt that everyone is free to experiment and corroborate his teacher's views. However, it is difficult to compare one's own experience with that of one's teacher or peers because it always involves subjective elements. Buddhist epistemology centers round one's own mind and feelings. It is closer to western idealist empiricism of Berkeley, Hume and others.

In western science a theory is based on hypotheco-deductive method which involves objective measurements of reality. Buddhism despite being empirical in a technical sense concentrates more on what your mind judges. The method of meditation for example, may be usefult in physiological psychology, or neurosciences but there seems to be lack of methods such as objective measurements. The mind-body complex seems to be the most important instrument. Of course, the main goal of Buddhism is alleviation of human suffering, and it will certainly have an important place in psycho-spiritual dimension of the integral approach to human problems (see chapter 31).

21.5 The Transcendent

Despite being rooted in agnosticism, Buddhism contains many elements which can be said to belong to the transcendent. The cycle of birth and death, the doctrine of *karma,* the concept of ultimate reality consisting of momentary insubstantial point-instants and many other topics discussed under Buddhist logic belong to the transcendent. They should be either accepted as unproved axioms or must have epistemic sources. The only method of reaching the mystical sources is either through meditation or yogin's direct perception.

While everyone is free to undergo the prescribed training to experience such states as *nirvāṇa, prajñā,* etc. it is difficult to treat such knowledge or states as *social knowledge.*

Again, while the existence of God is not posited by Śākyamuni, later Buddhist thinkers tried to deify the Buddha. It looks as if mysticism and the transcendent are essential to protect the human feeling of helplessness. There may be some truth in what Du Pré says "Science without a transcendent aspect seems cold, heartless and mundane, and it is becoming clear that transcendence is a basic human need." Du Pré adds, "What is required is a bringing together of religion and science so that religion becomes scientific and science becomes transcendent".[10]

But this is a different topic which we shall discuss in chapter 30.

Is Buddhism science? In the broader sense it certainly is a science. As we mentioned earlier any stystematic study of knowledge is science. Buddhism is certainly science in this sense. If you acquire the knowledge of Buddhism, its different schools, its beliefs, its rituals and so on you have every right to say that you have studied the science of a particular religion, viz. Buddhism. Similarly, knowledge of Christian scriptures including the old and new bible, different denominations found in Christianity would be called science in the broad sense. A

Hindu may believe in Viṣṇu's *avatāras*, a Christian may believe in biblical miracles. So long as you acquire an accurate knowledge of these religions, you are in the realm of science in the broader sense. This sense does not require that you, too, should have the beliefs of Hindus or Christians.

However, when scholars assert that Buddhism is science, they mean much more than this. They emphasize that Buddhism is based on scientific methods and have the six characteristics mentioned earlier in this chapter. There is no doubt that its rational outlook, agnosticism and freedom of thought and systematic experimentation in the field of psychology elevates it much above many religions from the viewpoint of science. Unfortunately some of its beliefs (the twelve-stage cycle) fail to meet the tests of modern science, while some other techniques (say, knowledge through meditation) cannot be truly called social knowledge. It does not satisfy Popper's test in some cases. For example, the existence of ultimate reality or the cycle of birth and death cannot be falsified.

However, there is one field, viz. psychology and neurosciences in which Buddhist contribution can be used in conjuction with modern western techniques. This will be considered at some length later, but we may briefly indicate how some scholars such as U. Aung Thein try to connect Buddhist meditation with bioscience.[11]

Thein quotes French physiologist Loeb to the effect that the ultimate objective of science is to predict.[12] According to him the method of deliverance through the eightfold path leading to *nirvāṇa* seems to satisfy the test of predictability.

The eightfold path is divided into three division – (1) a triplet ("virtue") consisting of right speech, right action and right livelihood (ii) another triplet ("meditation") right effort, right mindfulness and right, contemplation, and (iii) a doublet ("realization" or "wisdom").

All sentient beings are an integrated structure of five *skandhas*. They are "mentality, perception, sensation, mental activities and consciousness. It is the ensemble of those interdependent components which through the prescribed *sādhanā* lead one to *nirvāṇa*". According to Śākyamuni, "In this fathom long body lie all the mysteries and problems of the universe".[13]

Explaining that Buddhist attitude towards *skandhas*, Thein recalls that according to *Satipaṭṭhāna* and *Mahāsatipaṭṭhāna suttas* what we call MAN is a process in which participate the various organs in liquid and solid form. In *Milinda Pañha,* to a king's question the Master answers that the body is conglomeration of parts, there being no abiding entity.[14]

According to Thein the body is nothing but a composition of organic systems in which chemical processes are undergoing constant changes.

In *Visuddhimagga*, virtue is depicted as volition and non-transgression. The main hurdles in the path of virtue are anger, vanity, ill-will, hypocrisy, restlessness, envy and jealousy, craftiness, resentment, arrogance, idleness, lust, indulgence, vulgarity and lack of restraint. Drawing from modern medical sciences, Thein says that the harmful states release many unwanted neurotransmitters which can damage such parts as thyroid, adrenal cortex, digestive tract and reproductive organs. For instance, rage, anger and agitation produce epinefrin which may result in the rise in the blood pressure, cardial output and oxygen consumption. Fear and anxiety result in increased secretion of acids which may produce ulcers. When the state of nervous tension continues for a long time there is impairment of nervous autonomous systems. Before meditation is prescribed, the practitioner has to follow the path of virtue so that there is complete harmony among physical, emotional and mental systems. Once virtuous path is adopted the aspirant can enter the next stage, meditation. His ascent includes countering hindrances, contemplating reality and finally attaining liberation.

The author again borrows from modern science and asserts that meditation diminishes oxygen input and carbon dioxide output by 20%. Other effects are reduction of lactic acid in blood with attendant increases in pH and decrease in galvanic skin response. In general it decreases metabolic rate.

Buddhist scholars usually speak of four land marks or *jhānas* on the way to *nirvāṇa*. The first *jhāna* is attained when physical and mental peace pervades the meditator. The state of desirelessness is a mark of having conquered the first *jhāna*. The second *jhāna* is concerned with the mental plane, concentration or *ekāgratā* (one pointedness). Theing contends that a *jhāni* through concentration can produce beneficial changes in RNA and protein production (connected with short term and long term memory), generate electrical activity in different areas of brain and trigger off past memories. He even goes on to suggest "since sentient beings have existed from beginningless time, it is not improbable to conclude that the feature of recall of past lives can be achieved by one who succeeds in the second *jhāna* through this physical mechanism".[15]

The third *jhāna* is concerned with equanimity. The *jhāni* can watch and judge impartiality. He has reached a state where he requires the least energy for psychosomatic processes, where the entropy (a measure of disorder) is minimum. When he conquers the third *jhāna*, he is free from anxiety and restlessness.

The fourth *jhāna* takes the practioner to a state of complete purity. There is no pain, no pleasure. He is completely detached and liberated. According to Thein this state corresponds to the electromagnetic waves of about 7 to 13 cycles per second. Scientists have found that application of external electromagnetic waves of this frequency to the brain leads to efflux of bound calcium from the nerve cell membranes, facilitating neural transmission.

According to him recent experiences of astronauts in prolonged weightlessness suggest that they have a unique experience that may be called spiritual. He conjectures that the cause of meditator's feeling a spiritual experience and the astronauts having a similar experience should be attributed to the same physiological changes. He quotes Śākyamuni – "*Ehipassako.* Come and see. Experience for yourselves".

We have already mentioned that the Buddha asked his disciples to verify through their own experience, what he told them.

Undoubtedly the method described above is scientific in a certain sense; there is repetition of the original experience. However, the objective aspect of modern science lies in correlating this subjective experience with the brain states. But this science of correlation is still in infancy and much remains to be done to interpret or corroborate what the individual has experienced. Moreover, the final state of liberation is quasi-transcendental and is not testable. Finally, Thein's assertion that under certain circumstances, one can explore the forgotten memories of the earlier birth raises two questions :

(1) Who is the one who takes a rebirth if there is no ego, no *ātmā* and no identity.

(2) How can we objectively prove the process of rebirth?

We have already commented on both these points and will again address these dilemmas in later chapters.

21.6 Hard Science

It looks strange that despite many favourable factors such as rational outlook, freedom to challenge tradition and so on, hard science physics, chemistry, biology, etc. did not progress as they did in the West where the church authorities were generally against any scientific theory which clashed with Christian dogma. Actually, it was not so much the religion but the geography which seems to have played a major role in deciding the progress of science. Science in Buddhism merely reflected the general stagnation of scientific culture in India and Asia.

In astronomy India seems to have done well. Though geocentric belief in the planetary system prevailed. Āryabhaṭa in 5th century suggested that the earth revolved around the sun and rotated on its axis. But this remained only a speculation. However, medieval Indian astronomers knew with considerable accuracy the precession of the equinoxes, the Lunar month, the duration of the year etc. Eclipses could also be predicted and their causes were rightly understood. The lunar calendar was quite accurate and the astronomers knew how to reconcile it with the solar year. There were many eras and in Sri Lanka a Buddha Era (from 544 BCE) was used.

It was in linguistics, grammar, ritual science and mathematics that India was ahead of other nations in the world. The decimal system and the concept of zero are perhaps the most significant contributions India has made to the world of knowledge.

In physics and chemistry its progress was limited, mostly confined to speculation. Their ideas about elements and atoms have parallels in different schools of Greek philosophy. Buddhists believed in momentariness and their concept of atoms was a series of projections into the empirical world of vaccuous momentary (*kṣaṇika*) beings, which were non material, in the "real" world. According to many scholars including Basham Buddhist atoms resembled quanta of Planck.[16]

If hard science like physics could not make much progress, it was the Indians' inability to establish theoretical models even where they possessed practical knowledge (e.g. metallurgy). The main reason seems to be decline of mathematical progress they had made earlier. To be specific, it was the lack of knowledge of calculus which is a *sine qua non* of advanced physics and even other hard sciences. Despite being familiar with the notion of zero, infinity and even infitesimals, they could not proceed beyond algebra and arithmetic. I do not think that it is a mere coincidence that development of calculus (by Newton and in Europe Leibnitz) preceded the Industrial revolution and science which can truly be called modern. It is equally unfortunate that advanced mathematics of the West could not find its way to Indian mathematicians.

India was ahead of the West in many branches of mathematics till about the time of Bhāskara (12th century) after which it seems to have lost to the West and with the development of calculus, the West certainly made a quantum leap not only in mathematics but also in natural sciences.

In case of Buddhists in addition to the general cause mentioned above another factor was operative. Buddhism has roots in love and compassion and its main goal is amelioration of human suffering. The eight-stage path of the Buddha involved emphasis on the exploration of the inner universe, the mind. No doubt even their best brains were engaged in introspection and meditation rather than in laboratory experiments.

22

Relativity : Interpretation and Misinterpretation

22.1 Euclidean Space

We cannot perceive space, but we assume its existence. We observe that a material body can be removed and another object can be installed in its place. Thus space is that which can be occupied by a material body. It is doubtful if we will ever be able to prove or disprove its existence, but we can accept it as an excellent parameter or tool of physics which helps us in correlating different events.

In physics there is a concept of the rigid body. Poincaré was the first scientist to point out that the easiest changes we observe in the rigid body is the positional change by voluntary motion of the body. The most important feature of this change is its reversibility. The pre-relativity physics assumed that the laws of a rigid body followed Euclidean geometry. Suppose P and Q are two points on the rigid body. PQ is called an interval or length.

Most of us learn in school that a point P in space can be uniquely represented by three Cartesian coordinates (x, y, z) with respect to rectangular coordinate axes OX, OY, OZ where O is the origin whose coordinates are taken as (0, 0, 0). Suppose Q has coordinates (x', y', z').

The length PQ is given by

$$PQ^2 = (x-x')^2 + (y-y')^2 + (z-z')^2$$

The characteristic of the Euclidean space is that PQ is the same or invariant whatever the system of coordinates you choose. You may shift the origin or rotate the axes, PQ will measure the same so long as you use Cartesian system of perpendicular axes. This means that PQ is invariant with respect to all observers. Even to the layperson this appears obvious. If you have a rigid rod you may orient it in anyway its length, will not change.

A few remarks are in order. Like space, "points" are assumed to exist for our convenience. We really do not know if such dimensionless points do exist, but they have served us well in mathematics and physics. An event can be described in terms of four coordinates (x, y, z, t) where the fourth coordinate is the time coordinate.

Suppose two events P and Q take place at (x_1, y_1, z_1, t_1) and (x_2, y_2, z_2, t_2) with respect to an observer. In pre-relativistic physics time is believed to flow uniformly and the time interval $|t_1-t_2|$ between two events is invariant, i.e. the same for all observers in addition to the distance between the places where the events occur, being invariant.

One of the most important discoveries of the 19th century was that the velocity of light in vacuum is constant for different observers. This looks strange, for in practice if we observe a moving object, its velocity will appear less when we are moving in the same direction as the object and more when we are moving in the opposite direction. Electromagnetic waves of which the "visible" light occupies a small frequency band, is an exception. Their velocity is independent of the observers. The constancy of the velocity of light was detected by Albert Michelson and Edward Morley in 1887 in their famous experiment. This was mentioned earlier in chapter 2.

22.2 Special Theory of Relativity

Special theory of relativity was propounded by Einstein in 1905, and is based on the discovery that the velocity of light is constant.

If we consider several observers stationed in different Cartesian frames of references moving with uniform velocity relative to one another and ignore the gravitational effect, we find that space and time intervals (PQ and $|t_1 - t_2|$) are not separately invariant. It is the space-time interval which appears the same to all such observers.

Let us write $(x_1 - x_2)^2 = dx^2$
$(y_1 - y_2)^2 = dy^2$, $(z_1 - z_2)^2 = dz^2$ and $(t_1 - t_2)^2 = dt^2$

Then in the classical physics the space interval is

$ds^2 = dx^2 + dy^2 + dz^2 \ldots. (1)$

which is invariant, and so is dt. In special relativity the invariant space-time interval involves time too. In fact,

$ds^2 = dx^2 + dy^2 + dz^2 - c^2dt^2 \ldots.. (2)$

If we write $u = ict$ where $i = \sqrt{-1}$ (which is usually called an imaginary quantity), we get

$ds^2 = dx^2 + dy^2 + dz^2 + du^2 \ldots\ldots (3)$

This equation is similar to (1), but there are a few differences. We have now four dimensions x, y, z, u. Equation (3) characterizes what is called the Euclidian space in four dimensions. (x, y, z, u). The space in which we live is called "flat", a metaphor borrowed from a two dimensional flat surface in which $ds^2 = dx^2 + dy^2$. In special relativity equation (3) gives a Euclidian space-time or flat space-time having four dimensions. We should, however, point out at the outset that time does not directly appear as a dimension; the fourth dimension is *ict* and we must keep in mind that the time coordinate in this respect does differ from space coordinates. Note also that |dt| is not constant for different observers. This implies that the time lapses or time intervals between two events may be different for different observers.

We had mentioned a few corollaries of Einstein's theory in chapter 2. We recall them and add a few more effects :

(1) A length appears to shrink to an observer who is moving along the length.

(2) A stationary clock appears slower from the viewpoint of a moving observer.

(3) A stationary mass appears to increase for a moving observer.

(4) Under certain circumstance energy (E) can be converted into mass (m) and vice versa according to the relation $E = mc^2$.

(5) Two events which appear simultaneous to one observer may appear to take place at different times to another observer.

(6) There is no velocity greater than c.

(7) Of several observers moving with uniform velocities relative to one another, no particular observer or the system of coordinates can be called "stationary". The concept of absolute velocity is thus banished.

22.3 Spatial Symmetry

To have more insight into the relative nature of space-time. Consider two Cartesian systems S and S' : O-XYZ and O'X'Y'Z'. To simplify matters we assume that S' moves with velocity v with respect to S and the movement is only along OX. Originally OXYZ and O'X'Y'Z' coincide. An observe A is stationary in S and another, A', in S'. Both observe an event E whose coordinates are (x, y, z, t) and (x', y', z', t') with respect to S and S'. Initially, when the systems coincide, all coordinates for an event are equal for both A and A'. Suppose now S' moves along OX and the event E is observed by A and A'. If you recall your school physics you should not have any difficulty in correlating the observations of A and A' at time t in accordance with prerelativity physics.

$x' = x - vt$
$y' = y$
$z' = z$
$t' = t$

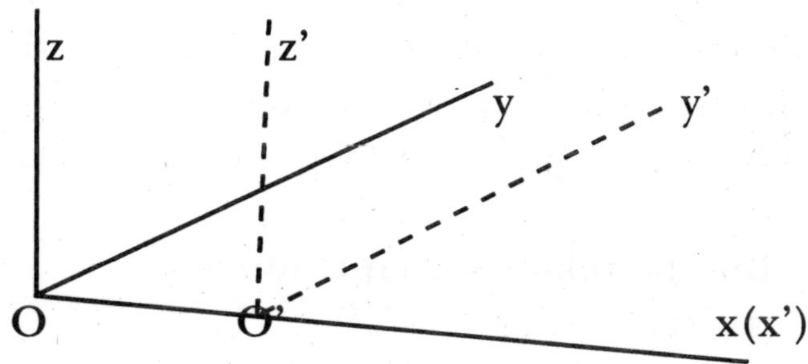

These equations are now modified in accordance with special theory of relativity.

$$x' = a(x - vt) \qquad \text{(A)}$$
$$y' = y,\ z' = z$$
$$t' = a(t - vx/c^2)$$
$$\text{where } a = 1/\sqrt{(1 - v^2/c^2)}$$

It is necessary to observe that $x \neq x'$ and $t \neq t'$. Note the additional multiplier *a* which is greater than 1. We cannot have $v \geq c$ because in that case v is either indeterminate or imaginary. This shows the c is the maximum velocity that can be attained. This is the velocity of electromagnetic waves. A material particle always travels with a velocity less than c. The time (t') is also modified. In fact all the consequences mentioned in 22.2 can be derived on the basis of this transformation equations which are called Lorentzian transformation equations.

If you consider S' as stationary, the S moves with a velocity -v with respect to S. The newly derived transformation equations appear as $x = a(x' + vt')$, $y = y'$, $z = z'$, $t = a(t' + vx'/c^2)$. This shows the spatio-temporal symmetry. The same equations are obtained when in (A) above v is replaced by -v and primed letters become unprimed and vice versa.

It is easy to see that if v is small compared with c, v/c = 0 and a = 1. The relativity equations then are the same as those in Newtonian physics. This is the reason why in day-to-day life we can make do with classical physics.

Consider three Cartesians systems traveling in the same direction S' travels with the velocity v with respect to S, and S'' with the velocity v' with respect to S'. What will be the velocity of S'' with respect to S? We should in classical physics, expect

$u = v + v'$

But the relativistic equation is

$u = (v + v')/(1+ vv'/c^2)$

which reduces to the addition u = v + v' if v, v' are small compared to c. It is now quite obvious that both space and time are relative.

Suppose the mass of a body in S is m_0 then if you measure this mass from S' it appears to be

$m = m_0/\sqrt{(1- v^2/c^2)}$

which is more than m_0. We call m_o the "rest mass" of the body.

22.4 General Relativity

We assumed in the special theory that the observer was located in any of the frames of reference travelling with uniform velocities relative to one another. These systems are called *inertial systems.*

Einstein argued that in general a system may not be inertial. We saw earlier that space and time were replaced by a single concept, space-time. Einstein conceived a space-time continuum in the universe. He maintained :

> Just as it was consistent from the Newtonian standpoint to make both statements, *tempus est absolutum* (time is absolute) *spatium est absolutum* (space is absolute), so from the standpoint of the special theory of relativity we must say, *continuum spatii est temporis absolutum* (space-time continuum is absolute). Here *absolutum* means not only physically real, but also independent in its physical properties, having a physical effect but not itself influenced by physical conditions.[1]

However, such thinking faced a few conceptual hurdles. This led Einstein to postulate the *principle of equivalence* which is the foundation of his relativity theory.

22.5 Principle of Equivalence

Most of us study the concept of inertia of a body. It is because of the inertia that a body remains at rest or continues to move with uniform velocity. In order to change its state we have to apply a force to it. Inertia thus represents a body's resistance to change its state. A measure of inertia is the mass of the body given by the equation

Force = mass × acceleration

$F = m\ a$

From this Newton's law, the mass can be treated as the ratio

$m = F/a$

We can call this mass inertial mass (m_a) We also study the behaviour of a body under the earth's gravitational force F_g.

$F_g = mg$, where g is the intensity of the gravitational field at the point which is usually treated as a constant. From this viewpoint the mass appears as the ratio $m = F/g$, which is called the gravitational mass (m_g) of the body. There is no *a priori* reason why the intertial (inert) mass (m_a) should be equal to the gravitational mass (m_g). But it so happens that both these masses are exactly equal. This was proved empirically through several experiments by Eotvos.

This equality of (m_a) and (m_g) has far-reaching consequences. It means that the acceleration is independent of the nature of the body. Consider a frame of reference S' which is accelerated with respect to an unaccelerated inertial frame S, the relative acceleration being g. Then the masses which are far away from each other from other bodies, will show no acceleration relative to S. On the other hand with respect to S' all masses will have equal and parallel accelerations, g. In fact they will behave in relation to S' in the same way as they would if gravitational field of strength g were present in S', and S' were not accelerated.

What this means is one cannot distinguish between an accelerated system and the system at rest with the equivalent gravitational field. This is the principal of equivalence. In Einstein's own words "the possibility of explaining the numerical equality of inertia and gravitation by unity of their nature gives the general theory of relativity, according to my conception, such a superiority over the conceptions of classical mechanics, that all the difficulties encountered in the development must be considered as small in comparison with this progress".[2]

This principle implies that there are no preferential "inertial systems" whose very concept involves circular reasoning : a body moves without acceleration if it is sufficiently far from other bodies, and we can know that it is sufficiently far away only by the fact that it moves without acceleration.

This does not mean that we totally rule out the use of inertial systems. There can be finite regions in space where there may exist a system with respect to which material particles move freely without acceleration at least approximately. We can use such a system as inertial and establish Cartesian coordinates as we did in case of special relativity. This is done for convenience. A region in which an inertial frame of reference can be used is called "Galilian region" or "flat".

However, the gravitational strength usually varies from point to point depending on the configuration of masses. In general relativity, therefore one considers an arbitrary system at least in theory. In such a case the interval

$$ds^2 = dx^2 + dy^2 + dz^2 + du^2$$

is no longer constant as in case of systems moving uniformly. The interval is replaced by

$$ds^2 = \Sigma g_{\mu\nu}\, dx_\mu\, dx_\nu \quad .....(3)$$

$ds^2 = g_{11}dx_1dx_1 + g_{12}dx_1dx_2 + ...$ where x, y, z, are replaced by x_1, x_2, x_3, x_4 and Σ shows the summation over μ, ν (which vary from 1 to 4) and $g_{\mu\nu}$ is called a tensor. Moreover the interval ds apples only to events which are infinitesimally close in space-time. We cannot discuss the mathematical aspect in detail. You may just remember tensors have some resemblance with vectors and $g_{\mu\nu}$ is a tensor of order two and dimensions four. The interval or metric in Euclidian space in four dimensions is

$$ds^2 = dx_1^{\,2} + dx_2^{\,2} + dx_3^{\,2} + dx_4^{\,2} \qquad .... (4)$$

This is only a special case of the equation (3) above.

22.6 Relativity-Reality and Myths

It is unfortunate that the word “relativity” appears in Einstein’s theory relating to space, time and matter. Relativity theory has been misinterpreted by common people, and stretched beyond credibility by some imaginative scientists. A brief account this aspect along with genuine parallels is furnished below.

Structure and Content

Epistemology and metaphysics are so entwined with each other that it is difficult to separate one from the other. When you gain more knowledge about the events in the universe, you feel there is a change in your perception of reality. This in turn enables you to have a different approach which may lead to the discovery of a new correlations between events in the world.

Generally we find there are two kinds of realities : one is related to structure and another related to the nature of existents. The history of physics teaches us that the second aspect is elusive and depends on such factors as human interpretation and the definition of existents. The first characteric is more important inasmuch as we feel we are on surer grounds. This is exactly why philosophers and scientists prefer to think of the universal phenomena in terms of events and their correlations, which is concerned with structure. Relativity and quantum physics have spawned innumerable conjectures that can be traced to speculation about metaphysical reality rather than events and their correlations.

Dimensions

The fact that the invariant space-time interval ds depends as much on time as on space coordinates has been interpreted to mean that we live in four dimensions and not in the three dimensional world.

We must realize that the word "dimension" should be used with circumspection. We always lived in the world of space and time, what we did not know was the fact that the time interval between two events was not the same for different observers. Although the invariant intervals ds and dt are replaced by combined space-time intervals, space and time parameters are not on par. First, there are three dimensions of space but only one dimension of time. We need three space coordinates and one time coordinate to describe an event. Second, space coordinates appear as the sum of three squares in ds^2 while the time coordinate appears as a negative square of time multiplied by *c.* Third, we know from our experience that "going through a time interval" is not the same as "going through space". In a spatial dimension we can move backward and forward while in case of time we can move only towards the future. Fourth, each of us has a personal time measured by a clock which is stationary with respect to us. This is the scale which gives us the feel for "time". It is necessary to understand that the word "dimension" is used figuratively or metaphorically to some extent.

The use of figurative language is even more apparent when we move from a "flat" space to a "curved space". The former is a Euclidean space with Cartesian coordinates. The second uses the Riemannian geometry; an abstract geometry developed by Georg Riemann (1826–1866) before relativity theory was born. We may say that the Riemannian geometry is a mere tool that is used in general relativity. From this viewpoint words such as "flat", "curved" appear mere metaphors. What this means is that metaphysical interpretation of space-time is a matter of taste and scientifically neutral.

According to Eddington we may call equation (4), as the natural geometry and equation (3) as the abstract geometry. Then "a field of force represents the discrepancy between the natural geometry of the coordinate system and the abstract geometry arbitrarily ascribed to it".[3]

Metaphysically, you may treat matter responsible for changing "the geometry of space-time" or remain old fashioned in the flat space and argue that it is the gravitational force attributable to the presence of matter which changes the behavior of the bodies. Scientists like E.A. Milne hold that there is no need to regard space as non-Euclidean and that the geometry we adopt can be decided entirely by motives of convenience.[4]

It is necessary to point out that physicists also introduce what is called *function-space* of n dimensions to study a system of n particles. Mathematicians have even constructed Euclidean spaces of infinitely many dimensions To summarize, the word dimension should not be literally translated as the dimension similar to the spatial dimension.

Relativism and Relativity

It is rather unfortunate that Einstein's theory embodying what is called the principle of equivalence is called relativity theory. This has created a misconception in the minds of intellectuals not familiar with relativity physics that "everything is relative".

In fact in philosophy there has existed a concept called *relativism* or *relativity* which denies objectivity. The fact that there exist several viewpoints in relation to concepts especially in social sciences and ethics indicates social relativism. A certain society permits polygyny whereas in most societies it is prohibited. In most western societies women have the same rights as men whereas in many eastern societies there is gender discrimination against women. Social customs and mores vary from society to society. What is "right" in one social group may be "wrong" in another. We shall revert to this topic when we consider *universal relativiztion.*

22.7 Jainism

We have discussed at length *anekāntavāda* and *syādvāda*. To some extent they contain philosophical relativity and to some extent they demonstrate how partial views can be mistaken for the whole truth. But they are only remotely connected with Einstein's theory. Ramji Singh's following comments clearly indicate a misconception harboured by non-physicists :

> Hence *anekānta* stands against all mental absolutism. We can stbstantiate this relativistic standpoint on cosmo-micro-physical ground supported by Einsteinian doctrine of relativity and Maxwell's equation of electromagnetism which go fundamentally against the notion of absolute truth.[5]

Ironically, Maxwell's equations have led to the discovery that the velocity of light c is a universal constant and not relative to different observers. Einstein's relativity again, uses this fact of constancy of electromagnetic radiation, based on Michelson Morley experiments.

Kothari has used an ingenious argument to connect *syādvada* with special relativity[6]. An object travelling with a velocity appears at rest to the person who is stationed on that object. Now according to *syādvāda* there must be a point of view which contradicts this proposition. In other words, there exists an entity with respect to which an observer cannot be at rest. This entity is identified with light or electromagnetic radiation which we know is the maximum possible relative velocity. But "syāt" is "may be" and not "should be". Nevertheless such an argument if made before the discovery of maximum velocity can be called one of those sources lying in philosophy which propels a scientist towards a genuine scientific theory.

22.8 Buddhist Logic

There are many paralles between Buddhist logic and physics. The things do not exist independently, their existence is relational. No thing can be studied in isolation there being interdependence. This is consistent with modern systemic view.

Existents interact with one another and are changing every moment. While the idea of causation appears strange, the basic concept of Dependendent Origin explains how the world is conditioned and subject to rules.

According to Upasaka Wu Shu in "Atom and *Anitta*", the *Diamond Sutta's* assertion, "when the Tathāgata speaks of universe he does not mean really universe; he calls them universes only nominally" is comparable with the finding of nuclear physics, viz. an atom is not indivisible. He contends that this assertion of sutta is analogous with the paradox – an atom is really not an atom; though it is called atom for convenience.[6a]

In Buddhist logic "Time and Space" cannot be separated from the things that exist in them.

> Every point instant may be viewed as a particle of time, as a particle of space and as a sensible quality. But this difference is the difference of our own mental attitude. The point-instant itself the ultimate reality cut loose from all imagination is qualityless, timeless and indivisible.[7]

The broad Buddhist idea of space-time on the whole idea of space-time is consistent with the relativistic view. Of course, we can only remain silent on the ultimate reality of point-instants.

Perhaps the best parallel between Buddhist logic and modern physics emerges when the Buddhist logician asserts that there is no matter but only flashes of energy (*saṃskāra-vāda*). This fairly agrees with mass-energy convertibility.

Again, the concept that "all things without exception are nothing but momentary events"[8] fairly agrees with the modern post-relativity scientists' view of perceiving phenomena as events rather than objects.

Buddhist scholars' conception of ultimate reality as chains of momentary beings each being efficient suggests the analogy of a field (such as gravitational, magnetic or electric field.) In physics the field theory was an advancement over the conventional "action at a distance theory in mechanics". As we shall see later that this concept is further extended to the quantum field.

23

Subatomic Particles

23.1 Classical Physics

In chapter 1 we barely considered the elements of quantum theory. In this chapter the quantum world will be considered in greater detail. The pre-RQ physics was first based on Newtonian ideas. There was an absolute space and also a uniform time which moved from the past to the future. In the space were material bodies whose movements were governed by the gravitational force one body exerting upon the other. The force was attractive and obeyed the inverse square law. Theoretically, material particles were regarded as mass points which are indestructible. Newton also developed the equations of motion which we study in school. It is to Newton's credit that he integrated the work of Copurnicus and Galileo relating to planetary movements and free falling bodies.

As we mentioned in chapter 1 the wave theories emerged to explain the phenomena like interference which could not be described by Newtonian mechanics.

The turning point in physics was perhaps 1905 in which year Einstein's special theory of relativity as well as his explanation for the discovery of discrete absorption and emission of wave-packets, now called quanta appeared. It was for this theory that Einstein received the Nobel prize though he is better known as the author of relativity theory.

Einstein's General Theory of Relativity appeared in 1915. These two theories (relativity and quantum) revolutionized many basic concepts in physics. This was briefly considered in chapter 1. An instance of what we have called RQ effect is found in what Heisenberg had to say :

> The violent reaction on the recent developments of modern physics can only be understood when one realizes that here the foundations of physics have started moving; and that this motion has caused the feeling that the ground would be cut from science.[1]

The discovery of X-rays and radioactivity led physicists to change their view that atoms were solid indestructible units. By 1920s a few models of the atomic structure were available, thanks to a group of scientists including Niels Bohr, Louis De Broglie, Erhin Schrödinger, Wolfgang Pauli, Werner Heisenberg, Paul Dirac and many others from different countries.

The crude picture of an atom we get is – there is a *nucleus* consisting of protons, positively charged and neutrons (no charge) Around the nucleus were the electrons in motion in different "orbits" or "shells". In an atom all protons are identical and all electrons are identical. In a neutral atom there are as many protons as there are electrons. In the hydrogen atom, the lightest element, there is one proton (p^+) and one electron (e^-). In Helium (He) there are two protons and two electrons, and so on and so forth. The number of protons determines the atomic number of the element. Thus hydrogen and helium have atomic numbers 1 and 2. The number of neutrons is not fixed. For example, the usual hydrogen has no neutron while its variant (isotope) has one neutron.

Although we stated that, electrons moved "round the nucleus" we really do not know the correct picture of how electrons are distributed. Physicists estimate that their speed is about 600 miles per second. With such a fantastic speed the atom appears as a solid though the volume of the nucleus and electrons is negligible compared with that of the whole atom. The atom is more of space than matter. When an electron "jumps" from a higher orbit to a lower orbit it emits energy as electromagnetic radiation and when the atom absorbs energy or quanta, an electron jumps to a higher orbit. When an electron is in the lowest orbit it is in the ground state which is the normal state. Neutrons and protons have approximately equal masses, and are about 2000 times as heavy as electrons.

The dual behaviour of electrons appears even when they are tied to an atom, they can be described as "standing waves" as are found in vibrating strings. Further, they are associated with integers called quantum numbers related to their energy level, the pattern of their equivalent wave, and their "rotation" which word should not be interpreted literally.

The attractive nuclear force which keeps protons and neutrons at the nucleus is extremely strong but extends to only twice or thrice the diameter of the nucleons. Beyond this the nucleons repel each other. Nucleons have a great speed about 40,000 miles per second. The net result is that the nucleus is dynamic but quite stable.

23.2 Building Blocks

For many centuries scientists have been searching for those fundamental substances – those bricks and mortar which are responsible for the entire edifice of the universe. The quantum phenomena have proved that the "ultimate stuff" is a will o' the wisp. Imagine the confusion of the scientists of the 20th century, when they were bombarded with incredible results :

> (1) Mass and energy are interconvertable (2) The list of "elementary particles" which started with electrons, protons and neutrons now exceeds two hundred. They can hardly be called "elementary".

The speeds with which nucleons and some subatomic particles move are so high that scientists have to use relativistic instead of classical physics. Dirac's prediction of the existence of the anti-electron having the same mass as an electron but equal and opposite charge was confirmed within two years of his prognostication. This has led to the discovery of many pairs of particles having opposite charges but otherwise the same mass. Scientists have been able convert energy into such particle-antiparticle duos. These pairs when they coalesce with each other, vanish totally, creating energy. Believe it or not, when we try to divide these particles using high energy what we get is not smaller pieces, but two original wholes. We can write the result symbolically

$$x + E = x + x$$

which simply means E (energy) is used up in creating an additional x. Capra writes : "The subatomic articles are *destructible and indestructible at the same time*".[2] This appears to violate the law of contradiction. Collision of two (high energy) particles is often used to study such phenomena.

Particle physics is now called high energy physics because one requires very high energy to deal with (especially collision) subatomic particles. Most of these created particles live for less than one millionth of a second. They seem to revert to their stable cousins : protons, electrons and neutrons.

23.3 Virtual Particles

It should be remembered that in case of high energy physics, scientists have to use relativistic equations on account of high speeds of subatomic particles. While some classical problems seem to vanish when these equations are used, new problems have cropped up.

The force between interacting particles has to be perceived as "an exchange of particles" These particles are called "virtual particles" the stronger the force, higher is the probability of exchangining virtual particles. It is conjectured that even a nucleon may emit such virtual particles. What we called field (force) seems to have its avatar in these virtual particles.

On the one hand, the quantum world appears complex with a plethora of particles called "elementary" which can fall into different categories based on mass, charge, behaviour and so on. On the other hand, the world appears simple though not predictable, simple in the sense you can use a simple epithet "everchanging". Capra captures the essence of this world in the following words :

> The high energy scattering experiments of the past decades have shown the dynamic ever-changing nature of the particle world in the most striking way. Matter has appeared in these experiments as completely mutable. All particles can be transmuted into other particles; they can be created from energy and can vanish into energy. In this world classical concepts like 'elementary particle', 'material substance' or 'isolated object' have lost their meaning, the whole universe appears as a dynamic world of inseparable patterns.[3]

The appearance of "virtual particles" means the boundaries between several categories, even broad categories, are vanishing : matter, energy, force, magnetic field, electric field, gravitational field. One should not be surprised if in the future any existent of type x is convertible into another type y and vice versa. By "existent" I mean any of the categories we use in physics. To quote Capra again :

> They show that the properties of a particle can only be understood in terms of its activity – of its interaction with the surrounding environment – and that the particle, therefore cannot be seen as an isolated entity, but has to be understood as an integrated part of the whole.[4]

The quantum world resembles a forest rich in flora and fauna with innumerable species and types. There is, however, a difference you cannot tell when a certain variety will suddenly disappear and when a certain member will suddenly emerge before you almost from nowhere.

You can have some idea of diversity if you know the characteristics on the basis of which the elementary population can be classified. Protons, electrons and neutrons were the only building blocks scientists knew about fifty years ago. Physicists later found that these particles consisted of different types of smaller particles called *quarks*. They can be classified according to the following properties[5] :

Flavor – of which at least six are known; up, down, etc.

Color – Each flavor has a "color" of which there are three red, green and blue.

Spin 0, 1/2, 1, 2, ..., etc.

Charge (Polarity) – positive, negative and neutral

Pairing – Every particle has its partner – antipartice – with opposite charges, but otherwise identical with its twin. (e.g. electron, positron) The antiparticle of a neutral particle is that particle itself.

Real-virtual – which we have already considered.

Size/mass – From zero (photon, nutrino), electron (the lightest mass), muons, pions, kaons (a few hundred times as massive as electron), cascade, omega, etc. (about a few thousand times as massive as electrons).

Life – From one millionth of a second (unstable) to comparatively long (stable) like neutron.

Of course you can think of innumerable combinations of these characteristics (subject to a plethora of rules) to imagine the variety.in the quantum world.

23.4 Reactions

This is not all; variety abounds in the outcome of collision of two or more particles. A few reactions are given below :

(1) $n \rightarrow p + e + \nu(a)$

This is called "beta decay" in which a neutron decays into a proton (+), electron (-) and anti-neutrino $\nu(a)$ (the twin of the neutrino). The last is massless and difficult to detect.

(2) $0 \rightarrow p + \pi + p(a) \rightarrow 0$

Three particles are created from "vacuum", proton, pion and antiproton and disappear.

(3) $n \rightarrow n + \pi \rightarrow n$

A neutron emits (under cettain conditions) a pion which is absored by the parent.

(4) $p + p(a) \rightarrow \pi^+ + \pi^- + \pi^+ + \pi^- + \pi^+ + \pi^- + \pi^+ + \pi^-$

A proton and an antiproton collide giving rise to eight pions. Usually these reactions are depicted using Feynman diagrams after Richard Feynman. However, I have used a simpler method and have not considered conditions under which these reactions take place.[6] This, of course, involves omission of secondary information, but our main purpose here is to indicae variety, uncertainty and dynamic nature of the quantum particles.

Example (2) is most astonishing, showing that a void hides an unperceived world.

23.5 Grand Unification Theory (GUT)

Force-carrying particles have been divided into four catagories :

1. Gravitational force is universal in the sense every particle experiences a force depending on its mass and energy. The force, so far as physics stands today, is only attractive and acts over long distances. Nevertheless it is the weakest type of force.

Physicists posit the existence of both virtual (massless) and real gravitons. The exchange of virtual gravitons is reflected in the gravitational attraction between two bodies even over a long distance. It is also hypothesized that real gravitons constitute gravitational waves. These weak waves have not been detected.

2. Elecromagnetic forces belong to the second category; these are attractive as well as repulsive and appear only between charged particles. The forces are strong and a force between two electrons is 10^{42} times bigger than the gravitational force.[7]
3. In this category lie weak nuclear forces responsible for radioactivity. They act on particles of spin 1/2.

4. Finally there is the strong nuclear force which hold quarks in the nucleus and also bind protons and neutrons. Its carrier is a gluon which interacts with itself and quarks. This force has a property called confinement according to which particles are bound in combinations that have no "color".

Physicists dream that all these categories would one day be brought under one single theory called Grand Unification theory. It is impossible to discuss here the progress towards this theory. We can only observe that physicists have not been able to amalgamate gravitational force with other three categores. In other words, a quantum theory of gravity is yet to be born.

24

Particle Wave Duality

24.1 Interference

In chapter 2 we introduced you to the quantum world. We must now consider a typical two-slit experiment which demonstrates the particle-wave duality in detail.

To understand the dual behavior of particles such as electrons or photons it is necessary to know something about interference, a phenomenon that occurs when two waves meet.

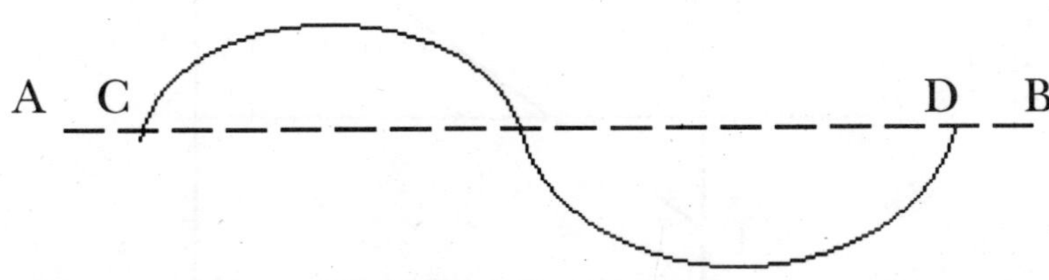

Fig. 24.1 A wave

A simple wave is shown in figure 24.1, which propagates in direction AB. The amplitude of a wave is the distance between the crest (or the trough) and the mean path AB. Its wave-length λ is the distance between the two successive crests or troughs or any two similarly placed points such as C, D on the path. If ν is the frequency or the number of cycles (such as CD) per second then

$\lambda \nu = c$

which is the velocity of the wave. In case of electromagnetic waves it is the constant *c*.

Suppose two waves are superimposed on each other. To simplify matters we assume that they have the same amplitude and frequency or wavelength. We say that waves are "in phase" when their crests (and also troughs) fall on each other. Such waves reinforce each other; the amplitude is doubled and the intensity or brightness (in case of light) becomes four times because the intensity is proportional to the square of the amplitude. The waves are totally out of phase when the crest of one wave coincides with the trough of the other. In this case, one wave "cancels" the other and the net intensity is zero everywhere. In the intermediate cases, the resulting wave gives a mixed picture : At the points where the waves reinforce each other, greater intensity will appear while at the points where they tend to cancel each other, the net effect will be the reduction of the intensity.

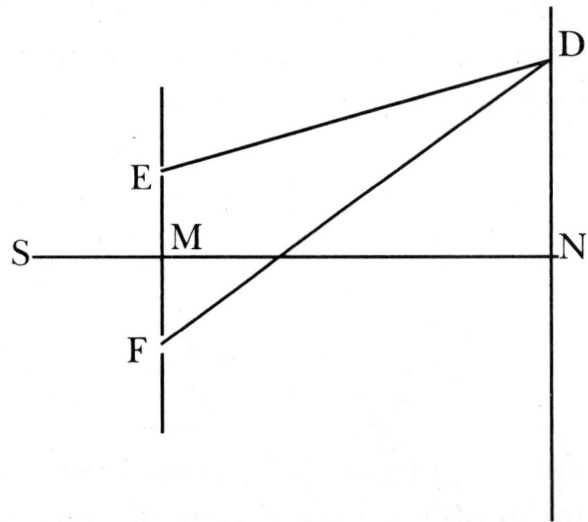

Fig. 24.2 Two-slit experiment

Fig. 24.2 shows the standard experimental set up. S is the source emitting photons (light) or elementary particles such as electrons, E, F (EM = FM) are narrow slits and DN is a screen perpendicular to the plane of the paper.

Suppose initially only one slit is open and we pass a beam of light (photons), through the slit, after passing through the slit the beam spreads out in different directions randomly, a phenomenon called *diffraction.* The screen is illuminated uniformly. We now reduce the intensity of light. We will find that the screen now shows spots. This explains the corpuscular property of light. The bright spots arise because dicrete photons hit the screen.

We now open the other slit. Remember we use monochromatic light which consists of a single frequency. For example, if the source is a sodium lamp it emits waves of the wave length 5×10^{-7}. If the light is sufficiently strong instead of the spots in the first part of the experiment we see a wavy pattern alternate bands of brightness and darkness. This clearly shows that the two secondary sources E and F give rise to two waves which *interfere* on the screen.

As we explained earlier the bright bands have four times the original intensity while the dark bands have zero intensity. Light now displays its wave properties. It is almost impossible to assert that a dark band can emerge when two corpuscular beams from E and F meet each other. If those beams of light consist of particles they cannot "cancel" each other.

It is easy to see that at the center N, both waves emanating from E and F have travelled the same distance. Hence they are in phase giving the brightest band at N (i.e. along the length perpendicular to the plane of the paper, in three dimensions). At any other point, the intensity will depend on the difference between two paths taken by these two waves, i.e. the difference between ED and FD.

If the intensity of source is reduced sufficiently it can be ensured that "not more than one photon at a time is passing the vicinity of slits".[1] According to Penrose the phenomenon of interference including destructive interference ("cancellation") arises even from one single photon. If only one slit is open the photon would travel through the slit; but if both slits are open it has two alternatives. Destructive interference suggests that the single photon has travelled through both slits. Has it divided itself into parts one at E and one at F and have these two truncated portions interfered with each other? Most physicists reject this possibility of "splitting a photon". Another interpretation is in terms of "alternatives" "each individual particle behaves in a wavelike way entirely on its own; and different alternative possibilities open to a particle can sometimes cancel one another out".[2] This is strange; it looks as if the photon has its own mind or a reflex (like human beings), or likes and dislikes If there is one route of escape it uses it, if there are more passages than one it says, "No I won't move unless you close one of the passages".

In order to test these two interpretations, the scientist can use a photon detector at one slit. This leads to a strange consequence; if the detector is placed either near E or F so that the experimenter can tell if the photon has passed through that particular slit, the interference pattern simply disappears. Ostensibly, it looks as if the lack of knowledge as to which slit the photon passed through is a precondition for interference to occur.[3]

Since physicists have decided that a photon cannot be split they present a weird explanation, "To get interference the alternatives must both contribute, sometimes 'adding'.... some times 'subtracting'...[4]".

Quantum physicists have developed a probability calculus involving i(√-1), which leads to two levels of reality : micro (quantum) and macro (classical).

We shall not consider the complex mathematics until a little later.

It appears to have been designed *ad hoc* to deal with this catch-22 position, for interference, both alternatives (slits) should contribute, but a photon cannot divide itself, so that its parts could use both alternative paths.

While we considered a photon-source above, use of electrons leads to a similar picture of particle wave duality.

24.2 *Catuṣkoṭi*

It is interesting to investigate if *catuṣkoṭi* can be used to explain the behavior of a photon or an electron. While *catuṣkoṭi* leads to the crisis of identity and breach of logical laws, it can be a good guide in the particle-wave duality.

Suppose *catuṣkoṭi* is applicable. In case of particles we should get four alternatives :

(i) x is a particle.
(ii) x is not a particle.
(iii) x is both a particle and a non-particle.
(iv) x is neither a particle nor a non-particle.

Actually physicists have come to the following conclusion :

(a) x is both a particle and a wave.

Unfortunately, they have been hasty in concluding that (a) is the same as the third option of *catuṣkoṭi,* viz.

(b) x is both a particle and a non-particle.

Their argument can be true if and only if wave ≡ non-particle.

There is no logical reason why this identity should hold good.

It is possible that x is neither a particle nor a wave; but a third type of existent that may be called wavicle or partiwave.[5]

The wavicle then may be said to possess its own properties to be determined empirically. We can then argue that physical existents are of three types – particle, wave and wavicle (or partiwave). The wavicle behaves like a wavicle and that is the end of it.

By creating a new identity, we have removed the violation of the law of contradiction and the law of the middle. Because if we do not create wavicles, we should have the following fallacies :

Light is both a stream of particles and a wave (non-particle).

Light is neither a stream of particles nor a wave (non-particle).

These violate the law of contradiction and the law of middle.

Buddhist and Jaina Logic

The above fallacies appear as the last two limbs of the *catuṣkoṭi*. We have already remarked that those who believe in *catuṣkoṭi* assume that these two alternatives exist only in transcendental phenomena in which case particle-wave duality will be banished from the mundane. The Buddhist logician can claim the behavioral changes of light are only apparent. To understand the inconsistent behavior we have to enter the supernatural world which is accessible to yogins and those who have practiced meditation to gain access to the transcendent. In any case, since the point-instant as well as its image is momentary or changes every moment, Buddhists do not face an epistemic problem.

Jaina logicians should have no major difficulty in demystifying the strange behavior of light. They should tell you "some of you have a viewpoint that light is a wave, some of you have a standpoint that it is a stream of particles. Your conclusion is based on your particle views. The only assertion we can make is that light – whatever it is – behaves like waves at one time and as particles at other; but these different behaviors do not occur at the same time". As we have remarked earlier Jaina logicians avoid entering the transcendent or the mystical world as far as possible.

For common people the behavioral pattern would appear strange, but since the opposite behaviors do not appear simultaneously, they would consider the phenomenon unusual, but not logically impossible.

24.3 Uncertainty Principle

This principle usually appears as Heinsenberg's inequality, viz.

$$\Delta x \, \Delta p \geq h/2\pi$$

where Δx and Δp are accuracies in position and momentum of a particle. To quote Penrose :

> According to this principle it is not possible to measure (i.e. to magnify to classical level) both the position and momentum of a particle accurately at the same time.[6]

I have purposely quoted Penrose because we find a strange linguistic equivalence in two expressions : “It is not possible to measure”, “i.e. to magnify to the classical level”.

This equivalence will be recalled later while discussing the interpretation of duality.

Heisenberg’s formula implies that the more accurately we try to measure x there arises greater inaccuracy in p; and vice versa. To give an example, if the position is measured with accuracy of one part in a nanometer (which is equal to 10^{-9}m) the ascertainment of the momentum would be so large that “one could not expect that one second later, the electron would be closer than 100 kilometers away”.[7]

24.4 Probability

Before we proceed to explore the quantum world a digression is necessary. In this chapter we shall discuss probability and chance without being technical. An elementary knowledge of probability theory is necessary to have some insight into how physicists look at this strange world.

The common person uses several words which appear to be equivalent : probability, chance, credibility, expectation and so forth. The following illustrations will appear quite familiar :

E1

(a) She will probably attend the board meeting tomorrow, she is rarely absent.

(b) If you toss a coin the chances that it will show heads or tails are equal.

(c) I think the probability that the US will win most gold medals in the next Olympics is very high, almost cent percent.

(d) “What is the probability that a square is circular?” “Zero, you fool”.

(e) I rate the probability of her passing the exam as 50%. But if she devotes one hour more to her studies, I would say her chances are 60%.

The common perception of probability is the degree of expectation which need not be defined. Whether we use the word probability or chance or odds we know what they mean. A few comments about the concept of probability must be made.

First, when we use the word probability of the occurrence of an event we are usually speaking from our experience of similar events. E1 (a) is an example which clearly shows this fact from the words "she is rarely absent".

Second, our hunches are based on our own knowledge or what the authorities in the field usually opine. However, we take into consideration several factors relevant to the occurrence of an event. This makes probability estimates vary from person to person. For example, all of us know that a certain hockey team is excellent and we assume that it will probably win the gold medal. Only three people know that an important player has suddenly developed pain in his knee-joint and is likely to be replaced by an inferior substitute at the last moment. These three people will have a better estimate of probability than others.

Most of us use a probability scale, though we may not be mathematicians or statisticians. The scale usually starts with zero (almost impossible) and ends with 1 (certain) or 100 (in case of percentage) E1, (d) and (e) illustrate this. However, even a savage who is not familiar with numbers has a non-numerical scale in which probabilities may be arranged in *order.* He may know that the probability of his son A defeating the wrestling champion X is more than the probability of his son B doing the same feat, though he may not quantify his hunch.

24.5 Extreme Probabilities

The knowledge of the external world, as we have mentioned earlier, is always probable. But the two extremes of the probability guesses "impossible" and "certain" appear to be easy to appreciate than the intermediate cases. For example, in E1(d) we know that the case is impossible because a square cannot be a circle. This may be considered a tautological impossibility. Similarly we can accept the statement "the probability that a bachelor is married is zero" as a tautological certainty.

But there are other extreme probabilities which we assume without misgivings and which only skeptics will challenge.

E2

(a) The probability that you will celebrate your *bicentennial* birth anniversary is zero.
(b) That the sun will rise in the east tomorrow is 100% probable.
(c) The chances that A, a marathon champion will run from Beijing to Moscow in one hour are zero.
(d) "I can assure you a cat can beget a dog. I have seen it happen twice". "Nonsense, it is impossible".
(e) "He is a brave man. I am told when he was just an infant of one year, he killed a tiger with his own hands". "Impossible. Do you think I am a kid?".

These examples illustrate occurrences which have probability zero (a, c, d, e) or certainly (b) However, these are synthetic statements and strictly speaking the probability figures cannot be proved. For example, pedants and skeptics can always argue that an infant may be so powerful that he can kill a tiger or that a cat may beget a dog once, say, in a thousand years.

24.6 Quantification

Those of us who are familiar with numbers often express their hunches as a fraction (0-1) or percentage (0-100). It would be interesting to find out the factors which enable us to express probability as a number.

Consider the simplest and oftquoted experiment; tossing of a coin. In absence of any special information you are likely to say that the chances of the coin showing heads or tails are equal. You may be more precise and assert that the probability that a toss will show heads or tails is 1/2.

What makes you so sure? There appear to be two reasons. First, you observe that there are only two alternatives head (H) or tail (T). You exclude the remote possibility of the coin landing on its rim. Second, you assume these alternatives as equally likely. This aspect is linked with what may be called our belief in the nature being impartial. Based on either our experience or the experience of the whole humanity for thousands of years which is embedded in our minds as innate logic, this belief is closely linked with symmetry with respect to time and space under identical conditions. Another way of saying this is "the coin is not biased". Unfortunately we cannot define bias, except through experimentation. If you toss a coin 100 times and find that it gives 49 H and 51 T, you will say that your hunch of the absence of bias was vindicated. If on the other hand, the pattern is 20H and 80 T, you might say that the coin is biased. Sometimes the "bias" may be apparent before you conduct an experiment. You might see that the coin does not have a uniform shape or one of its surfaces is very rough. But in absence of any visible irregularities you are bound to estimate that the probability of H as well as T is 1/2. This "prejudgment" is sometimes called "a priori probability". In real life we often encounter situations of "equal probabilities". Suppose in a game you are presented with ten boxes which look identical, and told that one of them contains a gold coin. The coin will be yours if you choose the right box. In absence of any visible bias you will reason that the probability that any given box contains the coin is 1/10 because

1. There are 10 alternatives which are mutually exclusive.
2. Each alternative is equally probable on account a natural law of symmetry. A sign of equiprobability is the dilemma you face when you have to make choices.

However, in real life apparent symmetry may not give us equiprobability or lack of bias. Conversely lack of apparent symmetry need not guarantee unequal chances. The probability estimated through experimentation is called "a posteriori probability". The dilemma we face is – how do we eliminate circularity in a priori probability -bias and a posteriori probability?

This leads to another question – what is the relationship between a priori and a posteriori probabilities?

It seems our concept of quantifiable chance is based on a statistical average. If a situation has the alternatives A and B, in absence of any special information we assume that (1) the occurrence A or B is equally likely, i.e. the a priori probability is 1/2, (2) when many experiments are conducted under the same conditions, on an average half will be in favor of A and half in favor of B.

Both (1) and (2) are prejudgments. But (1) is the a priori probability and the second is a prejudgment about a posteriori probability. That we accept two probabilities should be equal, again, is based on our intuition, symmetry and experience. But we cannot logically prove (2) from (1).

Our assumption that the nature is impartial is called the "principle of non-sufficient reason". Keynes calls it the Principle of Indifference. It is assumed, of course, that the Principle is valid when there is nothing to suggest any asymmetry or no visible evidence which should make us think that one option has greater chance than the other.

24.7 Non-numerical Probability

While we may express probability numerically, in certain cases there are situations where it is almost impossible to quantify the chances.

If you have a nagging mother-in-law, you may, at the beginning of the year, wonder what is the probability that she will exit from this world before the year is out. If you find her in the pink of health and bubbling with energy at the end of the year you might say in despair, "no chance" or "the probability is remote". But if you find she has been ailing for about a month and praying all the time, your hopes may soar and you might think it is highly probable that she will not live to see the next calendar year.

If you are a resident of Mumbai and someone asks you what is the probability that there will be an earthquake tomorrow your answer is likely to be "negligible", but if you are asked what are the chances that at least one person will commit suicide tomorrow, from your experience as a newspaper reader, you are likely to say "pretty high".

There are many situations when we estimate the probability only adjectivally "negligible", "low", "high", etc. but find it difficult to quantify it.

24.8 Probability Arithmetic

It is not difficult to understand simple probability calculations in practice. The treatment in this chapter is elementary, rigorous definitions are avoided.

1) Addition (or)

Suppose in a box there are 20 balls of the same size, of which 2 are white, 8 are black and 10 are red. You pick up one ball from the box without looking inside. What is the probability that the ball is (i) white (ii) black (iii) red?

Calling $p(w)$, $p(b)$, $p(r)$ the respective probabilities,

$p(w) = 2/20 = 1/10$

$p(b) = 8/20 = 2/5$

$p(r) = 10/20 = 1/2$

You can appreciate it intuitively. Now the ball you pick up has to be either white, black or red. It is easy to see that

$p(w) + p(b) + p(r) = 1/10+2/5+1/2 = 1$

This is as we should expect because you can chose only one ball, and either white, black or red, i.e. the total probability has to be 1 or certainty.

The events relating to $p(w)$, $p(b)$ and $p(r)$ are mutually exclusive. For example, the ball you pick up cannot be both white and black. The alternatives are also exhaustive, i.e. there are only three possibilities of the color, viz. white, black or red.

With the same data, let us ask ourselves what is the probability that the ball you pick up is either white or black. Since there are 10 balls which are black or white, the probability is 10/20 or 1/ 2 . If we write "black or white" as b + w, we have

$p(b + w) = 1/2$

It is easy to verify that

$p(b + w) = p(b) + p(w)$

since $p(b) = 2/5$ and $p(w) = 1/10$

2) *Multiplication (and)*

With the same data, suppose we pick up a ball, replace it and then have another pick. What is the probability that both will be white These two picks are independent events. Without going into the proof we will state the result. If the event white and white is symbolized as ww, we can write

$p(ww) = p(w).p(w) = 1/10 \times 1/10 = 1/100$

Similarly

$p(wb) = p(w).p(b) = 1/10 \times 2/5 = 1/25$

$p(bw) = p(b).p(w) = 2/5 \times 1/10 = 1/25$

$p(rr) = p(r).p(r) = 1/2 \times 1/2 = 1/4$

and so on. Note that wb is "first white second black" and bw is "first black and second white".

If you add up all possibilities the total will be 1 or certainty, as expected.

We add probabilities when we consider "or" and multiply when we want "and". However, conditions mentioned earlier should be present. Instead of repeating the picks you can have two lots of the same mix and pick up one ball from one lot and another from the second. You will get the same answers because both these cases are identical provided in the first case the first ball picked is replaced before the second ball is picked up.

A slightly complicated case is illustrated when we ask ourselves what is the probability that from two picks one will be black and the other white. Here the event consists of bw *or* wb. Their probabilities have to be added. The required probability is

$1/25 + 1/25 = 2/25$

24.9 Complex Numbers

All of us are familiar with real numbers which we use in our day-to-day life. For instance 7, 9.5, $\sqrt{2}$, π are all real numbers; the first two are rationals while $\sqrt{2}$ and π are irrational.

Mathematicians were once handicapped because in solving some equations, they came to a dead end. For example,

$x^2+1=0$

could not be solved because -1 does not have a real square root. The easiest way to tackle this problem is to assume that $\sqrt{-1}$ exists as an imaginary "number" symbolized by i so that $i^2 = -1$. However, when a new type of numbers is created, you have to integrate these numbers with real numbers in such a way that there is no inconsistency. Fortunately, addition and multiplication could be defined in the same way as in real numbers and the new type called "complex numbers" appeared to subsume real numbers as a subset. A complex number z is written as

$z = a + bi$

where a, b are real numbers.

For instance $2+5i$, $1-7i$, $-2+\sqrt{7}i$ are all complex numbers. They are added and multiplied as if they were real numbers. We only have to remember that $i^2 = -1$

For example,

(a) $(2+3i)+(1+2i) = (2+1)+(3i+2i)$
$= 3+5i$

(b) $2i(3+i) = 6i + 2i^2$
$= 6i-2$
$= -2+6i$

(c) $3+5i-2i = 3+2i$

(d) $3i(5)(8i) = -120$ $\quad (i^2 = -1)$

The transition from real numbers to complex numbers is seemless.

(e) $0 = 0 + 0i$

Hence 0 can be treated either as a real zero or complex zero. Similarly 5 can be treated as real or complex (5+0i)

(f) We can use most of the formulas we learned in school algebra

For exmaple, $(a+bi)^2 = a^2+2abi-b^2$

since $i^2 = -1$

(g) For division, we multiply and divide by the complex conjugate of the denominator

Thus

$(1+i)/(1-i) = [(1+i)/(1-i)]\ [1+i)/(1+i)] = (1+i)^2/1-i^2 = (1+2i-1)/2 = 2i/2 = i$

If z = a+ib, **z** = a-ib is called the complex conjugate of z. It is interesting to see that z**z** = a^2+b^2, which can be verified easily. This will be of considerable use to us.

Geometry

Complex numbers have extensive application in geometry and physics.

Consider two dimensional catersian geometry. (Fig. 24.3). A Point P is specified by two coordinates, say, (a, b). The complex number a+bi can be associated with P(a, b). It can be proved that there is a one-one correspondence between complex numbers z = x + yi and the points in the plane called z-plane or Argand plane such that for every complex number there is one and only one point in the plane.

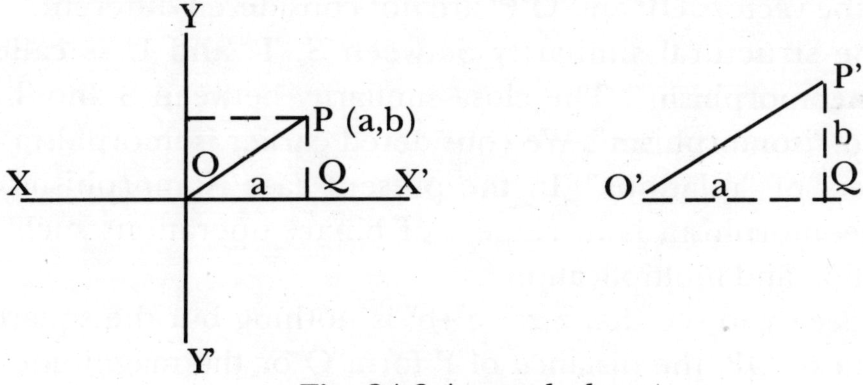

Fig. 24.3 Argand plane

In fact we can construct an algebra (addition, subtraction, etc.) for ordered pairs (x, y) which is not only consistent but is structurally similar to the algebra of complex numbers.

Vectors

Most of us are familiar with vector quantities which are specified by magnitude and direction. Complex numbers can be correlated to vectors in two dimensions. Thus in the above figure **OP** is the vector that can be identified with $z = a + bi$. It can also be identified with point P(a, b).

Vectors are added by the parallelogram or triangle law. Thus

OP = **OQ** + **QP** or **OP** = **a** + **b**

a, b are the components of **OP** along x and y axes.

Thus (a, b) can be identified with a complex number a+bi as well as the vector **OP**.

Again it can be shown that points in z plane, complex numbers and two dimensional vectors have structured similarity when we consider vector algebra with addition. Let us call these systems (points, complex numbers, vectors) S, T, U. These are similar for one operation called addition. S and T are also structually similar for another operation, multiplication.

There is however, one difference there is no one-one correspondence between either S and U or T and U. This is because a vector **OP** can be shifted elsewhere in the same plane such that its magnitude OP = O'P' and OP, O'P' are parallel and the vectors **OP** and **O'P'** are not considered different.

The structural similarity between S, T, and U is called "homeomorphism". The close similarity between S and T is called "isomorphism". We considered earlier isomorphism in respect of "relations". In the present case isomorphism or homeomorphism is in respect of binary operations such as addition and multiplication.[8]

It is easy to see that z **z** = a^2+b^2 is nothing but the squared length of OP, the distance of P form O or the magnitude of vector OP. We call this the modulus z or $|z|$

Thus $|z| = \sqrt{a^2+b^2}$

With reference to the point P, $|z|$ is called the radius vector. An interesting coordinate system is sometimes used in z plane : $P(r,\theta)$ are the coordinates of radius vector r and the angle θ it makes with x axis where θ is called the "argument". It can be verified that

$z = r(\cos\theta + i\sin\theta)$

In fig. 24.3 you can see $r\cos\theta = a$ and $r\sin\theta = b$.

24.10 Dilemma of Alternatives

How do we tackle the strange phenomenon of interference displayed by a single particle? Physicists have solved the problem only partially. They have developed a model indirectly based on probability arithmetic.

A quantum particle such as a photon or an electron is believed to be in a quantum state at any given time. It is associated with a wavefunction ψ which can be plotted as a function of x.$|\psi(x)|$ is the amplitude of this putative particle-cum-wave. But $\psi(x)$ is a complex function involving complex numbers. The probability of finding the particle at x is given by $|\psi(x)|^2$ which is a real number. (see section 9). This can be measured only when the parameters are enlarged to the classical level.

In the classical world a particle's behaviour is described in terms of its position and velocity (or momentum). Fortunately, quantum mathematical ψ also provides the information of (possible) momenta but the momenta too appear as amplitudes and not as simple probabilities.

To understand what this means a reference to musical terms would be helpful. A waveform can be decomposed and shown as the sum of various harmonics which are "pure tones" of different pitches. When applied to the wavefunction ψ, the "pure tones" are nothing but different possible momenta of the particle. The size of each component's contribution to ψ furnishes the amplitude for the particular momentum value.

These components or "pure tones" are called "momentum states".

If we plot a momentum state as a ψ function, it appears as a helix.[9] (right hand cork screw rule applies : when the momentum is along the positive direction the screw rotates clock wise.)

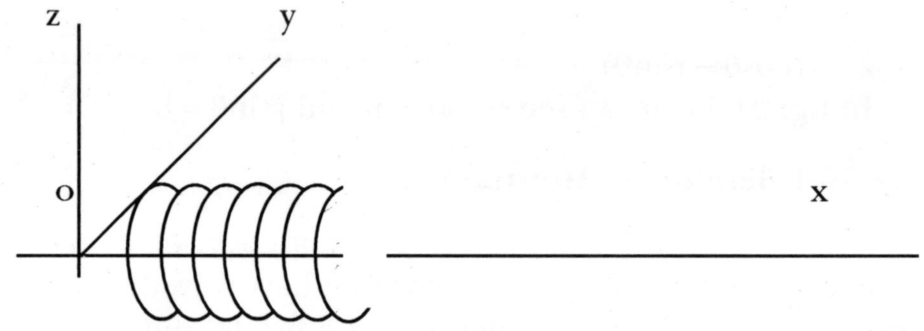

Fig. 24.4 A momentum state as ψ graph

Some of its characteristics are worth noting : tight winding shows high frequency or short wavelength, high momentum and high energy; loose winding shows opposite characteristics. In the extreme case, when the momentum is zero, the helix becomes a straight line. The distance between two consecutive windings is the wavelength.

Physicists have developed a related wavefunction ψ' based on momentum components. Thus ψ'(p) is the value for each p in what is called "momentum space". ψ'(p) actually gives us a complex value of the amplitude for each p of the particle.

There is a remarkable symmetry between ψ and ψ': they are Fourier transforms of each other.[10] In other words

(i) ψ when subjected to harmonic analysis gives ψ'
(ii) ψ' when subjected to harmonic analysis gives ψ

In case (i) the "pure tones" (helix in fig 24.4) now become position states, i.e. each x position corresponds to the pure tone in the momentum space whose contribution to ψ' shows the value of ψ(x).

In ordinary position-space picture a position state is shown in fig. 24.5. Its value is zero everywhere except at the particular point where it appears as a peak (strictly speaking its value here is infinite). It is called a "delta function" after Dirac, but in view of the sigularity involveded, it is a pseudo-function. Thus a delta function in position space under Fourier transform gives us a helix in momentum space and vice versa.

Fig. 24.5 Delta function

Physicists use the position space picture when they have to measure position which involves magnification of particle positions to the classical level (photo-cells for detection is an example).

When the particle's momentum (at the classical level) is to be measured momentum space description is useful. (diffraction from crystals provides an example at the classical level.) Before we proceed it must be made clear that at the quantum level though we use ψ and ψ' we speak only of their amplitudes. Probabilities appear only at the classical level when a measurement takes place and the probabilities are measured by $|\psi|^2$ or $|\psi'|^2$.

Let us go back to the two slit experiment (fig. 24.2) Consider a single photon emitted by S. This photon is associated with the wavefunction ψ. This can be considered as a combination of different momentum states in different directions. We do not know what happens physically, i.e. whether the photon splits or not. Most scientists prefer to think that it does not; but what emerges out of E and F are subsidiary wavefunction parts ψ(E) and ψ(F) each of them acting as waves in their own right. When they reach the screen DN they interfere with each other according to their wave properties as mentioned at the beginning of section l.

At this stage it would not be prudent to discuss different theories and views on what is happening in reality to the photon. Instead we consider Penrose's analysis of three cases of quantum states.

Consider the momentum state where the momentum is exactly stated. Here ψ curve is helical where every portion of the helix is at the same distance from the axis. In this case if the position is measured it will be totally uncertain since the amplitudes have equal squared moduli for all position values.

Consider now the position state where the location of the particle is completely specified. The particle should be precisely at the place where the peak of the delta function appears. The momentum amplitudes can be obtained from ψ' curve which is a helix in momentum space. We get a symmetrical result : the momentum amplitudes all have equal square moduli. Hence in this case the momentum when measured is totally uncertain.

In the intermediate case ψ as well as ψ' do not give helixes which are uniform, i.e. they may be almost straight lines for some distance and helixes of a reasonable width at others. This quantum state is sometimes called a "wave packet". It is this mixed bag or the wave packet which is usually taken as the best approximation to the particle in the classical world. This represents a case where positions as well as momenta are subject to constraints giving a limited range of variations.

24.11 Principle of Superposition

We shall see in the next chapter how the famous Schrödinger equation determines evolution of a particle's wavefunction with respect to time. A principle used in tackling the quantum puzzle in conjunction with Schrödinger equation is called the superposition or "quantum linear superpostion principle". Suppose $|\psi\rangle$ and $|\phi\rangle$ are two quantum states both satisfying this equation then the function

$w\,|\psi\rangle + z|\phi\rangle$

also satisfies the equation where w and z are complex numbers.[11]

For example, in the two slit experiment there are two possible routes for a photon to reach a point on the screen, $\psi(E)$ and $\psi(F)$ then their weighted combination will also be a possibility. Recall that in ordinary superpostion two waves are simply added (section 1). In the quantum state not only a linear combination is possible, but w and z are complex.

It is necessary to remember that the amplitudes are probability amplitudes. The experimenter can measure probability only *post facto* when the classical state is obtained.

You are likely to feel that ψ function is not only mysterious but its arithmetic dubious. This is partly true, but this complex mathematics seems to agree with observation at the classical level to some extent. We can briefly explain how probability theory is used in quantum mechanics. Refer to fig. (24.2). Consider the case when only one slit, say, E is open. Then the probability of a photon reaching D from S would be

$P(S, E) \times P(E,D)$ using "and" formula (section 24.8). Similarly the probability that the photon would reach D via F is

$P(S,F) \times P(F,D)$

We mentioned earlier that in quantum mechanics we can only speak of amplitude and not probability. Hence the two probability amplitudes we get are

$A(S,E) \times A(E,D) = A_1$, say

and $A(S,F) \times A(F,D) = A_2$, say

If you understand that these two paths are alternatives, you will also realize that, we have to use the 'or' formula to find the total prbability. (Section 24.8)

Hence the total amplitude for the photon to reach D from S is $A_1 + A_2$ or $wA_1 + zA_2$ in general considering weighted combinations.

We must, however, point out that (1) in the quantum state there are amplitudes (and not probabilites) (2) the superposition formula involves complex quantities.

Quantum Systems : Intrusion and Disturbance

25.1 Quantum Bonds

Physicists claim that the two slits in the experiment described in the last chapter need not be close to each other. The two parts ψ(E) and ψ(F) of the original ψ behave as if they still belong to the parent ψ. If we assume (one possible interpretation) that the photon splits into two parts, the bond between the split portions does not disappear. The following experiment is believed to demonstrate this strange phenomenon.

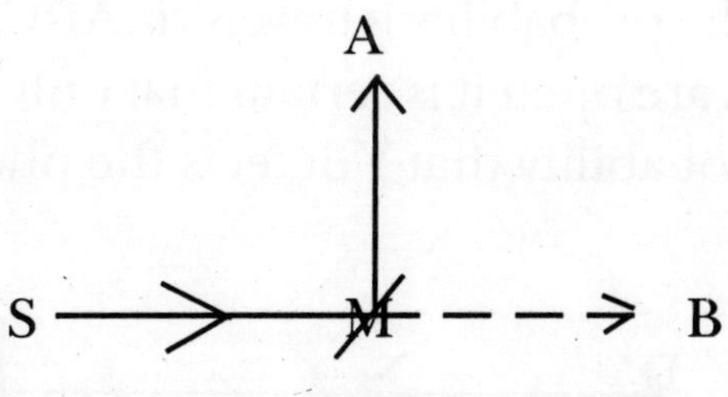

Fig. 25.1

In the above figure (25.1) a ray SM from S is incident on a half-silvered mirror. The mirror will reflect half the light in the direction perpendicular to SM and allow the remaining light to continue to travel along SM. We assume as before, that S is monochromatic and can send one photon at a time. As before at M, there are two split parts; $\psi(B)$ which continues to travel along SMB and the other $\psi(L)$ representing the reflected portion. Of course, both these parts will have their own peaks. As time passes, the distance between these will continue to increase rapidly. After one year, depending on your taste you can say

either (1) "The photon which struck M one year ago is now at two places separated by one light year".[1]

or (2) "the photon split at M one year go; its two parts are now at a distance of one light year from each other".

or (3) "The wavefunction ψ of the photon which struck M a year ago split into two wave functions which are now one light year apart. I cannot tell you what these wavefunctions are in reality, but if they come together again they will show the phenomenon of interference on a screen".

Consider a modified experiment (Fig. 25.2) in which S is the source of photons. A, B, C, D are mirrors (at 45^0). A and C are half-silvered while B and D are fully silvered. X and Y are particle detectors.

Case I

The beam of photons will split, half traveling via ABC and the other half via ADC. If these paths are equal, then theoretically the probability that a photon travels by one route ABC should be equal to the probability it travels via ADC. However, in practice if both paths are open it is certain that only X detects the photon while the probability that Y detects the photon is zero.

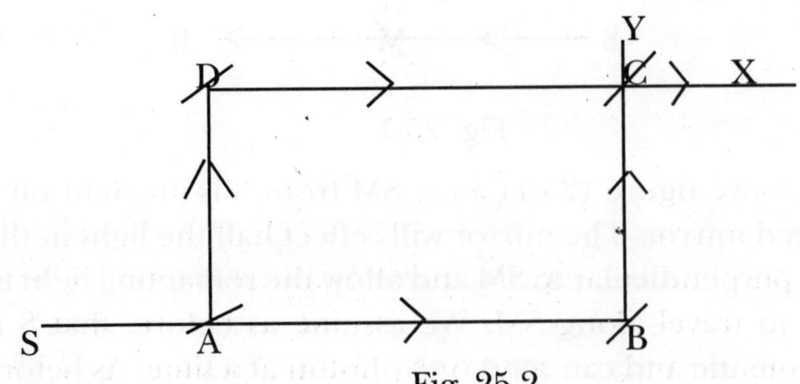

Fig. 25.2

Case II

Suppose we place an absorbing screen either on ABC or ADC then it is found that the probability of the photon reaching X and Y is equal, viz. 50%. This looks strange. According to Penrose this means a photon has travelled by both routes. In Penrose's own words. "Blocking of one of the routes allows Y to be reached! With both routes open the photon somehow 'knows' that it is not permitted to reach Y so it must have felt out both routes".[2]

Many scientists such as Niels Bohr contend that there is no objective meaning to the behavior of a photon between two measurements. Some other scientists treat quantum mathematics as a mere tool which should not be taken seriously when we consider the ontology of the photon's travel.

Penrose differs from these views. According to him the wavefunction describes the "reality" of the photon's behavior. He stresses that while ψ splits into parts, the state of the peaks of the ψ components decides whether they will strengthen each other or weaken each other. For the time being we can explain the two cases as follows.

Case I

When there is no screen in any of the paths, the photon reaches X. It is true that the paths ABC and ADC are equal but there is a difference in their orientations : The final journey of the photon CX is parallel to its original motion from the source, while in the other alternative the final journey (CY) is perpendicular to the original motion.

This difference could be responsible for the failure of our intuition that both X and Y should be reachable with equal probability.

Case II

When one of the paths is blocked, the case appears to be similar to "one photon passing through slits and interfering with itself" mentioned earlier. It is possible that the photon splits at A or B, it is possible that as a wavicle or partiwave it has properties which appear strange to us because we continue to think in terms of particle vs wave as we do at the macro level.

25.2 EPR Experiment

Another "thought" experiment due to Einstein, Podolsky and Rosen may now be considered briefly. The following is an adapted version from Bohm.[2a]

Earlier in chapter 23 we mentioned a characteristic called spin, which is in fact a rotational measurement of the particle's angular momentum (moment of momentum). Electrons and its antiparticles have a spin 1/2. However, the spin state of a particle is specified by spin measure as well as the axis of spin. Like mass-energy conservation spin is also conserved.

Suppose a zero-spin particle (such as photon) gives rise to a pair electron-positron These particles are assumed to move in the opposite direction. Since the initial particles had zero spin, the positron will have the spin axis opposite to that of the electron so that 1/2 + (-1/2) = 0 by conservation of angular momentum.

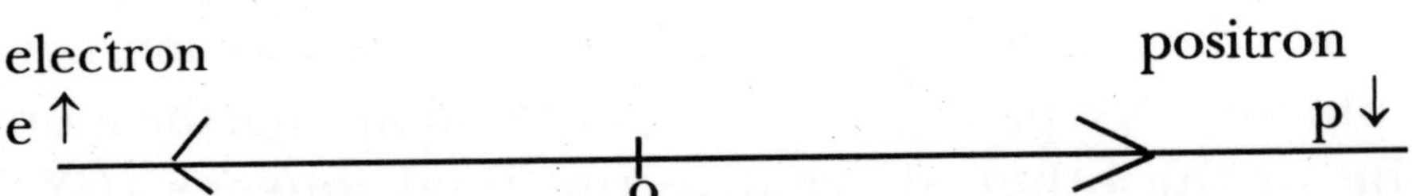

This means that if we measure the spin of the electron in a certain direction the positron has to spin in the opposite direction. For example, if the electron is measured as up ↑ the positron will instantaneously spin downwards ↓ (we use the right hand screw convention). In fact the particles may be many miles apart, their original bond is not severed. Suppose after some time you find the electron in the down state then the system has to jump to the combined state e↓ p↑ (p is up now).

If we had measured the electron spin in any other direction say ↗ we would find that the positron instantaneously jumps to the opposite state ↙.

It is difficult to expand the description further because a system of particles becomes more and more complicated as the number of particles increases. However, two aspects of this behavior should be kept in mind (1) Measurement of one particle's spin in a direction automatically changes the direction of the other particles spin consistent with $1/2 + (-1/2) = 0$.

(2) This effect is instantantaneous although the two particles may be separated by many miles.

One way of looking at this picture is that the system *knew* the directions of mutually dependent electron and positron, although the experimenter had no knowledge of this fact.

25.3 Schrödinger Equation

The behavior of the wave packet mentioned in the last chapter is usually treated as the best representation of the classical particle. It avoids the other two extremes – pure particle and pure wave. In fact the development of the wavefunction of the packet can be specified by Schrödinger's equation

$$\mathbf{ih}\frac{\partial \psi}{\partial \tau} = \mathrm{H}$$

We have written the equation in a much simplified fashion avoiding complicated symbols. The left side shows the rate of change of the wavefunction, H is a parameter called the Hamiltonian function, a measure of ψ, $i = \sqrt{-1}$ and $\mathbf{h} = h/2\pi$.

Roughly H determines how ψ will evolve. This is similar to the Hamiltonien function of a particle system in classical physics. You may remember its implication in a simple way. The equation asserts that "if we decompose ψ into momentum states (pure tones) then each of these components will move off with a speed that is c^2 divided by the speed of a classical particle having momentum in question".[3]

The evolution of ψ is wholly deterministic, there is nothing like quantum uncertainty. The problem arises when we make a measurement. It would help you if you remembered that such measurement implies human intervention and is bound to disturb the system. This aspect will be recalled later. Penrose calls the procedure relating to the deterministic behavior *U* and a completely different procedure (after a measurement is made) **R** (**R** is called state-vector reduction) It is necessary to emphasize that it is **R** which introduces uncertainties and probabilities into the quantum world.

To understand how the uncertainty enters, consider the wavefuntion ψ in a momentum state. We can measure its momentum at any stage and there will not be any uncertainty. Suppose now, we decide to measure the particle's position which implies magnification to the classical level. The whole picture now changes : we face a number of probability amplitudes whose squared moduli $|\psi|^2$ will give us the probability of the particle being at a certain point.

Again, if the wavefunction is initially in the position state, ψ will spread as we mentioned earlier. Though it is no more in the position state, it evolves deterministically. However, if we decide to measure its momentum we find there is complete uncertainty revealed by $|\psi|^2$ being equal for all amplitudes. The Heisenberg's principle has now entered the scene.

Finally, suppose we start with a wave packet, its evolution is deterministic in accordance with Schrödinger equation, but if we try to measure its position or momentum, uncertainties appear in accordances with Heisenberg's principle.

More than the particle-wave duality, it is the absence of a definite rule whether to select deterministic **U** or probabilistic **R**, that mystifies the quantum physicist.

25.4 Schrödinger's Cat

As explained in chapter 24 a characteristic of Schrödinger equation is that it is linear, i.e. the quantum principle of superposition applies.

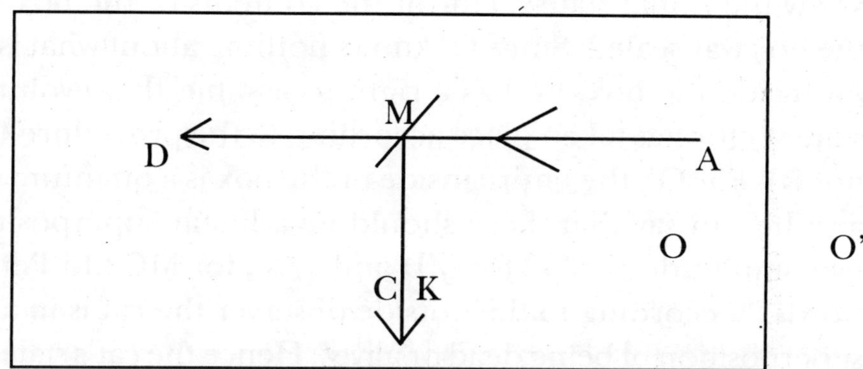

Fig. 25.3 Schrödinger cat

Erwin Schrödingers' thought experiment (1935) called "the paradox of Schrödinger's cat" is briefly described below. It contains the dilemma "**U** or **R**?"

Fig. 25.3 shows a completely sealed box. Photons from a light source A strike a half-silvered mirror M. The photon (or the wavefunction) splits at M; one part travels in the same direction MD, and the other is reflected along MC which is perpendicular to AM. C is a photo-cell with a device containing poison. If C registers a photon, a reflection has taken place at M. The device is activated and it releases poison which will kill the cat K. O is an (imagined) observer seated in the sealed box. If O observes the photo-cell's detection, the photon has certainly been reflected and the cat should be killed by the poison. On the other hand, no such registration is observed by O the photon has definitely travelled along MD and the cat will be saved. In any case, one of these events has taken place. This consistutes "measurement" as far as O is concerned. It is reasonable to assume that each event has a 50% probability. Our conclusion is that the procedure **R** has occurred because the event is observed by O.

O' is an outside observer who can neither pass on any knowledge into the sealed box nor can he receive any knowledge from inside the box. However, both O and O' are supposed to know the initial state-vector of the contents of the box before the box was sealed. Since O' knows nothing about what is going on inside the box, he has a right to assume that evolution of state vector has taken place according to the procedure **U** (and not **R**). For O', the entire inside of the box is a quantum system and he can say that there should be a linear superposition of two amplitudes; $1/\sqrt{2}$ for MD and $1/\sqrt{2}$ for MC.[4] In Penrose's words, "According to the outside observer the cat is in a linear superposition of being dead or alive". Hence the cat's state vector ψ can be shown as :

$$(\text{Cat})\,\psi = \frac{1}{\sqrt{2}}\{(\text{dead}+(\text{alive})\}$$

In fact O' can deduce many more combinations than the above, which we need not discuss here.[5]

For the insider O the cat is either dead or alive and the above guesswork is irrelevant for him. For many scientists this is a paradox. In fact Schrödinger the author of this imaginary experiment himself thought that something was wrong. How do we explain the discrepancy?

25.5 Interpretation and Reality

Since the quantum world is difficult to describe in the classical idiom, several opinions on the status of quantum mathematics have arisen. We may consider a few views on what actually happens at the quantum world :

(1) The entire quantum mathematics should be treated as a mere tool invented to agree with the results at the macro level when measurements are taken.

(2) The truncated ψ functions meeting again after a considerable lapse of time and interfere with each other. This cannot be tested. The phenomenon of the persisting fraternal bond looks like the apocryphal story that two identical twins though separated are bound to each other in a certain sense. If one of them is flogged the other suffers though he may be several miles away. Fortunately, experiments on ψ have been conducted only for a few meters.

(3) If what theoretical physicists tell us about EPR paradox is true, i.e. if the measurement of the spin of the -1/2 particle instantaneously effects changes in the spinstate of its antiparticle of the other, it would imply there can be a speed which exceeds c, the velocity of light, since this effect is instantaneous. This is not consistent with our present day knowledge of physics.

(4) To avoid our ridiculous result of the superposition of death and life of a cat some commentators have suggested that this discrepancy arises because there are conscious observers, one inside and the other outside. It is possible that quantum mathematics does not apply to consciousness.

(5) It may be contended that in case of "conscious" procedure a new or non-linear procedure needs to be applied.

25.6 Recapitulation

It is time to recapitulate the contents of chapters 24 and 25 (sections 1-5) before we proceed.

The quantum theory ostensibly applies to sub-atomic world. At the macro level it is either not applicable or its effects are too small to change our classical world. Thus we do not see apes or elephants producing interference effects.

At the quantum level there are alternatives and we have to use superposition employing complex numbers to obtain probability amplitudes of a quantum state. This reminds one of a similar confusion in case of Buddhist and Jaina logic of multi-value truths; there is a similar dilemma : should the alternatives be taken as real options or treated as part of the whole quantum state?

So long as a system is in the quantum state, it evolves in accordance with procedure **U**. The picture is purely deterministic. When different alternatives become large and the differences sizable, the system reaches the classical level. We may intervene to measure the parameters. The quantum system reaches the classical level : only one alternative is now possible in reality, though all alternatives are translated into probabilities in real numbers. In other words there is a collapse of ψ. **R** takes over from **U**. Uncertainty appears at this transition.

If a system is complex containing many entities, the situation becomes difficult to handle; some particles cannot be treated as independent and are entagled with others. Any disturbance effect in one will also disturb other particles with which it is "bound" displaying non-local effect. Can we See **R** objectively? This is what Penrose says :

> If **R** is considered to act in an objective way (and that would seem to be implied by objectivity of the quantum state) then the spirit of special relativity is accordingly violated. *No objectively real space-time description* of the (reducing) state vector seems to exist which is consistent with the requirements of relativity! However, the *observational* effects of quantum theory do not violate relativity.[6]

This shows that physicists have not been able to develop a theory which would describe the transition from the quantum state to classical state seamlessly. What's more, they do not know at what point ψ collapses and **R** takes over. Until a refined theory emerges which would coherently describe quantum to classical transition we have to make do with what is only a partial view involving **U** and **R**.

25.7 Nature of Uncertainty and Inaccessibility

U and R

It is often claimed by physicists such as Penrose that there is no uncertainty as far as U procedure is concerned.[7] The uncertainty arises when one switches from **U** to **R,** i.e. when an observation or measurement is made. Before we discuss the nature of uncertainty a simple experiment at the classical level may be considered.

Suppose you toss an unbiased coin. When in the air, the coin appears to spin and at any given time its state can be represented by a set of continuous variables. This can be done by photographing the coin and recording its parameters at a certain instant by necessary instruments. When the coin strikes the ground we can say that it can assume only two positions, head or tail. There is some similarity between the measurement of quantum to classical stage transition and the transition of the spinning coin to one of the stable positions. The difference is :

(1) In case of the quantum experiment the state of the system is theoretically certain but cannot be measured.

(2) In case of the coin, a theoretical prediction may not be possible because the initial conditions cannot be fully taken into account, but the measurement of any state is possible when the coin is in the air.

The quantum system operates, as it were, in total darkness inaccessible to the experimentor. Penrose concedes this inability to measure but says that the quantum state ψ is objective though not measurable.[8]

If **U** evolves in a determinate manner it should not surprise any one because the state vector is determinate only theoretically and the state is in fact indeterminate, i.e. not verifiable. According to the well-known verifiability theory the "meaning of a proposition is the method of its verification".[9] If our proposition is "The quantum states ψ evolves in a predetermined manner", what is the method of verifying the meaining of the statement? The meaning is nothing but the theoretical procedure **U**. It is doubtful that such trivial interpretation of the meaning devoid of any empirical content will be accepted by any serious student of physics who wants to know if the procedure **U** is determinate.

The general rule **R** is – "For a mesurement (or observation) requires that the different aspects of a quantum system that can be simultaneously magnified and between which the system must then choose must always be orthogonal".[10] We shall briefly explain the concept of orthoganality and the "jumping" of the system when measured.

25.8 Jumping in Hilbert Space

The space we use in two/three dimensional coordiante geometry is a Euclidian space in which we can draw vectors such as force, velocity, etc. Real numbers are called scalars. The axes OX, OY, OZ are perpendicular to each other. When two vectors **a**, **b** are perpendicular their scalar product **a .b** = abcos θ = o, θ being the angle between **a** and **b**. The following laws hold good for vectors (**a, b, c**,....) and scalars (x, y, z,...)

$\mathbf{a} + \mathbf{b} = \mathbf{b} + \mathbf{a}$; $(x+y)(\mathbf{a}) = x\mathbf{a} + y\mathbf{a}$

$\mathbf{a} + (\mathbf{b} + \mathbf{c}) = (\mathbf{a} + \mathbf{b}) + \mathbf{c}$; $x(\mathbf{a}+\mathbf{b}) = x\mathbf{a} + x\mathbf{b}$

$x(y\mathbf{a}) = (xy)(\mathbf{a})$; $1\mathbf{a} = \mathbf{a}$

$\mathbf{a} + \mathbf{0} = \mathbf{a}$; $0\,\mathbf{a} = \mathbf{0}$; $z\,\mathbf{0} = \mathbf{0}$

0 is the zero vector whose magnitude is zero and direction indeterminate, while 0 is the scalar, number zero. This space is called the "vector space". A "Hilbert Space" is similar but scalars are complex numbers. When this space has more than three dimensions, it becomes an imaginary space but retains its properties. In such a space orthogonality cannot be defined using perpendicularity. We have to resort to another definition **a.b** = **0**. We need not worry about what is meant by the scalar product when there are more than three dimensions.

There is, however, a problem to be solved in Hilbert space. If **a** is a vector z**a** is also the same vector where z is a complex number. For this reason we "normalize" the system. Take a simple case. Suppose **a** is a vector in two dimensions than a_x and a_y are projections of **a** on two orthogonal axes. We can write

$\mathbf{a} = \mathbf{a}_x + \mathbf{a}_y$

We divide both sides by |**a**| or a (the length of the vector)

$\mathbf{a}/a = a_x/a + a_y/a$

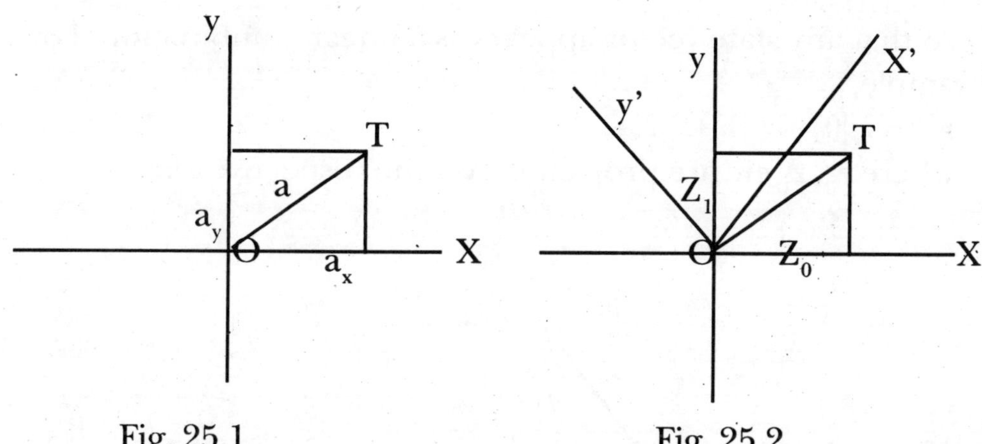

Fig. 25.1 Fig. 25.2

We have effected normalization; the magnitude of both sides is 1. Such a system is called *orthonormal.* Henceforth we will assume that the system is "normalized".

In Dirac's notation quantum states are written as $|\psi\rangle$, $|\chi\rangle$, $|0\rangle$, $|1\rangle$, etc. Suppose we want to consider the position of a particle. In a simple case (Fig. 25.2), the position vector OT is a linear combination of $|0\rangle$ along Ox and $|1\rangle$ along Oy. They form an orthogonal system and we can write OT as

$z_0|0\rangle + z_1|1\rangle$

z_0, z_1 are the orthogonal projections. Now this system of vectors $|1\rangle$ and $|2\rangle$ is called the "orthogonal basis" vectors for position. Suppose you decide to "measure" the position of the particle in the quantum state OT. Your action constitutes a distrubance, the quantum state collapses and OT jumps to $|0\rangle$ or $|1\rangle$. There is no definite rule for which axes it will jump to. Nature takes the decision. The probability values are given by squared moduli of probability amplitudes. For momentum measurement there is a set of other two axes OX' OY' which are orthogonal to each other and are actually obtained by rotating the system OXY.

We can generalize this picture. If some complete measurement is made on a system whose quantum state is $|\psi\rangle$, then the assumption is that there exists a basis

$|0\rangle, |1\rangle, |2\rangle, \ldots$

so that any state vector appears as a linear combination. For example,

$|\psi\rangle = z_0|0\rangle + z_1|1\rangle + z_2|2\rangle + \ldots$

where z_0, z_1 etc are projections on the respective axes.

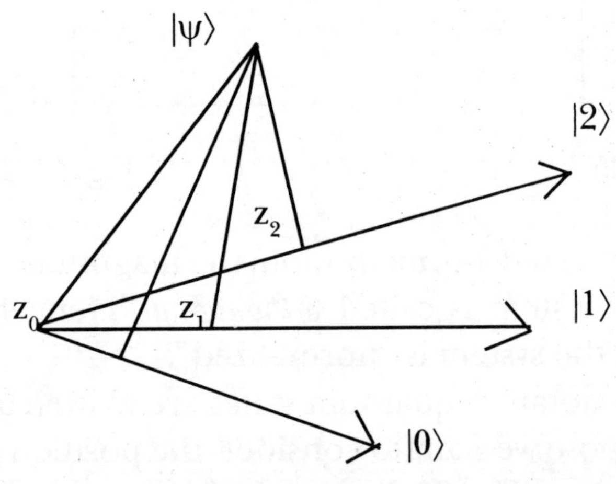

Fig. 25.3

The number of orthogonal axes depends on a particular case and can even be infinite representing an (imaginary) space in infinite dimensions.

We assume here that the system is normalized so that when measurement takes place z_0, z_1,... etc. are probability amplitudes. Their square moduli are different probabilities and the system jumps to $|0\rangle$, $|1\rangle$, etc. so that the total probality squared modulus of $|\psi\rangle$ is precisely 1.

25.9 Systems and Complications

It has been remarked earlier that modern scientists see a particle not as a single entity but an element in the entire web of interconnecting entities.

A system of particles can lead to an extremely complicated picture. Suppose a particle's quantum state or wavefunction has twenty alternative positions. Then it can be described as linear superpositions of twenty orthonormal states :

$$|\psi\rangle = z_0 + z_1|1\rangle + \ldots z_{19}|19\rangle \qquad (1)$$

z_0, z_1... being amplitudes for the particle to be at one point at a time. If we consider a system of two particles, we shall need $20 \times 20 = 400$ amplitudes or complex numbers. In fact the picture is much more complicated subject to a plethora rules. What we have to understand is that we cannot see one particle in isolation but a system of particles each exerting influence on the others. Fortunately there are some principles which prevent a system from going berserk. One such principle is the Pauli's exclusion principle. Its consequence for the structure of matter is that "all the principal constituents of matter are indeed fermions : electrons, protons and neutrons. Without the exclusion principle matter would collapse on itself".[10a]

We saw in chapter 24 that probabilities are added when we consider a *or* b and multiplied when we want a **and** b. When translated to probability amplitudes similar operations are needed. Consider a simple case of two particles, having states $|\alpha\rangle$ and $|\beta\rangle$ respectively. Then $|\alpha\rangle\ |\beta\rangle$ is the conjunction. The same rule applies to systems consisting or more than two particles. Let us apply the rules to a system of twenty particles. Equation (1) gives a state for one partice. When combined with the state of another particle, the combined state will be a combination consisting of 400 terms.

$|\psi\rangle = z_{00}|0\rangle\ |0\rangle + z_{01}|0\rangle|1\rangle + \ldots + z_{400}|19\rangle|19\rangle$. However, when the particles are identical different rules apply. We need not consider further complications.

25.10 Discreteness

Before we close this brief account on subatomic particles, two important characteristics of the quantum world must be mentioned. As we pointed out earlier classical physics assumes continuity in absorption and emission of energy. Discreteness, on the other hand, is the characteristic of the quantum phenomena. Planck's radiation law involves it

$E = h\nu$, which is the same as

$E = \mathbf{h}\omega$ where $\omega = 2\pi\nu$ is called angular frequency and $\mathbf{h} = h/2\pi$.

One of the earliest discoveries in nuclear physics was that in a simple (crude) model of the hydrogen atom, where an electron revolves around the proton; it is not permitted to move in any arbitrary circuit. This is because an orbiting charge would radiate energy and the loss of energy would ultimately lead to the electron spiralling to the nucleus and falling into it. Bohr postulated that only discrete orbits corresponding to discrete energy levels were permissible for the atom to be stable. This discreteness is reflected in several quantum phenomena. For example, an angular momentum of an electron in a circular orbit can be written as $l = n\mathbf{h}$, $n = 1, 2,...$ Notice how positive integers assume importance in quantum theory.

Another result pertains to Balmer's researches in 1885 when he found that radiation emitted by the hydrogen atoms were given by a discrete set, viz.

$\omega = N(1/2^2 - 1/n^2)$. $n = 3,4,5...$

Many advances have been made during the last 120 years and many "laws" have been modified. Nevertheless, discreteness as such remains the hallmark of the quantum world.

25.11 Groping in the Dark

So far we have refrained from mentioning certain characteristics in quantum theory either because they belong to the mathematical apparatus or because they are harder to appreciate conceptually. We should briefly mention these features because they reveal certain axioms of a theory which is partly shrouded in mystery. This account will also throw some light on how the physicists ever thought of a weird theory involving complex numbers, and how groping in the dark quantum world they ever came out into the real world. Of course, their hunches led them only to probabilities and not certainties as to where they would reach when they returned to the classical world. In a way the following account is an approach slightly different from what we described earlier.

(i) *Discreteness*

We have already discussed this feature in last section.

(ii) *Observational Operation*

An observation can be as simple as looking at the shining light which involves bombardment of a surface by photons. It has been already pointed out that a quantum system being delicate is bound to be disturbed. Hence this disturbance is also reflected in quantum theory. It has been found that with each type of operation a set of numbers is associated. Some of these operations are – measuring momentum or position of a particle or measuring the energy level of the system. In classical physics the measuring numbers vary continuously but in quantum theory the set of numbers is discrete.

(iii) An operation can be denoted by A, B, etc. Suppose we make two successive operations in different orders BA (A followed by B) and AB (B followed by A) each operation leads to a disturbance. The question arises as to whether AB = BA. In practice this commutative property holds good in many cases but not always.

A clockwise rotation about the same axis by two successive angles is commutative at the classical level. At the quantum level, this is not so. It is usually assumed that two successive disturbances do not cancel each other or

$AB - BA \neq 0$

Researchers in this field correctly assume that this difference is connected with Planck's constant h.

Interpretative Postulates

Those working in quantum physics have devised appropriate operators useful in quantum theory. To understand what this implies we briefly explain what an operator o(x) means. An operator converts a function of x into another function. For example, o(x) may "cube" the function. Thus if $f(x) = x + 2$, an operation by o will give us $(x+2)^3$. Similarly, o(x) would mean the function is multiplied by x. Thus $x + 2$ would become $x(x+2)$. There is a most interesting category of operators. We shall denote this type by o'. A characteristic of this type is that each operator is connected with discrete values of n. For example, in case of o'

$$o' u_n(x) = a_n u_n(x)$$

What this means is when o' operates on functions $u_n(x)$, i.e. $u_1, u_2, \ldots$ these functions are simply multiplied by values a_n, i.e. $a_1, a_2, \ldots$. These functions u_n are called "eigenfunctions" and the corresponding a_n called "eigenvalues". Note the discreteness of a_n and u_n.

Thus "the eigenfunctions of an operator are thus those special functions which remain unaltered under the operation of the operator apart from multiplication by eigenvalue".

This category of operators o' actually shows that the physical properties of observations correspond exactly to the mathematical properties of operators.

With each operator is associated a set of numbers n in such a way that there is one operator for each observable characteristic (position, energy, momentum, etc.) The functions operated are called "state functions" (or wave functions) and represent the state of the system. If the state pertains to an eigenfunction it is called an "eigenstate". There are three assumption made by quantum physicists :

1) The possible results of an observation o' are the corresponding eigenvalues a_n.
2) If o' is the observation in an eigenstate $u_n(x)$ certainly leads the result a_n
3) The average value of o' involving repeated observations on a set of systems, each one in an arbitrary state $\psi(x)$ is given by $a(\psi)$ which involves a method of averaging in integral calculus and depends on $\psi(x)$, and its complex conjugate $\psi(x)$ and o'(x).[11]

Remember that these axioms are based on observation, hunch and internal consistency. But this does not rule out the possibility of another set of interpretative postulates.

It should be mentioned that a property similar to observational operations is assumed. If o'and o'' are two operators, then in general the commutator [12] $[o', o''] \neq 0$

There are also two other axioms called physical postulates:

(a) The Correspondence Principle

This principle is based on the assumption that when the system becomes large and disturbances become neglibible, the system should obey the classical laws. The formal law is

"The essential definitive relation between physical variables in quantum mechanics (which do not involve derivatives) are also satisfied by the corresponding quantum operators".[13] Note that there is a correspondence between physical variables and the corresponding quantum operators.

(b) The Complementary Principle

This is based on the previous hunch that the difference o'o''- o'' o' should be connected with h.

This hunch is suggested by de Broglie matter waves (chapter 2). His equation (not mentioned here) immediately leads to a conjecture.

$[x', p'] = i\mathbf{h}$

where x', p' are position and momentum operatores. In fact a more general postulate is : any position observable, χ and its corresponding momentum π are said to be complementary and they are commutable[14], i.e.

$$[\chi', \pi'] = i\mathbf{h}$$

where primes indicate corresponding operators.

It is necessary to remember that classical observables such energy H, momentum p and position x retain their relationships in quantum mechanics provided they are replaced by corresponding operators H', p', x'.

26

Life, Cognition and Consciousness

26.1 Introduction

Induction, which in the broadest sense includes spatiotemporal extrapolation, is not only used in physics and chemistry but also in biology. Biological systems have features which differ from physical systems – we have not been able to bridge the gap between life and non-life in the sense life has not been created in laboratory abiogenically. It is necessary to know something about life and consciousness as well as evolution. This is essential to understand the scope of extrapolation in biology and compare the inductive methods in physical and biological sciences. Some knowledge of life and consciousness should also help us understand if the animate and the inanimate influence the quantum world differently.

26.2 Life

In school all of us study certain characteristics of living organisms – intake of food, excretion, reproduction, etc. Most of us are aware that life appears to be a continuum from the lowest bacteria to the highest mammal whom we call a human being. We also have a hunch that concurrent with the evolution of life there are other concomitants which evolve – consciousness, intelligence and so on. In our discussion we may assume this ascending continuum. However, there are two questions which are difficult to answer. First, at what stage an organism feels consciousness. Second, and a more difficult question, at what stage life begins?

Modern scientists regard "cells" as the most important sign of life. The simplest life manifests as unicellular bacteria. The complex life-systems are believed to have evolved from bacterial cells. The simplest bacteria are mycoplasm which are spherical. Even such ostensibly simple forms of life, however, have a complex metabolism or biochemical processes that are characteristic of life.

26.3 Cells

The bacterial cell contains two types of very large molecules or macromolecules; proteins and nucleic acids (DNA and RNA). There are also two types of protein molecules which form the cellular structure and enzymes which are catalysts facilitating metabolic process. The DNA contains the coded information. The RNA molecule is a messenger which carries this information necessary for the synthesis of enzymes. This molecule is a link between the genetic and metabolic aspects.

It is often believed that the DNA is "life" because it facilitates the replication of a cell. However, the DNA is necessary but not sufficient for life, you can find the DNA molecules even in the organism that is dead.

A cell is separated from the environment by the cell membrane which is semipermeable. It selectively admits certain substances and allows others to exit. The membrane is the hallmark of what philosophers call individuation. In higher organisms whose cells have a nucleus and even in some bacteria one observes many internal membranes. In fact all these membranes constitute one single system called "endomembrane system" which regulates molecular composition.

It is necessary to mention that new cells are produced only from living cells. When a nucleated cell is about to divide into two cells, the nucleus changes to form rod shaped bodies called "chromosomes". When the cell division is complete, the daughter cells are identical, each having a nucleus and the same number of chromosomes as the parent, the cell division is called "mitosis".

The cell membrane is only one of the signs of life. The other is internal metabolism. As Lynn Margolis observes in *Symbiotic Planet,* metabolism, the incessant chemistry of self-maintenance is the essential feature of life. "Through ceaseless metabolism, through chemical energy and flow, life continuously produces, repairs and perpetuates itself. Only cells and organisms composed of cells, metabolize".[1]

Most modern scientists have a systemic or network approach to life – organisms are networks of cells, organs and organ networks; cells, in turn, are networks of molecules. According to Capra, "Wherever we see life, we see networks".[2] The dynamic constituents of the metabolic system transform, and replace other components and in the process the entire structure regenerates itself. Biologists Humberto Maturana and Francisco Varela have introduced the concept of autopoiesis ("self making") which integrates the functions of the membrane and metabolism. As Pier Liguigi Luis has pointed out, "Life cannot be ascribed to any single molecule component (not even DNA or RNA) but only to the entire bounded metabolic network".[3]

Some biologists recognize two distinct systems in the cell, (1) metabolic networks (2) epigenetic network; the latter not only includes but also transcends the genetic level. However, the two networks should be seen as a whole autopoietic system. It is important to understand that in cell reproduction there is a transmission of the entire autopoietic network with its paraphernalia such as DNA, enzymes and so on.

Paradoxically the living autopoietic system is also an open system in the sense it receives matter and energy from the environment. It is not in equilibrium. Left to itself it would die. Such structures are called dissipative structures which have been extensively studied by Ilya Prigogine and other scientists. The dissipative structures focus on spontaneous emergence of order at certain points of instability. These structures are studied with the help of nonlinear dynamics and have provided new insights into self-organization, development, evolution and what is called morphological complexity. Scientists now define complexity not just in terms of structural intricacies but also the complexity involved in the process of the structural emergence.

There are a few models of what is called prebiotic stage. There is no need to consider these models in detail, but it is necessary to remember that scientists seem to agree that there is a continuum from the inanimate to the animate. This thinking is reflected in the following words :

> It is clear that the process leading to life is a continuum process, and this makes all unequivocal definition of life very difficult. In fact there are obviously many places in Oparin's, pathway where the marker 'minimal life' can be placed.[4]

26.4 Evolution

Today the starting point for the discussion of life seems to be bacteria as a matter of convenience. Despite the continuum, there appear to be some cases which baffle us. The virus being noncellular is not a living organism. It lacks its own metabolism. Outside living cells, viruses are nonliving entities containing proteins as well as nucleic acids. They thrive in host cells and produce new viruses. But these baby viruses (if such a term can be used) are not produced inside it, they are outside the parent virus and in the host cell. Nevertheless the language used in medical literature creates an impression that the viruses are living organisms. We often hear people saying , "Viruses attack", "I am suffering from viral infection", and so on.

Existents like virus (and even DNA) raise some epistemological questions. Do viruses violate the law of the excluded middle? An existent can be either living or nonliving. There are two solutions which can save the law. First, we arbitrarily draw the line and say that all prebacterial existents are non living, since such existents like viruses do not live independently. The second solution is to add a new temporal dimension to life. We then will have to describe life at a given time. For example, "This virus was dead at 9 a.m., living at 10 p.m." and so on.

Evolution from the bacterial stage appears to proceed in three directions. The first is through gene mutation. This is attributed to a random error in self-replication of DNA. However, such errors are not significant except in case of bacteria who divide and spread rapidly.

The second road again seems to be probable only in case of bacteria. Bacteria spread rapidly and are believed to exchange herditary traits "in a global exchange network of incredible power and efficiency".[5]

This phenomenon is called "DNA recombination". On account of this "free exchange", scientists often wonder whether we should classify bacteria according to species.

The third mode of evolution explains the vast variety of creatures, especially of higher forms. It was Lynn Margulis who discovered this avenue now called evolution through symbiosis. Symbiosis is a phenomenon in which different organisms live with one another or one inside another providing, as it were, mutual life support. The full-fledged theory developed by Margulis is now known as "symbiogenesis".

Symbiogenesis explains the evolution from the lower forms of life to the higher forms. Bacteria sometimes live inside larger cells symbiotically as organelles. When they merge with the cell over a long time, the process of complex forms begins. Larger organisms absorb bacteria and incorporate from them genetic material necessary for a higher form of living cell. It is this process of absorbing bacteria which unleashes an ascending chain of organisms of higher complexity leading to creatures we can see and which reproduce sexually.

These three avenues coupled with natural selection has led to the diverse and complex flora and fauna found today. It is also believed that the process of evolution is not smooth. First, there could have been periods of quietude followed by sudden jumps. Second, there could have been catastrophes and extinctions followed by rapid regeneration.

26.5 Cognition, Mind and Consciousness

We have already made references to the human mind and consciousness earlier. It is interesting to view them from evolutionary point of view. Like life, mind and consciousness may be treated as a continuum because from animal behavior we perceive degrees of awareness and intelligence. Most scientists now reject the Cartesian view that the mind is a thing. They regard it as a process connected with the brain though the exact relationship between the brain and mind is not yet clear.

Santiago Theory

Cognition means knowing. The Santiago theory of cognition authored by Maturana and Varela contends that cognition is coëxtensive with self-generation and self-perpetuation of living network; life and cognition cannot be separated. A living network has some distinct characteristics. The living system interacts with the environment continually and its structure undergoes constant change. However, in one sense even this change has the potential inside the organism. As Maturna and Varela point out, you can never direct a living system; you can only disturb it.[6]

From the various stimuli from the environment the organism "decides" which stimulus it will react to. The stimulus merely triggers off the structural changes in the organism; the direction of change seems to be determined by the autonomous system itself. The Santiago theory emphasizes that the structural changes themselves constitute cognition. The Santiago conception of the notion of cognition differs from what the layperson means by cognition. For us cognition is associated with consciousness. The Santigo theory almost brackets cognition with life. Consciousness will emerge at a certain point in the ascending scale of evolution. Nevertheless consciousness is cognition though the converse is not true.

Consciousness

Modern biologists appear to view consciousness, like life, as an emergent phenomenon. "Experience emerges from the complex nonlinear dynamics of neural networks and can be explained only if our understanding of neurobiology is combined with an understanding of those dynamics".[7]

Since consciousness is felt, scientists feel that any investigation of consciousness should proceed from two directions : the external, which involves the systemic analysis using nonlinear dynamics, and the internal or knowing what the conscious organism feels. However, the subjective .approach is possible only in case of humans and perhaps higher primates like chimpanzees.

There are many "schools" relating to consciousness. The first is called "neuroreductionist school" by Varcla. This school describes consciousness in terms of neurons. It accepts that it is the emergent property of the brain but does not use the techniques of the complexity theory.

The second school is based on functionalism. Its adherents assert consciousness as patterns of causal relations in the neural network. They are aware of the role of nonlinear dynamics and thus somewhat differ from the neuroreductionists. However, they do not agree that consciousness is irreducible to functional relationships. There is another school of "mysterians" who believe that consciousness has mysterious or rather transcendental depth that can not be fathomed by human intelligence.

Another little known school led by Varela is called "neurophenomenology". Phenomenology is a philosophical school founded by Edumd Husserl who held that "the object of cognition does not exist outside the consciousness of the subject focussed upon it".[8] While he set out to found a science based on this philosophy, his "idealism" ultimately led him to criticize science and scientific thinking. His thinking is reflected in the philosophy of several existentialists particularly Heidegger. However, today's "neurophenomenonlogists" try to combine the "science" of lived experience and the analysis of neural networks. Needless to say, this approach which tries to correlate personal experience with neurobiology is possible only in case of human beings.

There are two subschools of this thought, one headed by Varela and the other by Tonani and Edelman. Varela treats each consciousness experience as arising from a specific cell assembly in "resonance". Elderman and Tonani, too, regard a conscious experience as emergent involving synchronization of neural activities. While both subschools use slightly different idioms, the gist of both the branches seems to be nonlocalization of consciouness and emphasis on patterns of neurons.

Those who speak of consciouness being patterns or an emergent process may be correct but the vagueness inherent in such phrases as each pattern is unique and "the exact dynamic varies from person to person" introduce considerable imprecision in their models. If I say that my thought process and feelings are reflected in a unique neural pattern not found at other moments or in other people, I am only admitting that it is not possible to analyze the correspondence between the state of the brain and mind in general. Those who contend that we should have a systemic view of the brain-mind will not add much to our knowledge unless they establish a correlation or some theory which enables us to translate neural patterns into mental states and vice versa.

Science as we know today involves classification, abstraction and predictability. So long as we are not able to understand neural patterns in terms of mental parameters even in statistical or probabilistic terms, we cannot say that we have understood the "science" of consciousness. Words such as "consciousness consists of emergent patterns", "consciousness cannot be resolved into components", etc. will then appear as mere jargon used to conceal our lack of knowledge.

26.6 Socio-cultural Dimension

The mind is not only a biological but also a socio-cultural product. It has been found that domesticated animals behave differently from their wild relatives – a pet dog's responses radically differs from those of a wild dog and a plow horse's responses contrast with those of the horse in a wild herd. Of course, we implicitly assume that the mind is inseparable from behavior even in case of animals.

All of us know that the way we feel and react to situations depends to a considerable extent on our cultural background. If an aboriginal living in an isolated tribe is "transplanted" into a modern society he is likely to feel uprooted, become sick and yearn to go back to his tribe.

In an extreme case two Indian children were found living in a den of wolves. They behaved like animals, "walked on all fours, made howls like wolves, wolfed their food, and had other reactions similar to wolves".[9]

It is usually believed that non-human higher animals form a bio-social system while humans form a socio-cultural system. Humans are not only social animals they have something more, viz. culture. Our language, artifacts, literature, everything humankind has created for thousands of years which is passed on from one generation to another constitutes culture.

A socio-cultural system differs from a bio-social system in that the members belonging to the latter form societies, but are not able to pass on their knowledge to the next generation which has to start almost from scratch. Their behavior is predominantly instinctual. However, recent studies in higher apes, especially chipmpanzees tend to show that culture does exist at least in higher primates albeit in primitive form.[10] It is possible that life, cognition, consciousness and culture appear in the ascending fashion in what is essentially a continuum connecting the inanimate to the animate. The appreciation of the socio-cultural factors in the formation of the mental apparatus makes us realize that we cannot consider the individual mind in isolation. Our mind is not only shaped by our cultural milieu, we constantly interact with it, and are capable of changing the culture. This socio-cultural "group of minds" must be viewed as a dynamic system.

26.7 Structural Varieties

While discussing relations and isomorphism we looked upon structure as purely an abstract form. We broadly classified structure into static and dynamic types. While studying human society it is convenient to use the idea employed by those who have studied or analyzed social structures extensively.

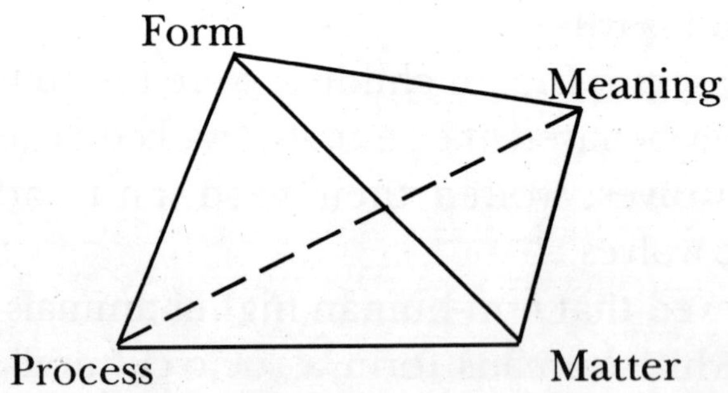

Fig.26.1 Cultural Tetrahedron

I have found Capra's nomenclature quite convenient to discuss different types of structures.

Capra speaks of three perspectives of life. The first relates to the study of form or pattern organization. The second is concerned with the study of matter or material structure. The third deals with the study of process.

He treats form, matter and process as three interconnected vertices of a triangle. A living system from these three perspectives can be described as a self generating network (form), a dissiptive structure (matter), and a cognitive system (process). Capra maintains that the distinction between a living and nonliving system is that in the latter matter is considered as basic and pattern as emergent or secondary. In the former it is the pattern that is most important. For example, it is the structural changes in this pattern which are identified with cognitive process from which emerges consciousness at some stage. "All these cognitive phenomena are nonmaterial, but they are embodied, they arise from and shaped by the body".[11]

Capra later converts this triangle into a tetrahedron by adding a hermeneutic dimension which he calls "meaning". For him meaning means a short hand notation for the inner world of reflective consciousness which contains a multitude of interrelated characteristics.[12] We may call this complex of four perspectives cultural tetrahedron.

26.8 Epistemology and the Cultural Tetrahedron

In wake of what modern scientists have found about life, consciousness and society do we need to change our epistemological tools?

The mind opens up a new dimension. We have seen in chapter 21, that one of the requisites of a body of knowledge to be science is that it should constitute social or public knowledge. If the mind can be understood only in terms of pattern which vary from one person to another two question arise :

1. In what sense can the mind be used as a tool of knowledge?
2. How do we obtain the knowledge of mind itself?

For the time being the first question is not difficult to answer. Where objectivity is well defined, as in case of physical sciences and mainstream biology the condition of social knowledge is easy to attain, especially with the help of modern instruments. My location in the cultural tetrahedron may be different from yours, but we can nevertheless have objective standards in most sciences. An exception is psychology when treated as science, which is related to the second question, viz. how do we obtain the knowledge of mind. There is also another area, viz. sociology treated as science but here our difficulties are not acute : despite individuality and uniqueness of the mind, we can have broad classifications in any society.

26.9 Brain and Quanta

We have already discussed consciousness, we now have to connect it to quantum world. Our observation of higher animals; strongly suggests that they too possess consciousness, though this assertion cannot be proved. However, it is safe to assume that consciousness or rather its quality or degree follows the evolution of life. We cannot surmise at what point consciousness appeared in the evolutionary process, but one can think of the consciousness continuum, its highest degree appearing in human beings.

But how is consciousness connected with quantum theory? Penrose has tried to established a connection which given the state of physics today appears tenuous.[13]

Locus of Consciousness

Where does human consciousness reside? We may ignore the many pre-scientific and metaphysical theories and safely assume that it is somewhere in the brain. The only point on which modern neuroscientists agree is that there may not be a single part of the brain which contributes to the phenomenon of consciousness. If you decide to walk from one place to another, you need not plan out the whole journey. A considerable part of your walk is automatic, you need not be conscious of how your limbs are moving or even uninteresting objects you encounter. You are partly controlled by your cerebellum (little brain). Similar automatic reflex actions appear without conscious effort and are controlled by the upper part of the spinal column.

This strongly suggests that it is the cerebrum (the main large brain) whose contribution to consciousness is the greatest.

Wilder Penfield, a renowned US-Canadian neurosurgeon, who performed numerous brain operations and was responsible for mapping sensory and motor areas of the brain concluded that the seat of consciousness is in the upper brain-stem which includes thalamus and midbrain. His inference was based on the fact that the brain-stem is directly in contact with the cerebral cortex (the surface layer of the cerebrum), in fact it is in communication with different regions of the cortex, associated sensations, thoughts, memories and so on, which are linked with consciousness.

Some scientists believed that it is the "reticular formation" where consciousness resides. If this part is damaged, unconsciousness results. However, the curious fact is that this part is active in the conscious state when you are awake. When you are asleep and dreaming it is not active.

According to some scientists the hippocampus a part of the brain which is responsible for recording long term memories, has a role to play in conscious awareness.

A few scientists feel that, cerebral cortex, the human being's most precious treasure itself is responsible for consciousness.

A few neurologists feel that it is the language center on left side of brain which is the seat of consciousness.

Split-brain Experiments

Experiments with patients whose left and right hemispheres of the brain had to be severed have yielded perplexing results. The two hemispheres appeared to behave as independent individuals and the experimenters could establish communications separately with them with some limitations. This is similar to identity crisis we came across in quantum mechanics as well as in Buddhist conception of ever-changing world. Does one person's consciousness give rise to two independent conscious entities? No definite answer can be given because there are contradictory results. Some researchers claim that both hemispheres share common emotions. Those who believe that language determines consciousness believe that the language center (which in majority of human beings is located on the left-hand hemisphere) is concerned with consciousness. They seem to be vindicated in some respects. If you ask the hemispheres, "Are you conscious?", it is only the left hemisphere that can answer "yes". An experiment conducted by Donald Wilson and others in 1977 has yielded interesting results : while the left hemisphere could speak, both the hemispheres showed comprehension and consciousness. Even the right hemisphere could speak at a later stage. The hemispheres expressed different wishes. The left wanted to be a draftsman and the right a racing driver.[14] According to Penrose, it is possible that both hemispheres shared common memories before the brain-split, the dichotomy of consciousness appears after the split.

Self-repair and Regeneration

It is interesting to consider how life and possibly consciousness appears in some lowly creatures. "If a flatworm is cut transversely the head-end will grow a new tail and the tail-end will grow a new head; even if cut into six or more slices, each slice can regenerate a complete animal".[15]

This is an example of self-repair. As we go from the lower level to the higher level of the evolutionary ladder we find that scope of self-repair mechanism dimishes. Neelham has called this regeneration "one of the more spectacular models, pieces of magic in the repertoire of living organisms".[16] In man the physical repairing has a limited scope; but humans have compensatory assets, the intellect. It is human intelligence which has made vast advances in medical sciences. If an amputated part of the human body cannot regain its original form, transplantation of organs is now possible in many cases : What they were not endowed with by nature, humans are able to achieve through science. Recently developed techniques of using stem cells to harvest other tissues and organs are still in infancy. It may be possible to grow and store vital organs in the future.

Quantum Connection

The visual cortex is one of the most interesting sensory centers in the brain. It receives inputs from the retina, but some information processing is already done before the data reaches the cortex.

Suppose we draw a generally well-known figure (such as a triangle or a rectangle) which has discontinuities on its contour a person who sees the figure without the knowledge of broken lines may not notice the gaps. For him it is the whole figure. Most of us have experienced such illusions. The reason usually attributed to this phenomenon is that our mind/brain perceives the world through inference from the unknown to the known.

What is surprising is that experimenters have found cells in the secondary visual cortex which can register the positions of the absent, but inferred lines. These cells are specialists – they are sensitive only to certain angles or orientations.[17] The retina is usually treated as a part of the brain. It has been found in case of toads that under suitable conditions, a single photon striking the dark-adapted retina can trigger a macroscopic nerve signal.[18] In case of human beings about seven photons are needed for a dark-adapted retina, to be aware of the photons' arrival.

Penrose wonders whether such cells which can be activated at the quantum level exist in the brain. So far no such evidence has been found. But let us assume that such cells do exist in the brain.

Penrose imagines a scenario somewhat similar to experiments involving silvered and half-silvered mirrors.

> Suppose that a photon arrives at the retina, having been previously reflected off a half-silvered mirror. Its state involves a complex linear superposition of its striking a retinal cell and of its not striking the retinal cell travelling, say, out of the window into space.[19]

He contends that at the time at which it might have struck the retina there should be a linear superposition of a "nerve signal" and "not a nerve signal". It is of course assumed that **U** procedure is still applicable. When the superposition (whatever it may mean in reality) strikes the one-photon sensitive cell, only one of the alternatives will appear to take place, and the other procedure **R** would have been effected. Calculation based on the one *graviton criterion* suggests that the disturbance created by the signal is not significant but a secondary effect of the signal creating a field in the surroundings could generate enough disturbance. What this implies is that "procedure **R** could have been effected well before we perceive the flash of light or not as the case may be".[20] Penrose concludes that the viewpoint leads to the conclusion that our consciousness is not needed to reduce the state-vector. This is in contradiction to the conventional quantum theory that "observation" is a *sine qua non* of the disturbance at the quantum level. We cannot pursue this topic further since it leads to many conjectures. Penrose's important conclusion is that "there is a essential non-algorithmic ingredient to (conscious) thought processes".[21]

27

Violation of Logic

27.1 Identity Crisis

It is time we addressed the important question : Do RQ theories violate the three laws of western logic discussed in chapter 20.

We found that the concepts of "identity", "individual", "numerical diversity", etc. are often tailored to meet practical problems.

The pure identity appears in A = A. Since modern science teaches us that even sheer passage of time changes an entity, the pure "identity" is a concept not of use in practice.

Usually we employ the biographical identity. Thus Newton remains Newton throughout his life. The river Ganga remains Ganga though its appearance, purity, mineral content and even the course may have changed over thousands of years.

Since we need classification for various purposes, we use a common noun, say, "cat" to indicate a broad class of quadrupeds. The classical approach to classification is a property or a set of common properties. In chapter 6 we studied how classification is carried out on the basis of "differentiation and integration" and CCD. This leads to classes, sub-classes, superclasses and so on horizontally and vertically.

In chapter 6 we saw the mathematical, technique of forming "equivalence classes" so that two elements in the same class may be considered identical for some purpose. We also considered how on the basis of one-one correspondence numerical equivalence or numerical diversity can be defined.

In Buddhist logic, inferential knowledge is based on identity or causation. The identity may relate to the content or reference.

In brief, the concept of identity itself is relative for pragmatic reasons. The concept based on the "essence" is rejected both by Buddhists and modern western philosophers.

Nevertheless, we do use the word "identity", usually it is the pseudo-identity during the life of what appears to be distinct, whether your dog Tommy or your shirt which you have been wearing for the last two years.

In the quantum world the subatomic particles may appear and disappear in a fraction of a second. For example, a zero-spin particle may suddenly give out two half-spin particles, say an electron and a positron.

Despite the identity crisis we mentioned earlier, the law of identity holds good in a certain sense. For example, two particles x and anti-x may suddenly emerge from void. We can identify them as x and anti x as long as we track them or they do not change into something else. We may discover many thousands of new particles (usually created in laboratories), but each particle has its own identity albeit for a short time. The very fact that we can use classification in science proves that, the law of identity is not violated. Even, say, two protons which appear to be identical will be treated as different on account of their separate locations.

We have already considered "identity" in Buddhist logic. In the world where an entity lasts only for a moment there is no identity except the pure identity A = A at a given moment. In fact in Buddhism law of identity is not considered important.

In quantum statistics sometimes we come across a few cases where identity presents a confused picture.

Suppose we have two balls A and B and receptacles having two compartments. Let us see how many arrangements are possible. It is assumed that one compartment can accommodate one or two balls.

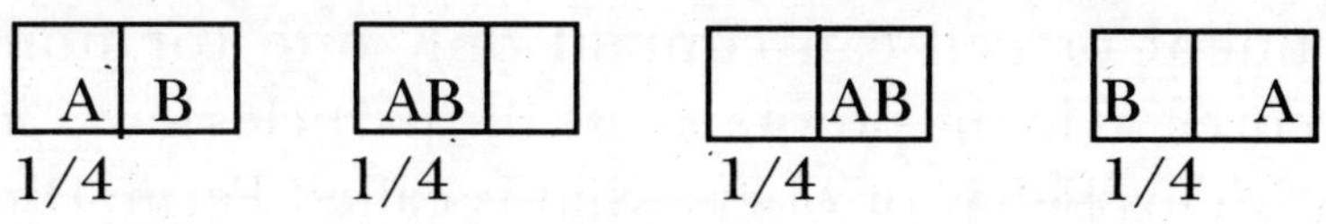

Fig. 27.1

There are four arrangements each having probability of 1/4 (Fig. 27.1). Suppose instead of the balls we have what are called "bosons" from the quantum world. These particles have a "spin" which is a numerical multiple of $h/2\pi$: 0, $h/2\pi$, $2h/2\pi$, $3h/2\pi$....

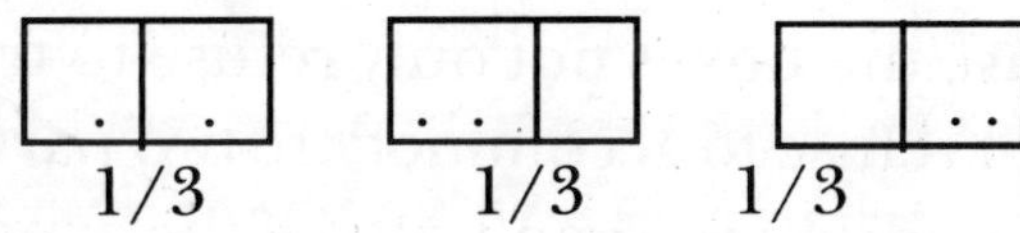

Fig. 27.2

It is found that there are only three possibilities, each having probability 1/3 Fig. 27.2.

This appears shocking to us. In the above arrangement "bosons" have lost their identity in the sense A and B are not distinguished. The first and fourth arrangement in Fig. 27.1 is now replaced by a single receptacle or the first arrangement in Fig. 27.2. We really have a baffling problem of individuation. The statistics involved in the behavior of bosons is called *Bose-Einstein statistics* (S.N. Bose was an Indian physicist).

In certain cases Bose-Einstein statistics needs to be modified in the wake of constraints imposed by Pauli's exclusion principle, according to which only one electron in a system can have a given quantum state. Using the above metaphor we can say that there is only one arrangement possible as shown below.

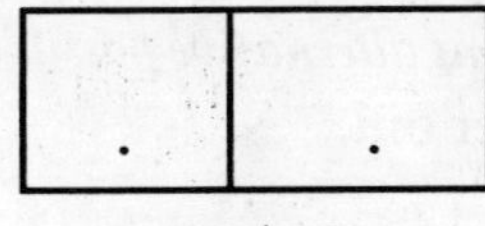

Fig. 27.3

A compartment or cell can contain only one (or none) particle. Moreover, as in the previous case the particles have "lost their identity". This behavior obeys what is called Fermi-Dirac statistics. This example shows that the laws relating to the micro (sub-atomic) world may differ from those pertaining to the macro world. However, it is difficult to draw a definite conclusion from these two aberrations. In case of two balls A and B may be treated as different because they cannot occupy the same space at the same time. In case of bosons the boxes have rejected one of the options of particle-box pairing. In case of the balls there were two pairs out of two balls and two boxes. It looks as if the boxes cannot differentiate between one boson and another. In the third case the boxes not only refuse to treat the particles as different but refuse to accommodate two particles at a time. The identity conundrum is complicated if the experimentor can keep track of the particles, so that according to him the particles are distinct. We, may keep this problem "open" for the future scientists who may be able to explain the paradox when physics advances further.

27.3 Law of Contradiction

The usual law of contradiction is that

x cannot be both A and -A

This law which was supported by Kant enthusiatically and extended to epistemology was accepted in western logic almost universally before the quantum dilemma appeared. Scientists have become more cautious and express some reservations on the accuracy of the law. This is clear from what Penrose says in case of particle wave duality :

> It is really not that light behaves sometimes as particles and sometimes as waves. It is that *each individual particle* behaves in a wavelike way entirely on its own; and *different alternative possibilities open to a particle can sometimes cancel* one another out.[1]

This argument is based on the premise that "particles" and "waves" are both mutually exclusive and also exhaustive categories.

Interference is a phenomenon which was observed in waves historically for the reason that in our macro world we can easily detect this phenomenon. This does not preclude the possibility of interference being present even among what we call things or particles. It is the characteristic of the quantum world that subatomic "particles" display interference, a phenomenon which could not be detected earlier because physicists did not have the required tools to probe the micro world.

As pointed out earlier, we may call subatomic existents as partiwaves or wavicles having certain properties which are not displayed by objects or waves at the macro level. An object of a metal of a definite shape is called "solid". When it is heated it begins to melt and becomes liquid at a high temperature. In the transitioal stage it appears to have both characteristics, it becomes soft and begins to spread, but you cannot call it liquid because though its parts are gradually moving, there is no "flow" of a liquid. The thing is both a solid and a liquid at the same time. But scientists do not show any surprise or shock because they are fairly familiar with this world. This also involves the concepts of identities, viz. "solid" and "liquid". For practical reasons we may define these terms in a certain manner so that at a certain point the "solid" is transformed into "liquid" which could save the law of contradiction. But this is only possible by an arbitrary definition.

If we introspect a little, we realize that there is no reason why a photon should not "split" or "spread" so that interference can take place. I am using the words as metaphors. In fact most quantum phenomena are described metaphorically unless their effects reach the classical level. Has anyone seen a photon or a neutron? We identify these particles on the basis of their effects at the perceptible level. We can only describe events at the macro level though they may be caused by quantum particles. If human physicists were inhabitants of the quantum world, perhaps they could describe an electron, a proton or even a photon accurately. But if they happened to visit the macro world they would bc shocked to find that many of their laws (belonging to their quantum world) are violated. If we stop viewing the subatomic world through projection of the macro world we live in, the quantum world will appear less mysterious.

There is another law of contradiction which is exactly opposite to what we call the law of contradiction. In Europe it existed before Aristotle. "Reality consists of mere contraries because all things proceed from contraries and the corresponding thought is nothing but contradiction".[2] This has some resemblance with Buddhist idea of contradiction and the importance of the "negative".

As explained in earlier chapters we may treat the paradox of duality by re-lebeling quantum particles as wavicles or partiwaves. It summary it appears that the law of identity in its purest form A = A at a given moment is not violated. All other notions of identity, diversity, equivalence, cardinal number of a set, etc. are based on our own definition of what constitutes identity for pragmatic reasons and so long as we adhere to the criterion consistently no violation of the concept of identity should occur.

27.4 Excluded Middle

We mentioned in the earlier chapter that western logic retains the law of excluded middle to save the law of double negation. Like the law of contradiction, the law of excluded middle, too, is not violated in the quantum mechanics when the concept of partiwave is introduced.

Because now options or alternatives are not merely "particle" or "wave", a not-particle need not be a wave and a non-wave need not be a particle.

In Buddhist logic, too, contradiction implies excluded middle. As Dharmakīrti observes "Contradiction is complete mutual exclusion", which implies exclusion of everything in the middle. The law of middle is not vitiated in the quantum world because particle and wave do not form an exhaustive system in the sense a partiwave shares common properties with particles as well as waves. Since the options are now increased from two to three, the conventional bivalent logic is no more applicable.

It should be clear to you that none of the following, viz. 1. multiplicity of particles, 2. uncertatinity, 3. thought experiments described earlier violate any of these three laws. In case of thought experiments (chapters 24 and 25) assertion regarding bifurcation of ψ and the assertion that their meeting again even when they are separated for hundreds of miles and then display interference is purely theoretical. Even it is true, it can be contended that two parts of the same entity were separated and then united again, and hence interference after re-union is not a perplexing phenomenon because wavicles do display internal interference.

There is another putative violation, not of western deductive logic but the epistemic rule that an object cannot be at two places at the same time. In chapter 24 it looks as if the particle (photon or electron) appears to be at two places (slits) at the same time. Once we understand the nature of partiwave, this objection disappears. The partiwave has some wave-like properties. If a wave of a large wave-front say 50 feet in length strikes a shore do we ever ask a physicist at which point the wave has struck?

27.5 Numerical Diversity

If you compare the paradox of one photon passing through two slits (chapters 24, 25) with the behaviour of particles obeying Einstein's or Fermi-Dirac's constraints you will find an interesting contrast :

1. In the first case a particle appears to split into two entities. Thus there is an increase of numerical diversity (one entity → two entities).
2. In the second case there is a decrease in numerical diversity in Fig. 27.2 the numerical diversity has decreased and all bosons are treated as one. In Fig. 27.3 the capacity of the locus too seems to displaya decrease in diversity.

The conclusion we can draw is that the number of combinations has decreased in Bose-Einstein and Fermi-dirac constraints.

In discrete mathematics mathematicians have created quasi-sets called "multisets".

Consider

{a, b}, {a, a, b}, {a, a, a, b}

We know they represent the same set {a, b}. However, qua multisets they are different their multiplicity (number of repetitions of a) being 1, 2 and 3. If we denote bosons by a, we can have the following interpretation in case of {a, a, b} :

It is a set of three particles – two bosons and one non-boson, denoted by {a, a', b}.

However, their quantum behaviour sometimes makes them a set of two particles, its multiset being {a, a, b}.

This incidentally confirms that numerical diversity is dependent on which view you take or the context. Recall the importance of context mentioned in section 6.3 while discussing numerical diversity.

28

The Concept of a Field

28.1 Nature of Fields

We saw in chapter 9 that the ultimate reality for Buddhist scholars consists of the sequences of momentary beings. These beings ultimately create the world of phenomena for us. These existents are not material or substantial. But to account for the efficient moments, modern commentators often compare them with flashes of energy, force, field and so on. Paradoxically, these moments are described as unique without "qualities". However, the idea of a field seems to be quite appropriate since the chains of moments have creativity – they are able to create the phenomenal world – although this world is an illusion for Buddhist. It would be very interesting to examine if such a conception is consistent with quantum phenomena.

The western concept of fields is comparatively new. Michael Faraday (1791–1837), and James Clerk Maxwell (1851–1879) are the major contributors to the classical field theory. Newton's magnum opus *Principia* published in 1687 is one of the greatest treatises in science. His mechanics deals with material objects and how they react with each other. His work borrowed from the earlier thinkers such as Galileo Galilei, Rene Descartes and Johannes Kepler. However, his theory was inadequate because it could not explain the "action at a distance" a concept involved in the attractive force between two material bodies. Newton's corpuscular theory of light was also inadequate to account for such phenomena as "interference". As we mentioned earlier Huygene's wave theory was more appealing.

The concept of fields is related to the waves historically but can be discussed independently.

We are all familiar with the ubiquitous "inverse square law". For example, in case of gravitation the force between two masses m, m' at a distance r from each other is given by the equation

$$F = G\,mm'/r^2$$

where G is the gravitational constant. The force is attractive.

A similar law exists in magnetism and static electricity. In school we learn that a magnet attracts certain metals like iron. The inverse square law also holds good. If m and m' indicate isolated pole-strengths the force is given by

$$F = k\,mm'/r^2$$

where k is a constant which can be reduced to 1 in vacuum by suitably choosing the units. However, the force is repulsive when m and m' are like poles and attractive when they are unlike poles. It must be pointed out that magnetic poles do not exist in isolation. Like many other parameters in physics magnetic poles are conceptual entities which help us in physics. Every magnet has two unlike poles, conventionally called N (north) and S(south).

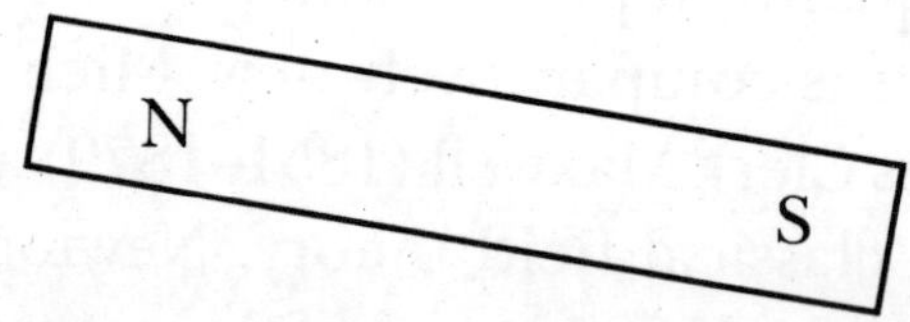

A bar magnet when freely suspended becomes stationary, its length being approximately parallel to the earth's north-south axis. It is assumed that the earth itself is a magnet with the magnetic south pole located near the geographical north pole and the magnetic north pole near the geographical south. Thus the magnetic south pole of the bar magnet approximately points to the geographical south and the north pole of the bar points approximately to the north.

The space surrounding a magnet where it is able to show magnetic properties is called its magnetic field. Theoretically the inverse square law suggests that the field is boundless because the force is zero only when the distance r is infinite.

The concept of field can be explained better in case of static electrical charges which can exist independently. The rule "like charges repel each other and unlike charges attract each other" is well known.

The inverse square law is the same as before

$F = qq'/r^2$

where q and q' are magnitudes of charges.

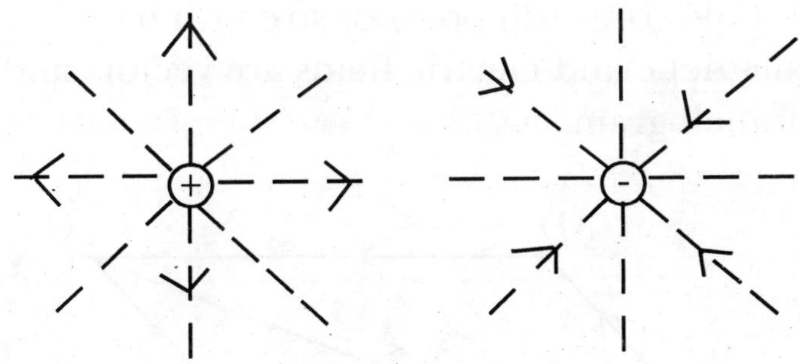

Fig. 28.1 Electric field

As before, theoretically, the field due to a charge extends to infinity. For the sake of avoiding ambiguity we assume that the measure of the field is the force experienced by a unit positive charge at a point (isolated positive pole in case of a magnet). Fig. 28.1 shows the electric field due to positive and negative charges. There are a few points which should be remembered clearly. The lines (arrows) showing the direction of the field are called lines of force. The lines of force can be quantified. When the field strength is multiplied by the area of a plane perpendicular to the lines the product is called the flux passing through the plane and is a measure of magnetic or electric quantity across the plane.

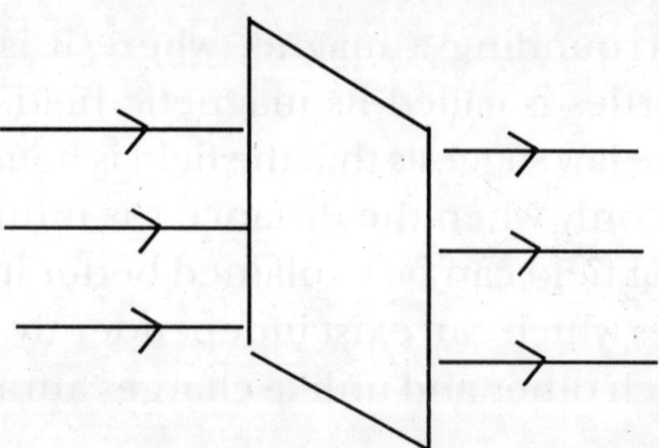

When the units of the field strength are properly chosen we can prove that 4πq is the flux emanating from an isolated positive charge q and equal flux enters the negative charge q. In case of magnetic poles 4πm is the magnetic flux going out (or entering) the north pole (or south pole) of strength m.

Both magnetic and electric fields are vectors and are added by the parallelogram law.

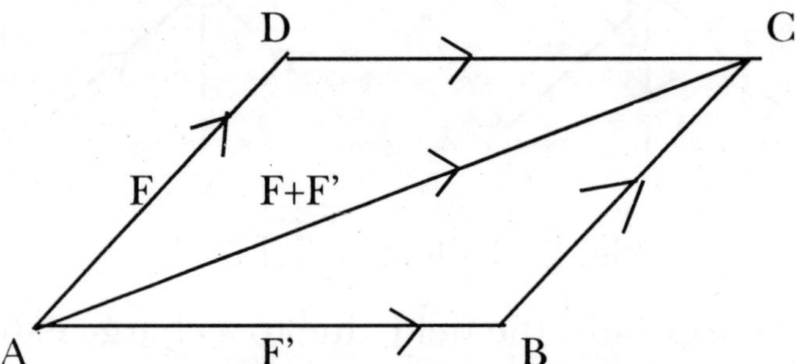

In the above figure for example, if two fields F and F' are superimposed, the resultant field is F + F' along the diagonal AC of the parallelogram ABCD.

It is necessary to remember the following points :

1. The concepts field, pole strength, quantity of charge, polarity (north or south) and the charge sign are conventional. These parameters cannot be directly perceived, but can be inferred through their effects. We really do not know the ontological status of a field or the lines. It would not be wrong to say that we are familiar with the epistemology relating to these concepts, but their

ontology is elusive and is likely to remain a mystery for ever.

2. It is assumed that the fields are continuous – there are no gaps in the "lines" of force. This also implies that one and only one field strength is associated with any point of space containing the field.

28.2 Electromagnetic Fields

Electric and magnetic fields are interrelated. When an electric current passes through a conductor it establishes a magnetic field around it. Similarly when a magnet is plunged into a coil or taken out of it it induces a current in the coil. Similar effects are observed when a conductor moves with respect to a magnetic field. Two current carrying parallel conductor repel or attract depending on the directions and strength of the currents. In fact the physics of electromagnetism provides many examples of how one type of energy can be converted into another type. It also affords ample scope to prove the law of conservation of energy when one type of energy is converted into another type.

28.3 Maxwell's Theory

While magnetic and electric fields have been known to physicists, their existential status appeared to be controversial. Before Michel Faraday, a field was treated as something abstract, non-material which would activate or affect a substance placed in it depending upon the nature of the substance and type of the field. Faraday experimented extensively on varying current and associated magnetic fields, moving coils in magnetic fields, and so on.

He came to the conclusion that electric and magnetic fields did have some "stuff".

Faraday even conjectured that light itself might consist of fields. Note that Huygen's concept of light as waves required a medium of transmission called ether. This new thinking of propagation of a wave without any medium was revolutionary.

Andre Marie Ampère (1775–1836) and James Clerk Maxwell, the former a great Scottish physicist and the latter a mathematician could be credited with effecting seismic changes in the perception of what electric and magnetic fields are. Ultimately it was Maxwell who suggested a few changes in the equations relating to electromagnetic phenomena. The final set of equations appeared as

(1) $1/c^2 \times \partial \mathbf{E}/\partial t = \text{curl } \mathbf{B} - 4\pi \mathbf{j}$

(2) $\partial \mathbf{B}/\partial t = \text{curl } \mathbf{E}$

(3) $\text{div } \mathbf{E} = 4\pi\rho$

(4) $\text{div } \mathbf{B} = 0$

The constant c was identified with the velocity of light. What's more Heinrich Hertz a German physicist showed that these electromagnetic waves can be produced artificially.

The first two equations show how the magnetic field **B** and electric field **E** are related. "Curl **B**", "curl **E**" are functions of **B** and **E** which we need not discuss, while **j** is the current density.

$\partial \mathbf{E}/\partial t$, $\partial \mathbf{B}/\partial t$ indicate the rate of change of **E** and **B** respectively with respect to time.

With knowledge of school physics you can appreciate (3) and (4). Suppose you surround any point by a closed surface S where the density of electrical charge is ρ. div **E** is an expression of the total flúx which goes out of the sphere less the flux entering the surface. In other words it is the net flux which is obviously due to ρ, and 4πρ is precisely the flux emitted from ρ. In case of a magnetic field there are no isolated poles. Hence the net flux out of S is zero. This is precisely what div **B** = o shows.

In fact, similar equations hold good for any field obeying the inverse square law, where we assume continuity.

Note that light as an electromagnetic field is a moving field with velocity c.

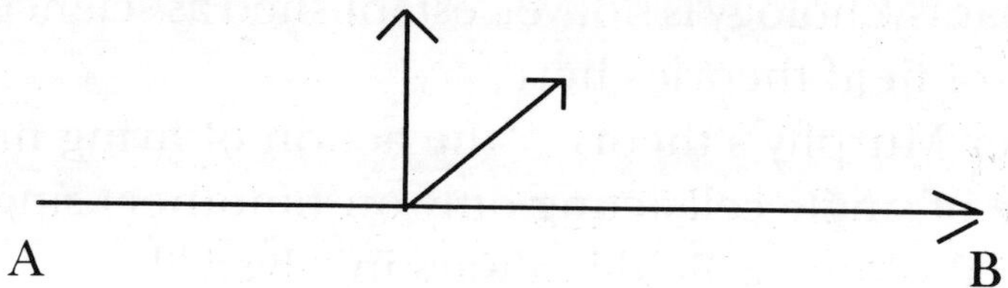

The above figure shows the progress of an electromagnetic field in the direction AB.

Magnetic and electrical oscillations are perpendicular to the direction of propagation.

These two field vectors are sometimes conditioned. For example, a plane polarized light is one in which the electric field oscillates in a plane perpendicular to AB. The magnetic field vector oscillates in unison but in a plane perpendicular to that of the electric vector. In a circular polarization both vectors rotate about AB but are always perpendicular to each other. In elliptical polarization the electric field vector traces an ellipse.

28.4 Field in Psychology and Sociology

The concept of field has also been borrowed by psychologists and sociologists. One can think of an individual having a field which we normally call his sphere of influence. An individual's psychological field can influence us in several ways : it can induce fear, awe, love, peace, hatred and so on. It also follows the standard rule prevalent in magnetic or electric field : the closer you go towards the source the greater is the intensity of the field. But since each individual has her own field there is interaction of individual fields. The net result is the emergence of a social field which we usually call "social milieu", and which reflects customs, mores, fads and so on. In fact we are not only influenced by the socio-cultural field in which we move, we in turn influence the field. The views of interdependence in Buddhist logic appear quite appropriate in a socio-cultural system.

Though parasychology is not yet established as science, there is no dearth of field theories here.

In Gardner Murphy's theory , "the action of living matter is never a case of single cell acting only on (another) single cell. The structural whole or field is always involved".[1]

The theory also contends that the psychic field moves backwards and forwards in time. According to Murphy, "all personal activities are constantly changing context and interacting with those of others, and it may be that each one becomes part of cosmic process".[2]

Another parapsychologist C.D. Broad contemplates the survival of the *psi* component after death. According to him :

> We need no longer suppose that although a surviving *psi* component may be bodiless, it is necessarily unextended and unlocalized, for we are nowadays well accustomed to such phenomena as electromagnetic fields which cannot be called bodies, but which still have structure and definite properties and dispositions.[2a]

It must however, be mentioned that parapsychology is not recognized as science since parapsychology includes ESP (extra sensory perception) and psychokinesis. Clairvoyance, prognostication and telepathy are some of the powers claimed under the first category. Psychokinesis is the supernatural power to manriputate (e.g. move) an object at a distance. In fact any phenomena for which no scientific explanation exists can be studied under parapsychology. Fortunately most subsets of *psi* phenomena can be falsified under Popper's test. I have discussed its status elsewhere.[3]

In early 20th century parapsychology acquired some respectability when research was conducted under Dr. J.B. Rhine at Duke university, North Carolina. Later attempts by S.G. Soul and others to repeat Rhine's experiments seemed to have failed. Rhine's claims are no more considered authentic.

28.5 Field in Buddhist Theory

The Buddhist logic postulates that ultimate reality consists of instantaneous moments, which give rise to the illusion of empirical reality. The theory of cognition, though it recognizes only two sources, perception and inference, depicts the process of cognition in such a way that one is tempted to compare it with the field theory of modern science. The relevant similarities we have are :

1) The instantaneous beings are "point instants" and not material.
2) They are efficient.
3) They activate the mind to construct an image in the empirical world.
4) Every point instant arises as a results of the combination of all preceeding point-instants in the wake of the doctrine of dependent origination.

Interdependence and functional dependence are the terms used in connection between two point instants or the relationship between the corresponding images. There is no harm in assuming that cognition takes place through a field which is the same as the electromagnetic field when the object in the empirical world is at a distance from the perceiver.

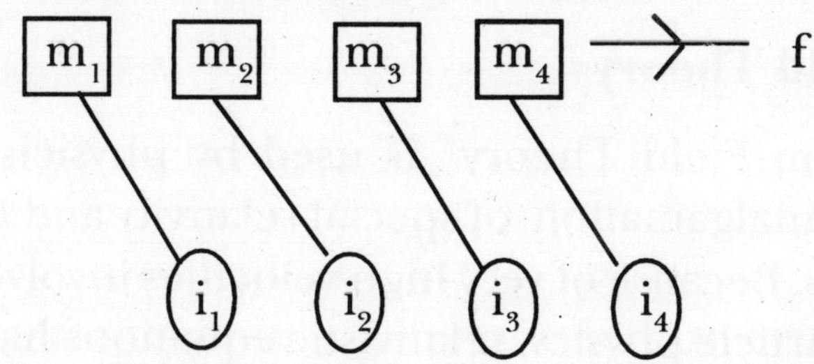

Fig. 28.3 Field-like *kṣaṇikas*

In Fig. 28.3 are shown the chain of instantaneous beings m_1, m_2, m_3,... giving rise to images i_1, i_2, i_3,...

However, such depiction appears audacious because the moments (m) belong to the transcendental and are indescribable. The depicted images however have greater credibility. These are the images we see in the empirical world. All of us perceive them in similar manner except for differences due to our spatial position and our minds insofar as they may "construct" slightly different images.

We can easily see that Russell's postulates (chapter 24) do not violate basic conceptions in Buddhist law. The postulate of quasi permanence helps us convert our series of perceptions into an object an illusory "thing" and its states in the empirical world. The postulate of separable causal lines helps us connect different causal chains. The postulate of spatio-temporal continuity, however, contradicts the notion "discontinuous motion" in Buddhist logic. We may either reject the Buddhist theory or assume that discontinuity is infinitesimal and does not create any "jerks" in our perception. The structural postulate is vindicated by our empirical knowledge. It is also similar to Buddhist idea of *sārūpya.* The analogy postulate may be ignored since it has no place as a separate source of cognition. However, this postulate is not sufficient to build a theory even in modern science. This postulate only suggests a possible solution by observing parallels. But any new theory developed on the basis of an analogy has to be verified empirically.

28.6 Quantum Field Theory

The term "Quantum Field Theory" is used by physicists to indicate a possible amalgamation of special relativity and (old) quantum mechanics. Because of very high velocities involved in of the sub-atomic particle physics, relativistic equations have to be used in place of Newtonian physics. The quantum field theory not yet fully developed makes many assumptions.

First, the number of particles of any particular kind need not be constant. Second, in every type a particle has an antiparticle (see chapter 21) though in some cases the antiparticle is of the same kind as the particle itself, e.g. photon. Third, a massive particle in collision with its antiparticle leads to mutual destruction leading to the creation of energy. Fourth, linear superposition of states is widely allowed (creating as, it were, a bonded family). This requires that even the number of particles need not even be definite. A little introspection will convince you that this bonding leads to confusion as regards identity and numerical diversity. I am not sure how the term quantum field arose, but it seems to have the origin in the fact that out of a void can emerge a pair of particle-antiparticle a process of creation as opposed to the reverse process of destruction. Physicists certainly need an ominipresent field which can conjure up such pairs.

Quantum electrodynamics is called the supreme quantum field theory, a theory of photons and electrons, because it makes a few accurate predictions. However, Penrose calls it untidy because physicists encounter many initial apparently absurd results The following words from Penrose correctly describe the status of quantum field theories.

"I should make clear that compatibility between quantum theory and special relativity provided by quantum field theory is only partial referring only to **U**...".[4]

The problem is the quantum field theory cannot explain the "quantum jumps" the procedure **R** leads to in such cases as EPR thought experiments. It has also failed to incorporate gravity in the physicist's search for a grand unification theory.

However, assumption of an omnipresent quantum field has spawned many kindred hypotheses in almost all the branches of knowledge. It would be worthwhile to furnish a brief account on what Deepak Chopra, a well-known writer, has to say about quantum theory and health.

28.7 Quantum Bridge

Deepak Chopra is an American endocrinologist of Indian origin. He is also an immensely popular writer who has authored many best-sellers such as *Ageless Body, Timeless Mind* and *Quantum Healing*. His books fall in such categories as "self-help", "spiritualism" and "mind-body medicine". He heavily borrows from quantum and relativity theories, Indian philosophy and medicine. He also attempts to present a theory which tries to bridge the quantum world and the body-mind unity. His ten principles covering a new world view are as follows : [5]

1. The observer being part of the world affects it. We do not only have experience, we create our own bodies. You can change the world by changing your perception. Consciousness can control the so-called involuntary functions such as heartbeat, digestion and respiration.
2. Although our body appears solid, in reality it is information and energy. This in turn is only a part of the infinite fields of energy which we call the universe.
3. The difference between the body and mind is superficial. At the deeper level they are the same-part of the universal field.
4. Our beliefs, thoughts and other mental processes can give rise to chemical changes which we call the biochemistry of the body. This is present in every cell of the body.
5. Perception is not automatic : it is learnt. What's more if you change your perception you change your somatic experience and your world.
6. Your intelligence and impulses change your body every moment. You are the totality of the thoughts. If you change the pattern of your impulse you change yourself.
7. The doctrine of non-dualism is true : our body and mind are only an aspect of the cosmic body-mind.
8. There is no absolute time. In fact there is only eternity. The events and change create an illusion of linear time; hours, days, months, etc. With sufficient practice we can learn to feel the changeless time. This should open the path of no change leading to immortality.

9. Our senses are only apparent. Deep inside lies the non-changing eternal being which creates an illusion of body, mind and senses.
10. That eternal being is the seer, the spirit. Aging, sickness and death are illusory. Chopra's quantum worldview resembles *advaitism* of the nondualists.

Unfortunately, he claims that this philosophy is "grounded in the discoveries of quantum physics made almost a hundred years ago. The seeds of this new paradigm were planted by Einstein, Bohr, Heisenberg and other pioneers of quantum physics, who realized that the accepted way of viewing the physical world is false".[6] We have already mentioned Capra's views on modern physics and mysticism. The only difference between Capra and Chopra is that while the former draws parallels, the latter treats implicit advaitism (monism) as nothing but modern quantum science.

As a physician Chopra has come across many cases of miracle cures that can be attributed to the patients' mental strength rather than medicine. He calls this phenomenon of sudden upward jump, quantum healing. This is usually attributed to faith, suggestion, hypnosis, etc. Based on our latest knowledge of neurotransmitters, neuropeptides, enzymes and self-generating characteristics, Chopra like many modern thinkers feels that our entire body contains intelligent molecules, metaphorically, our body has its own mind.

He builds a conceptual framework incorporating the mind-body unity which is somewhat similar to the particle-wave unity.

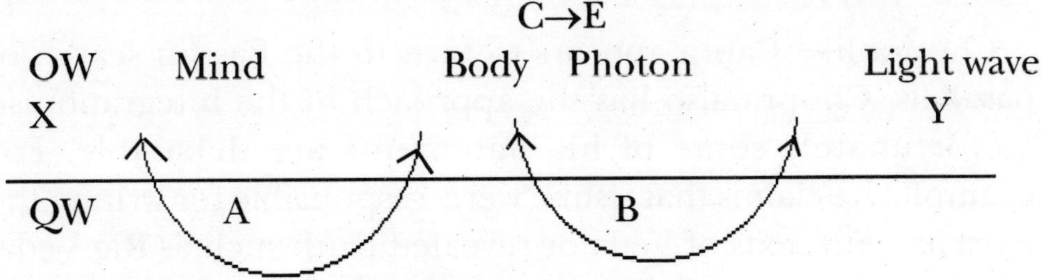

Fig. 28.4 Quantum field

In fig. 28.4, XY shows a border which separates our world OW from the quantum world QW. Matter and energy (B) appear distinct in the world above XY. Similarly mind and body are distinct (A). In our normal world the chain of cause-effect can be shown by a simple arrow above XY (CE). For example, a person throws a stone at you and you receive a blow on your head. This is a cause-effect chain which can be perceived by us. However, when matter is converted into energy and vice versa the causal chain is mysterious and has to pass through an unknown territory. Thus there is a gap between the cause and the effect which can be explained only with the help of all-pervading quantum field.

Similarly the fact that neuropeptides can be created by the mind or emotional changes will have to be shown by a path which joins OW and QW. Such a path would indicate conversion of thought into molecules.

The region QW is actually an epistemological void because we are not aware how the conversion (mind-body or particle-wave) occurs. Nevertheless, the all-pervading quantum field seems to take care of this conversion. In case of the mind-body it is the "intelligence" which is omnipresent that is responsible for this conversion. Chopra calls the intelligence above XY "active intelligence" and that below XY "silent intelligence". Chopra explains particle-wave phenomenon in a slightly different way :

> .. a photon is a form of light as is a wave, but both arise from a hidden field. On the surface of reality we see either photons or light waves, but the reason why both can exist in one reality is that they preexist as mere possibilities in the quantum field.[7]

Chopra like Capra appears to turn to the East in search of parallels. Chopra also has the approach of the integrationist. Unfortunately some of his statements are debatable. For example, he claims that rishis "were responsible for writing the most ancient texts of Veda or revealed truth such as Rig Veda, which may predate the Egyptian pyramids by several thousand years".[8] Most Indologists agree that the Rig Veda was composed around 1500-2500 BCE.

Chopra also mentions how the rishis used a new approach to know the fundamental nature of reality.

When the rishis closely inspected the states of waking, sleeping and dreaming they found that each of this states has its own reality. Moreover when we move from one state to another there is a gap in transition. "..it is like a little window into the field that is beyond either wakefulness or sleep".[9] He compares this gap with the mysterious region below XY in fig. 28.4. He also likens yoga, which literally means union, with Einstein's quest for a unifield field theory. "The major difference between the two is that the rishis not being theoretical declared that the unifield field exists in the real world; it is an experience and not merely a mental construct".[10]

A few comments need to be made on Chopra's views. First, Chopra's way of looking at apparent dichotomies seems imaginative. By creating *ad hoc* gaps he tries to bridge the chasm between the cause and effect. However, from the viewpoint of epistemology these gaps must be regarded as the gaps in our scientific knowledge, to be filled by a plausible unified theory at a future date. Second, Chopra seems to be going in the same direction as Capra. Some parallels between Indian mysticism and modern science are only apparent : the rishis, yogis and others who practice esoteric disciplines will tell you that what they experience is indescribable, which can at best be conveyed by such oxymoron as "space is and is not". The universal 'field' of the sages need not be the same as that which a physicist calls "quantum field". Nevertheless, Chopra's holistic approach in the mind-body medicine cannot be exaggerated. We will see in chapter 31 that such integral approach allows us to make useful changes at the psychological level if not at the transcendental level. It is also true that belief, suggestion, or hypnotism can have psychophysical effects which can be used for healing a patient.

In terms of the different stances described by Wilber (see chapter 31), Chopra seems to have views similar to Wilber – a belief in overlapping magesteria of science and religion and an integral approach to human problems. However, unlike Wilber, Chopra has definitive positive views – he appears to believe in advaitism and tries to explain scientific phenomena in terms of an all-pervading field which the scientist may call quantum field and which the monist calls Brahman. It is necessary to realize that despite its practical utility such integrationist views are beset with the pitfalls mentioned later in chapter 31 and also have a hard core of nonscience that cannot be separated from mysticism and religion including nondualism of *Vedānta.*

Universal Relativity

29.1 Motivational Source

We have seen that relativity and quantum theories have some parallels in Buddhist logic, but despite many similarities Buddhism does not qualify for the status of hard science especially because it involves transcendental concepts not amenable to scientific scrutiny. It has the right environment, rational approach and scope for revising a theory, at least theoretically. These feature can inspire a scientist to propound a new theory, but the status of Buddhist logic here is only that of a motivational source. Since the major goal of Buddhism is alleviation and eradication of suffering and attainment of *nirvāṇa*, it is preoccupied with the area which in modern sense may be called nonscience. Even the most promising department, investigation of deeper levels of the mind through meditation has neglected the empirical side which could transform personal experience into social knowledge and then to a hard science. It is only recently that researchers have undertaken studies which may shed considerable light on the mind-brain or body-mind connection.

Śūnyatā identified with relativism is one of the pillars of Buddhist logic along with the doctrines of dependent origination and momentariness. There are two dimensions along which Buddhist logic can integrate itself with science. The first relates to what is called wholistic or integral approach and the other the concept of universal relativity. We briefly consider the second dimension in this chapter deferring a discussion on the other to a later chapter.

29.2 Generalization of Relativity

Buddhist logic incorporates the philosophical conception of relativism which has been discussed by many other schools of philosophy, eastern as well as western. We pointed out in chapter 21 that one of the features of science is generalization. Ostensibly it appears that the philosophical relativity lacking precision and advanced mathematical tools and entwined with mysticism is a far cry from relativity physics. However, Finkelstein's approach based on the analysis of Segal, Inonu and Wigner shows that the concept of relativity can be enlarged to fit both physics and philosophy into one universal concept. It is possible that both physics and Buddhist logic (as part of philosophy) will stand to gain.

So far as possible we shall follow Finkelstein in briefly describing the process of relativization. The technique will be called SIW (after Segal, Inonu and Wigner). The method of identifying a false absolute has its own idiom. "Relativity" is the term used to indicate that a theory implies that a phenomenon's appearance is dependent on the observer. An "absolute" is a property or an existent which is not observer-dependent. "Reification" means false identification of something as an absolute which in reality does not exist. An "idol", the word first used by Francis Bacon, is an entity which is misperceived as an absolute through reification.

A "simple" is an entity if it does not include any other entity. It is called "semi-simple" if it is simple or a collection of simples. A "nonsimple" or "compound" is an entity which is not semisimple. It may also be called a "complex". When one simple is subordinated to another dominant simple, there being no total integration, the resultant is a compund. Frankelstein provides an excellent example; a snake which has just swallowed a pig[1]. This is a one way coupling; the relation between the snake (dominant) and pig (subordinate) is not symmetric.

In Galilian mechanics space does not exist without time. Galileo thus treated space/time as a compound; space as nonabsolute and time as absolute. Time here is thus a potential idol. Now the task of relativization is to hunt for a "coupling constant" which would make Galileo's space/time symmetrical. This constant is precisely c, the velocity of light. When this constant is incorporated into Einstein's special relativity, the coupling becomes two-way. In other words we can call it a new absolute space-time.

However, special relativity has an idol. Newton believed that there is no standard rest, but there is a standard of nonaccelaration. Einstein's special relativity retains this idol in inertial systems moving uniformly with respect to one another. The principle of equivalence, however, is an advance which incorporates matter into general relativity making matter-space-time symmetrical, i.e. establishing a two way coupling between matter and metric (spacetime). The "coupling coefficient" is usually taken as G. (Newton's constant). It is worth mentioning here that in the process of relativization from special to general relativity there is a transformation of the idol, viz. Euclidean spacetime into a complex non-Euclidian space-time that has absorbed matter. Compare the equation :

$$ds^2 = dx^2 + dy^2 + dz^2 + du^2$$

of the Euclidian geometry with

$$ds^2 = \Sigma g_{\mu\nu}\, dx_\mu\, dx_\nu$$

of non-Euclidian space-time.

29.3 Quanta and Relativization

The uncertain and bizarre quantum world has changed the physicist's epistemology. In pre-RQ physics there was a definite place for the concepts such as an isolated entity with a set of properties (*svabhāva*); moreover an entity or a system is not dependent on the observer. Scientists soon realized that in the micro world the behaviour of an entity not only depends on its own (putative) properties, but the configuration in a system whose separate entities interact and almost lose their identities.

This fairly agrees with Mādhyamika view of functional dependence, and the concept of *niḥsvabhāva.*

However, the quantum physicists needed relativization beyond the conventional interactivity. The experimenter or observer should be included in the set of actors in a quantum phenomenon. This perception is based on Heisenberg's uncertainty theory. The classical theory has a compound doing/ knowing which needs to be fused into a simple. In order to introduce symmetry in the coupling physicists use "h" Planck's constant as the coupling coefficient.

According to Finkelstein this approach of eliminating the idols has been successful. However, a new idol now appears on the scene. One of these idols is "Not". According to many quantum physicists predicates and classes (or sets) are defined selectively by specific actions stripping them of generality. This involves a peculiar problem : unlike in classical physics, a sequence of two selective acts need not be a selective act in quantum world. However, quantum physics still recognizes absolute negation : a proposition p has a unique negative ~ p. For "x is A", one and only one negative "x is not A" exists. Classically, an experimenter can manipulate his object (the system constituting the experiment). She has sufficient time to monitor the feedback of her action and then decide the next action, according to her "flow chart". At the quantum level this is not possible; the time available to the experimenter after one act is not sufficient to make adjustments through a second act.

A polarizer for a photon affords an excellent example. Once the polarizer detects a photon the latter cannot be used again. Unlike in classical physics we cannot repeat the experiment on the same photon. (This is tantamount to saying that the photon's identity has changed or vanished.)

Suppose a photon is allowed to pass through A, the first detector and then through B, the second detector. After being detected by A we have the following options :

If A then B

If A then not-B

At the quantum level it is found that If A Then Not B can be judged easily. We can even use an uncaliberated null detector. The positive assertion If A Then B requires a complex process. After detecting that a photon has passed through filter A we have to ensure that it also passes through filter B. This needs a calibrated instrument or counting; a null detection will not do.

The present Quantum Theory believes that some physical processes respect negation. According to Finkelstein "...when predicates evolve under these processes the negation of the evolute of the predicate is the evolute of the negation of that predicate".[1a] These processes are termed unitary in "quantum" idiom.

According to Finkelstein almost all quantum processes have no respect for negation. They are negation violating and are called "nonunitary". Quantum intervention such as input, selection and outtake provide good examples. This is in contrast to classical theory, according to which all systems respect negation.

In other words the Absolute Negative of the classical physics is not totally banished in quantum mechanics. For instance "quantum logic has a fixed negation that all dynamical evolutions of isolated systems are supposed to respect". Thus this idol still persists despite the scientist's efforts for its relativization.

There is another absolute idol which appears when we go from special to general relativity. This is the one-way coupling between field and space-time. A field is characterized by associating every point with a vector. When we attempt a transformation of coordinates from a frame of reference to another with relative acceleration or curvilinear coordinate system there is asymmetry. One has to know the point, but its converse does not hold good. In other words space-time coordinates of a point couple into a field, but not vice versa. In the field theory space-time is the idol.

Finkelstein's hunch is that a coupling agent will have to be introduced for symmetry. This should be a small time called ψ "chronon". There are a few hurdles, one of them is the "locality principle" in Einstein's theory which appears as an alien when we try to incorporate it in quantum physics. According to Finkelstein it is these absolutes, space-time and locality principle, incorporated in most theories of quantum relativity that need to be relativized before the incomplete theories relating to quantum gravity, super gravity, grand unified theory, string (and super string) theory, etc. appear satisfactory.

There is another absolute called "dynamic" law or dynamic which influences a quantum system, but the converse is not true.

What is unfortunate is that when you try to relativize an idol, a new idol appears on the scene. The lesson physicists have learnt is that the search for any final integrational theory is an endless persuit. We can only define a theory which still remains approximate, and further revision is needed sooner or later.

What is true of relativization in physics is also true in other branches of knowledge. For example, a school student considers her teacher as a genius, but when she joins a college the erstwhile hero becoming a false idol, and a new absolute say, a mathematics professor may appear on the scene who in turn will be replaced later by another absolute, say, a Nobel laureate.

It is in this sense that the scope of relativity can be enlarged to cover almost the entire phenomenal world.

Before comparing relativity with Buddhist logic, it is necessary to consider the profound implications of universal relativity in science itself.

29.4 Implications of Universalization

We saw that most idols are false in physics, and that when one idol is relativized another idol appears. How do we interpret this experience?

The first idea that strikes us is that there is no absolute or constant in physics; the so called universal constants, the velocity of light in vacuum (c), Planck's constant (h), gravitational constant (G) all are variable. This means even the universal laws are not fixed; it is possible that these constants/laws change gradually. A few western scientists such as Newton, Mach and Whitehead subscribed to this view.

On the other hand, some scientists especially Laplace and Einstein believed that, the march of science was progressing towards a grand fixed law.

If you introspect a little on "the old idols disappear but new ones replace them" you could come out with a diffrent interpretation : there are (apparent) constants, but as science progresses they appear to change because of newer and sophisticated techniques of measurement.[2]

It is difficult to prove any one of these alternative interpretations. When we find scientists wrestling with the problem of Grand Unification Theory (GUT), we can either say that such theory cannot exist or that scientists will ultimately arrive at GUT and absolute constants. There is no logical reason to adhere to one view or the other.

29.5 Comparison with Buddhist Logic

We have already discussed philosophical relativity in Buddhism in connection with the doctrines of *pratītyasamputpāda*, momentariness, *śūnyatā*, *catuṣkoṭi* and so on. It was pointed out earlier that Buddhist logicians often tread the territory of the transcendent despite Śākyamuni's silence on the fourteen metaphysical questions. Buddhist philosophers use the method as most philosophers use, namely; an attempt to reconcile the opposites.

Two worlds are created, the phenomenal and the ultimate ; one condidtioned reality and other unconditioned (ultimate) reality. Relativity appears only at the phenomenal level while the ultimate truth is that "all things are *śūnya* devoid of their own natures".[3]

Nevertheless, the real (ultimate) and the empirical are not separate. The phenomenon apears at a different level, but it pertains to the same noumenon. However, this attempt to reconcile two worlds often creates new problems. In such cases different schools may appear on the scene for solving new problems. This often creates hierarchical realities, levels of comprehension or different standpoints.

One of the methods of reconciling contradictions is ambiguous statements. A few quotations will indicate how different compartments are created from reality which is *one* in the ultimate sense.

"The *tathatā* (the true nature) of things is of two kinds, the specific nature and real nature".[4]

"*Śūnyatā* as the mundane truth of things means this nature of change and relativity, and in this nature, things are one, indistinct and undivided, while as specific forms of becoming they are distinct, many and different".[5]

"The *Śāstra* thus distinguishes three kinds of *tathatā*, the lower the middle and the superior".[6]

"The indeterminate nature is the true nature of all things. Determinations and divisions are the constructions of imagination".[7]

One of the consequences of creating different realities is that one term has several interpretations depending on the context. On the other hand apparently different concepts are equated.

For example, *nirvāṇa* can mean extinction of suffering, death of clinging, eternal joy, ultimate goal of all beings, ultimate nature of all things, non-apartness from *saṃsāra* and so on.

On the other hand concepts *nirvāṇa, śūnyatā, tathatā,* ultimate reality are used equivalently while referring to the ultimate One.

To summarize, Einstein's relativity is a theory in physics unlike relativity in many philosophies. But the concept of relativity can be enlarged so that we can speak of universal relativity. The Buddhist concept of relativity is based on the philosophy of momentariness as well as the comprehension of different levels of reality. At the mundane level, this concept fairly agrees with the recent findings in quantum world. However, the gulf between science and Buddhist logic is difficult to bridge because of the transcendental concepts (ultimate reality, *nirvāṇa,* etc.) in Buddhism.

30

Eastward Ho !

30.1 Mysticism

Mysticism is hard to define. It has a close connection with what we call the supernatural. When we explain a phenomenon which our forebears considered mysterious, in scientific terms, we say that the phenomenon is demystified. To some extent mysticism is antithesis of science.

Those who believe in mysticism can be theists, agnostics or even atheists. The theist seeks direct experience of God and this is what he calls spiritualism. But there are a number of people who do not believe in God as the word is understood in traditional religions, but may speak of "hidden wisdom", "peak experience" and other states of mind or emotion which cannot be called normal. This may be called spiritual experiences in a broader sense. It is worth quoting Rabindranath Tagore, "Man has a feeling that he is truly represented in something which exceeds himself".

Mysticism fascinates most of us especially when we are children or when we are very old and tend to believe that life cannot be described in terms of science on the one hand and morality on the other.

"Nothing" and "pairs of opposites" characterize the language of mysticism and inconsistencies, relativism and nonsequiturs often live happily together in the world of mystics.[1]

Russell mentions four characteristics of mysticism.[2] First, a mystic has intuition and insight through one of his indescribable experiences, which we have already mentioned. A closely associated with the "revealing experience" is the belief that the reality is different from what appears to us on the surface. There is, therefore, a search for the Ultimate Reality (or the noumenon behind the phenomenon). It is necessary to mention that every believer in mysticism is not a mystic, I may believe in one of the yogas, tantra and other methods of attaining liberation from the cycle of birth and death, but you cannot call me a mystic unless I claim to a have that "unique experience" and people who believe in mysticism are convinced about my claim.

The second characteristic of mysticism is that it treats the universe as a whole and usually a conscious whole. To some extent this holistic view enables one to reconcile the pairs of opposites; good-bad, hot-cold, poor-rich, etc. The mystic can find a solution to our lack of understanding of the entire connected universe. In fact while we may take the universe *as a whole* we do not give up the habit of splitting its connections into the pairs of opposites. The mystic on the other hand can see that the ostensible contraries are only illusions. Mystics often use oxymorons and contradictions to explain that we need insight to reconcile the contraries. For example, "we step and do not step into the same river", "Brahman (the Ultimatate Reality) exists, and does not exist", "reality is neither void nor nonvoid". The very contradictions are believed to give them the feel for that which is real behind the apparent.

The third characteristic of mysticism is denial of time as reality. This often arises because the speed with our subjective time passes is not constant. When we are happy or fruitfully engaged, time flies while when we are sad or unoccupied it crawls. Moreover, time is measured in terms of intervals between two events and the question that haunts the intellectuals is whether there is anything like time independent of events we perceive.

Fourth, mystics treat evil as unreal. This is especially necessary if we believe that God is just and good. However, in certain eastern philosophies, evil is not a special category – both evil and good may be considered as mere illusion.

30.2 Need for Mysticism

There are many reasons why we turn to mysticism or are fascinated by it.

As children we feel helpless in the midst of the world of giants, our parents and other adults, big animals and huge buildings. At the same time the very same world is magical, many events pleasant or disquieting occur without our knowing how or why they happen. Invisible forces, God, demons, fairies, sprites and a host of good and bad elements inhabit our world. This world is also attractive because we can indulge in fantasies for the solution of many of our problems.

Even when we grow up we retain our childhood in the unconscious. Moreover, even when we become adults we know that we cannot control the world. We may become engineers, doctors, scientists or dictators, yet we know that there are many things which happen whether we wish them or not : disease, financial problems, failure in love or career and of course the ultimate exinction or death. As children turn to their parents to allay their anxiety we turn to mysticism which may be theistic or not.

When we are in deep crisis we turn to magical thinking and mysticism whether it appears as religion, spiritualism, our good parents inside or our dead heroes. What we called nonscience earlier has great relevance in mysticism. It is nonscience which makes mysticism immortal. Nonscience like god, afterlife or rebirth forms the indestructible core of mysticism. Whether we believe in God or not, whether we consider spiritualism as a legitimate dimension of human existence or sheer nonsense, we do believe in our heart of hearts that we cannot be

Omniscient and what lies beyond our knowledge certainly belongs to the mystical world.

However, how we manifest our fascination or dread of mysticism depends on our personality.

One finds a strong trend, overt or covert, to mystify science and a drift towards eastern mysticism. Eastern mysticism appears especially attractive to western intellectuals because neither science nor conventional religion has solved the problems of the affluent and technologically advanced West. There is therefore, a desperate search for inner peace in the eastern religion and mysticism, and we know that when our efforts to solve our problems in our cultural milieu fail we turn to the exotic which in any case fascinates us. The second reason why science is drifting to eastern mysticism is that there are a few parallels between modern science and what the ancient Indians and Chinese sages speculated. These parallels can be elevated to the level at which we can see science in mysticism and mysticism in science. This identification of mysticism and science possibly has several benefits : there is a great reconciliation and we can see the whole connected universe, and the mundane contradictions disappear, pleasure and pain appear to be two sides of the same coin. We have already considered mystical areas of Buddhism, viz. ultimate reality, liberation, survival of consciousness after death, etc. and we will again recall them in chapter 32.

30.3 Mystification of Science

However, one can mystify science even without going to the East. As we explained earlier, one can speak of the four-dimensional space-time as if it had a separate ontological status apart from the old world of space and time. In cosmology there are what are called string theories. According to stephen Hawking, "String theories have a bigger problem, they seem to be consistent only if space-time has either ten or twenty-six dimensions".[3] We can take one step further and interpret the metaphor "dimension" in string theory literally. Such ontological mystification seems to be quite common.

An offshoot of relativity theory is the proposition that one can go back in time. This is based on the fact that "all successful equations in physics are symmetrical in time".[4] While Penrose conjectures that "our physical understanding actually important ingredients other than just equations of time evolution – and some of these do indeed involve time-asymmetries".[5] But there is no dearth of scientists and science fiction writers who take time symmetry to interpret that it is possible for us to journey back in time.

In quantum mechanics the uncertainty principle is often used to project our world as something mysterious. We have discussed enough about the nature of this mystery and need not comment further.

One also sees an aura of mystification around such concepts as computability, consciousness, Mandelbrot set and logical formalism. I have discussed consciousness in earlier chapters. Other topics have been discussed elsewhere.[5a]

30.4 Eastern Mysticism

The Vedas are considered most sacred by Hindus and are believed to have been revealed to the sages called rishis. The Upaniṣads are texts written later and contain the philosophical aspects of Vedas. There is a maxim to the effect that the Vedas and Upaniṣads have to be "properly interpreted". Since there are hundreds of commentaries on Indian scriptures, it is usually possible to interpret any ancient scripture in a convenient manner.

Some Indian scholars feel that these scriptures not only contain rituals, mantras and philosophy but even advanced science. You only have to interpret the Vedas and Upaniṣads in the right way. The ancient Indians built airplanes and missiles, used television and radio, and even knew the techniques of cloning.

The Vedic society had advanced knowledge of nuclear science and astrophysics. They had discovered antimatter and black holes. They not only knew the Euclidean geometry but also Riemannian geometry and were possibly familiar with Einstein's Relativity Theory. The well-known *nāsadīya sūkta* in the Ṛgveda has been interpreted to contain the Big Bang Theory.[6]

While it is jingoism and ancestor worship which impel Indian intellectuals to see modern science in the Vedas and Upaniṣads, the western intellectuals in search of a solution to the problems created by advanced technology, riches and boredom, have seen extraordinary parallels between eastern mysticism and science.

According to modern science there is no real void or emptiness. According to A.W. Thirring :

> The field exists always and everywhere; it can never be removed. It is the carrier of all material phenomena. It is the void out the which the proton creates the pi-mesons. Being and fading of particles are merely forms of motion of the field.[7]

Since what we call void can create innumerable varieties of elementary particles which can vanish in a fraction of second, Capra argues that this kind of void has a close resemblance with the living void of the eastern mysticism. It is what the Indians especially nondualists call Brahman and to which Chinese referred as ch'i, Capra's view is tantamount to saying that the modern scientist's quantum field is nothing but what the eastern sages called the One.

There is undoubtedly some parallel between what modern scientists tend to feel, viz. that behind these innumerable manifestations of the field and matter there may ultimately be only one "stuff", and what the eastern mystics thought about Brahman, the One. Both views reflect one ultimate reality behind the apparent multiplicity. However, the parallels appear to be only superficial. The eastern mystics make it clear that the One is ineffable. Their description of Brahman is only partial since the Ultimate Reality is indescribable. For example, "there exists neither void nor voidlessness" (*Avadhūta Gītā* 1–76), or "there is no space or absence of space" (*Avadhūta Gītā* 5–5).

When the One is neither void nor non-void, how can we compare it with the void containing the quantum field?

We have already explained that in relativity the fourth "dimension" time is not on par with the three space dimensions. Capra quotes Lama Govinda to elucidate another parallel, viz. space-time unity :

> An experience of higher dimensionality is achieved by integration of experiences of different centers and levels of consciousness. Hence the indescribabilty of certain experience of meditation on the plane of three dimensional consciousness and within a system of logic which reduces the possibility of expression by imposing further limits upon the process of thinking.[8]

The world of relativity and that of Lama Govinda cannot be compared. The relativity theory is objective, public and testable. Lama Govinda's mystical experience is unique, it is not social knowledge. It can have scores of interpretations. If a mystic could articulate his mystic experience in a language which is intelligible to others, he would cease to be a mystic.

30.65 The World as a Whole

What has fascinated the western scientists most is the fact that the eastern mysticism sees the universe as a whole. According to Capra, "In the Eastern view then, as in the view of modern physics everything in the universe is connected to everything else and no part of it is fundamental. The properties of any part are determined not by some fundamental law, but the properties of all other parts".[9] According to Capra, what we require is "not a synthesis but a dynamic interplay between mystical intuition and scientific analysis".[10] However, epistemologically this does not seem to be practicable. Even if we take "spiritualism" as a valid dimension of investigation, by its very nature a mystical experience is indescribable and hence it can never be social knowledge and hence cannot be science. Capra is aware of this and says that "the multidimensional experience transcend(s) the sensory world, and therefore almost impossible to express in ordinary language".[11] For resolving this dilemma he turns to Taoism of the Chinese in which there are two principles, yin (complex, female, intuitive) and yang (clear, rational, male, intellect). Tao roughly means "the cosmic process in which all things are involved; the world is seen as a continuous flow of change". According to Capra the interplay between science and mysticism has not been possible because our attitude is "too yang"[12] displaying our partiality for rationality and aggressiveness of the male. What we need is its complement yin which had been ignored in scientific investigation preventing us from experiencing the whole as unity; with which we live in harmony.

While appreciating Capra's insight into the parallels between eastern mysticism and science one only has to observe that the dynamic interplay between science and mysticism can only lead to a kind of polycentricism in which each individual has, his or her own perception of reality. The situation is in a way similar to Leibnitz's monadism – the universe is reflected in each monad, but a monad cannot communicate with another. This may be a good "way of life" or "an art of living", but can it be called a reliable epistemology in modern science?

That our world is "connected" in a certain sense is indubitable. Humankind during its development of thousands of years has created innumerable cultural products. The earliest societies produced more intangible or nonmaterial products; religion, philosophy, mystical cults and so on. Unlike scientifically advanced societies the ancient societies had plenty of leisure time to create mental products including speculation, fantasies, meditation, etc. Some of these intangible products did anticipate the scientific advances, purely in the form of ideas such as the idea of flying. Of the innumerable mind-products these societies created, a few are bound to have parallels with modern scientific theories. We have to understand that the speculative mind is absolutely free and is not trammelled by the laws of the real world which imposes several constraints on science and technology. We have to be careful when we compare the cultural products – ideas or objects which are rooted in wishful thinking and mysticism, and those which are born in scientific milieu.

It is worth mentioning a recent publication (Verma, 2008), the author contends that the Vedas when viewed through Sāṅkhyan angle reveal RQ theories and can even provide answers to unsolved questions. What you need is the right interpretation. The merit of the book is, that it is scholarly and shows the author's command over Sanskrit. It is the richness and flexibility of this language which enables him to interpret words and expression in the way well-known translators have never thought of. Undoubtedly, through hermeneutic techniques he has produced a treatise which is "internally consistent". This in itself is a feat. It is doubtful however, whether his hypothesis will be accepted by the scientific community. Collateral evidence such as the general condition of Vedic society, total absence of any quantification due to lack of knowledge of advanced mathematics in Vedic times weigh heavily against his thesis. A similar book *Vedantieel Vidnyan* by Dhananjya Deshpande was published in Marathi, an Indic language in (2001). The author in this book uses, the same technique of "interpretations" which radically differ from standard translation. I have commented on his work at greater length elsewhere.[13]

31

Integration

31.1 Holarchy

We have seen that Buddhist scholars reject the concept of essence and replace it by a more inclusive conception of functional interdependence. It views the universe as a whole in which no part functions independently. This is in tune with the modern thought. This notion of integration leads to a systemic approach, or a holistic approach.

In chapter 29 we used the method of relativization to eliminate false idols; we found that idols cannot be destroyed totally since new idols appear in due course. Nevertheless the technique of relativization effects generalization in which Buddhism has a rightful place. In this chapter, we use an intergral approach whereby Buddhism and Buddhist logic are "fitted" into the web of interconnections which we call the universe. We shall use the concept of "holons" which are the constituents of various systems – cell systems, tissue systems, organ systems, biosocial systems, socio cultural systems and so forth. We have to remember that systems spread horizontally as well as vertically and are entangled with one another.

According to Capra, "All these entities from molecules to human being, and on to social systems, can be regarded as wholes in the sense of being integrated structures, and also as parts of larger wholes at higher levels of complexity".[1] Arthur Koestler coined the word "holon" to describe the world of systems. A holon is a whole that is part of other wholes : a whole atom is a constituent of the whole molecule which in turn is a holon that is part of the higher whole, a cell, and so on. According to Koestler, a growth hierarchy is a holarchy. Ken Wilber expresses the philosophy of holarchy as, "Reality is composed of neither wholes nor parts, but of whole/parts or holons. Reality in all domains is basically composed of holons".[2]

To modern thinkers no source of knowledge is a taboo and no evidence can be dismissed as rubbish – astrology, mysticism, seances all have their own realities which are only part of the whole reality.

I shall closely follow Wilber whose book *A Theory of Everything* makes a fascinating reading, though you may not agree with everything that Wilber says.

31.2 Human Development

Clare Grave, Don Beck and Christopher Cowan have developed an eight-stage model of human progress. In this theory called "Spiral Dynamics" a general stage is called a "meme". Memes are not rigid but flow as waves overlapping and interweaving. Every individual is believed to have all these memes as potentials. One is reminded of Haeckel's biogenic law according to which ontogeny (the development of the individual organism) recorpitulates phylogeny (the development of the species). However, the Spiral Dynamics is more flexible and depicted as a spiral.[3] The stages are also recognized by "colors".

First Tier

1. Beige – This is the lowest archaic-instinctual stage having the greatest survival value.
2. Purple – This characterizes the tribal society, also called magical-animistic stage. Spirits, ethnic tribes, black magic, kinship, etc. are a few features.
3. Red – At this stage the person's own distinct ego emerges.

Power gods, heros, good and bad forces, feudal empires, mythology are some of its indicators.

4. Blue – Also called Mythic Order. The principle of absolute right and wrong, law and order, emergence of guilt, self-control, penal code, etc. are some of its characteristics.
5. Orange – This is characterized by scientific achievement, individualism, personal achievements, reason, corporate world, winners and losers.
6. Green – At this stage society is more important than individuals, based not on force but cooperation. Feeling, holding, respect for earth and life, resurgence of spirituality, cultural diversity, etc. are its main features.

Second Tier

According to Wilber after the sixth stage there is a quantum jump, which leads to the second tier thinking which appreciates the necessary role that all of the various memes play. At this stage the integral and holistic approach begins.

7. Yellow – Also called Integrative meme. The world is seen in terms of systems and holarchys. Awareness of equality, interdependence are some of its features.
8. Turquoise – This is the truly universal holistic system. According to Wilber this stage represents the possibility of a "grand unification" which will incorporate theory as well as practice. At this echelon, one finds reconciliation of different levels. One also comes across nonlinear dynamics and complexity theory. According to Wilber, this stage reflects Mahatma Gandhi's and Nelson Mandela's pluralistic integration. He also feels that further progress to higher echelons is possible.

31.3 Spirituality

Many modern intellectuals regard spiritualism, along with introspection, and exploration of the unconscious mind as an important dimension of the integral approach. In Latin *spiritus* means breath. In many religions, especially the eastern, and in mysticism breath has a vital role. Some Indic religions, most yoga systems and *tantra* incorporate breathing and meditation as essential components. Called *prāṇa* in Sanskrit, it is often equated with Brahman, the Ultimate Reality.

Capra maintains that, "since respiration is indeed a central aspect of the metabolism of all but the simplest forms of life, the breath of life seems to be a perfect metaphor of metabolic process that is the defining characteristic of all living system".[4]

Spiritual experience is difficult to define. It is usually regarded as moments of heightened awareness, the feeling of the unity of body-mind, indescribable joy, a peaceful state, the experience of "aha" or revelation, oneness with the whole universe, immeasurable love and compassion for the whole world and so on, depending on your religious belief. In *tantra* it may be ecstasy characterizing the final stage when the worshipper of the Mother mereges with *śakti* (Power), or it may be a trance-like state where the meditator lives in a unique world and so forth. In Buddhism, spiritualism culminates in complete quescence, *nirvāṇa.*

Spiritual and religious practices in which the mind is directed inside is believed to open up a new world not accessible to the common person. For example, Māṇdukya Upaniṣad describes four states of the mind – waking stage, sleep with dreams, dreamless sleep and still beneath is *turīya*, the state where there is perfect freedom, a state identified with Brahman.

However, similar states of peace and love can also be described in the psychological idiom. One may say in the language of psychoanalysis that such a state indicates freedom from the oppressive superego or conscience. A transactional analyst might suggest that the state reflects approval from the inner Parents or a good "stroke" by them.

Whatever the interpretation of such a spiritual state, the modern intellectual treats it not only as a dimension of feeling but as a possible source of knowledge. Acceptance of religion and spiritualism as valid epistemological avenues has far reaching implications for the concept of science.

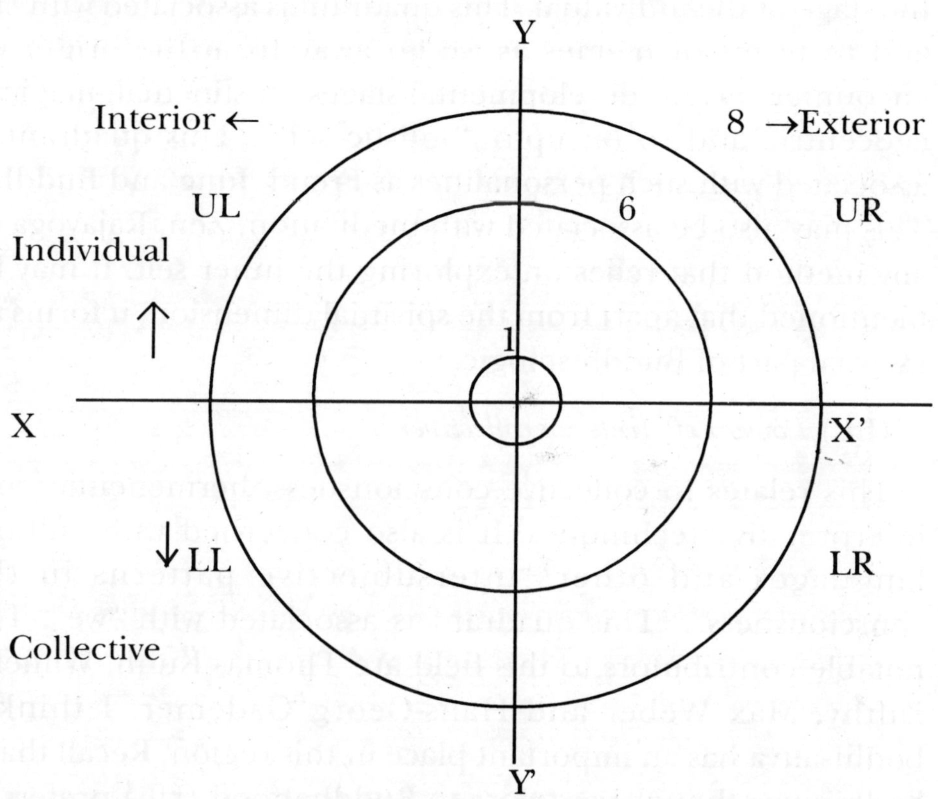

Fig. 31.1 Quadrant Analysis

31.4 Quadrant Analysis

Ken Wilber has an interesting approach to human possibilities. His "integral map" or full spectrum approach is extremely complicated and we can only briefly discuss its gist. I have used a simple figure for depicting the essentials. The eight circles (of which only three are shown) represent the (fluid) eight stages; the lowest (1) is the archaic stage (beige) while (8) is the universal holistic stage (turquoise). The portion above XX' is the region relating to the "individual" and that below XX' is "collective". The region left to YY' is the interior region and that on the right is the exterior. The significance of the four quadrants is as follows :

(UL) *Upper Left (interior individual)*

This pertains to the individual consciousness depending on the stage of the individual. This quadrant is associated with "I", and in terms of memes as we go away from the origin we encounter various developmental stages; instinctual, magical, egocentric and so on upto "holistic self". This quadrant is associated with such personalities as Freud, Jung and Buddha. This may also be associated with meditation, Zen, Rājayoga or any method that relies on exploring the inner self. It may be mentioned that apart from the spiritual dimension, it forms an essenial part of Buddhist logic.

(LL) *Lower Left (interior collective)*

This relates to collective conscionsuess, hermeneutics and interpretative techniques. It is also concerned with culture, languages and other "intersubjective patterns in the consciousness".[5] This quadrant is associated with "we". The notable contributors to this field are Thomas Kunh, Wilhelm Dilthy, Max Weber and Hans-Georg Gademer. I think a bodhisattva has an important place in this region. Recall that a bodhisattva though very close to Buddhahood (UL) prefers to be a spiritual guide for the wayfarers.

Its developmental stages from the innermost circle are archaic, animistic, magical, power gods, mythic, rational, pluralistic (where the first tier ends) and hence to integral and holonic.

(UR) *Upper Right (exterior individual)*

This is related to the brain, organs and the whole (physical) organism. It is associated with "It". Its developmental stages would be cellular, organic states, limbic system and so on probably ending with neocortex.

The quadrant is related to empiricism, positivism, behaviorism, physics chemistry, biology, neurology, etc. Its major contributors are John Watson, Newton, B. F. Skinner et al.

(LR) *Lower Right (exterior collective)*

It is related to systems analysis, nonlinear dynamics, ecology, complexity theory and so on.

It is identified with "Its" and its developmental stages are clans, tribes, etc. right upto the holistic interconnected network.

Those intellectuals who have contributed to this field are Talcott Parson, Karl Marx and Auguste Compte. Wilber calls this region interrogative realities or social systems.[6]

31.5 Knowledge and Application

The map of Kosmos is much more complicated than the brief account given above. According to Wilber a few points need to be kept in mind for correct interpretaton of the map and its application in practice :

1. Each meme or quadrant has its own reality and necessity. A particular society may have advanced to the highest or 8th stage, nevertheless the infant born in this society has to start at beige or stage 1. (Recall Haeckel's law)
2. The fact that individuals are at different "points" on the map implies that we cannot have a standard solution for all. Whether it is integral politics, integral medicine, integral business or integral education or any other integral approach, we have to take this factor into account. For example, when viruses kill people, the remedial measures do not just involve elimination of viruses but should include such socio-economic tools which are appropriate for a particular society. The virus is only one cause, the other causes such as poverty, hygiene, etc. need to be addressed. Again, an integral approach to education would mean the right approach suitable for a particular section of society. A group which is in the third stage will have to be gradually elevated to higher stages, any accelerated program of education calculated to skip the intermediate stage can only inflict irreparable damage to

the psyche of the group. All stages are important to some extent for development, and there are no short cuts.

3. Spiritual experience is not the prerogative of the higher memes. Any person can have such peak experiences whose nature will depend on the meme which he rides.

31.6 Science and Religion

Since modern thinkers use an integral approach to knowledge and its application, their worldview has far reaching implications for epistemology. In particular we have to investigate whether we need a radical change in paradigm or a totally new epistemology. Since our focus is on science, we shall discuss the integrationists' views on science and its apparent antithesis, religion and mysticism.

We have already considered major features of science in chapter 21. It is worthwhile to briefly discuss what according to Wilber are different stances of science-religion relationship :

1. The most important school considers religion as at best a survival gimmick used for the propagaton of species, and at worst a superstitious legacy of our ancestors. In other words "science denies religion".[7]
2. The second school is exactly the opposite; science is heresy. This school is rapidly vanishing. Since everyone has to use (if not believe in) science and its application it is difficult to downgrade science at least openely and adhere to the literal meaning of scriptures.
3. The third school reflects a reconciliation of science and religion : both science and religion can coexist peacefully since their realms complement each other.

Wilber believes that there are two subschools, the first he calls *epistemological pluralism.* Both science and religion have a place in the theory of, knowledge. Religion considers higher topics such as soul, spirit, etc. while science deals with the mundane phenomena. Kant and Whitehead are typical representatives of this school.

The other subschool called NOMA ("nonoverlapping magisteria") is led by Stephen Jay Gould. It is similar to the first, but believes that science and religion belong to different realms. He does not subscribe to the idea that both science and religion are two necessary dimensions of the "whole". In other words religion and science are watertight compartments that can be considered, analyzed, deprecated or deified according to your own taste, but you have to keep them apart.

4. The fourth school contemplates the possibility of scientific explanation of many religious beliefs including soul, spirit, gods and so on. "For exmaple, the big bang theory seems to require some sort of Creator principle".[8] Many intellectuals are turning to the East beacuase science has failed to solve their emotional problems. The recent drift of science to mysticism reflects the attitude of many laypersons as well as scientists. However, such attitude often stems from glorification of the past or an attempt to solve at one stroke scientific phenomena which baffle us. Since even those who adhere to this school know that their beliefs cannot be proved, this school can hardly change the classification of science-nonscience.
5. The fifth stance represents the postmodernists. This school believes that scientific knowledge is one interpretation of the world. We can have other interpretations : art, social norms, poetry, psychology and so on. All interpretations are equally valid. According to Wilber these thinkers are usually found among popular writers in science and religion. This thinking is also popular "among the academic and cultural elite, who are not dedicated to constructing any sort of integration, but deconstructing anything of worth that anybody else has to say on the issue".[8a]

6. Wilber's own thesis is that we cannot compartmentalize the regions of science (dealing with matter, and body) and religion (concerned with soul and spirit). He believes that we can learn from each quadrant about science as well as religion, He believes in overlapping magisteria. What's more he stresses on the direct spiritual experience.

It should be remembered that direct spiritual experience is a *sine qua non* of most Indian philosophical schools including Buddhism. In fact the experience forms an inalienable component of Indian epistemology. However, this raises a few questions which we shall address in a few moments .

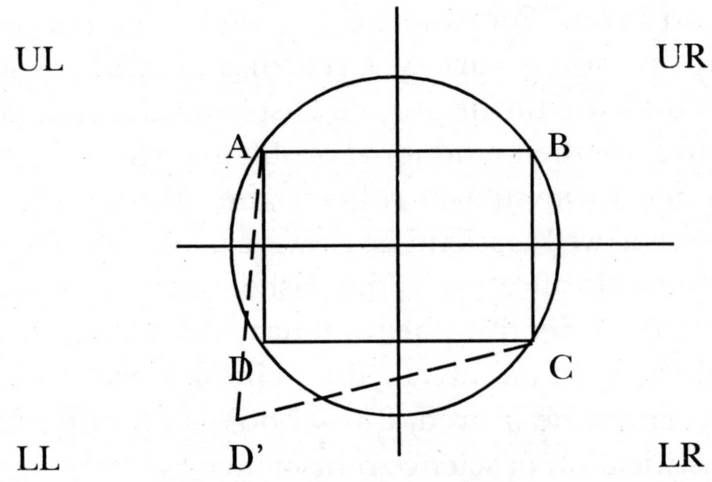

Fig. 31.2 Variation from the Average

If I have understood Wilber properly, at a given level of development (the circumference of any one of the circles in fig.31.1) the societal stage or a phenomenon has four correlates.

Consider fig. 31.2 in which the circle represents a certain stage, then A, B, C, D are correlates corresponding "I", "It", "Its" and "We".

Suppose A's brain is mapped by EEG (electroencephalogram), then if A is a meditator then his personal feeling such as peace, expanded consciousness, etc. will have a correlate at B, say delta waves (usually indicating dreamless sleep). Thus we may say that the person has a spiritual experience (A) which has a correspondence with the brain state (B). Similarly we can learn something from other correlates C and D. The whole information obtained from these corresponding points in the four quandrants constitutes science.

One of the greatest merits of such integral approach is of course, its practical utility. For example, in integral medicine the physician's prescription will depend on the all-quadrilateral information. The patient may suffer from anxiety or a certain phobia (UL); his brain mapping may indicate some abnormality (UR); he may be a tribal (LR) and belong to the animistic-magical mode of thinking. His physician is bound to take all these factors into consideration. But this is not a new mode of treatment; enlightened physicians have always given weightage to the patient's personal likes and dislikes and his socio-cultural background, apart from the physical symptoms (UR), while treating him. The correlation quadrilalteral is only a general average depiction. In a certain case it may happen that there are deviations in a particular case. For instance, in the case of the above person this particular patient may belong to a higher order in the "LL" quadrant (D') which will provide the physicain valuable input for the treatment.

One of the major problems that pertains to UL-UR correlation may now be explained. An important problem is the mind-brain correlation. There are several methods of brain-mapping – X-ray, CAT, MRI, FMRI, EEG, PET, SPECT and so on.

CAT – Computorized axial tomography
MRI – Magnetic Reasonance Imagery
FMRI – Functional MRI
EEG – Electroencephalogram
PET – Photon Emission tomography
SPECT – Single photon emmission computerized tomography

Some of them like CAT give us only information relating to anatomy, some like EEG provide information relating to electrical activity, while those like SPECT, PET, FMRI reveal physiological processes. Theoretically if brain and mind are two aspects of the some entity it should be possible to establish a perfect correlation between the mind (what the person feels) and the brain (mapping). This science is still in infancy. It is doubtful that we can read the mind from the brain map and vice versa. As we have seen earlier consciousness is defined in terms of "patterns" and nobody seems to know exactly how to describe these patterns. Secondly, their is apparently no 1-1 correspondence betwen the mental state and the brain map. For example, a person who putatively has spiritual experience and the person who is in dreamless sleep could show the same electrical activity in the brain.

In what sense can UL quadrant be believed to have scientific significance? I think, the significance is purely psychological. If a meditating person feels "I am peaceful", "It is heavenly bliss", "I am ecstatic", the only science it reveals is psychological. It is in this sense that certain feelings may be called "spiritual". Unfortunately not all people experience such states and spiritual experience seems to be confined to select individuals. We shall point out serious epistemological problems relating to the contribution of the UL to science after we consider Wilber's perception of what "science" means.

31.7 Scientific Inquiry

According to Wilber three factors are involved in a scientific inquiry whether the concerned science is hard (physics, chemistry, etc.) or soft(psychology, sociology, linguistic, etc.):

1. The first step is a practical injunction or exemplar, which simply means if you want to know something, you have to go through it or do that which will lead you to knowledge. According to Wilber, Kunh's conception of "paradigm" precisely means this exemplar or practice, it does not connote a supertheory.

2. Once you perform the experiment or follow the injunctions, you experience something which may have several facets. According to William James "datum" is immediate experience.[9] The data could be physical, mental or "spiritual". According to Wilber the four-quadrant analysis takes into account both objective and subjective aspects.
3. The last step is that after a series of experiments and data collection, the result is subjected to the scrutiny of community peers or those who have already gone through steps 1 and 2 for rejection or confirmation.

These criteria apply to what he calls all "good science". For him the region on the right side of y axis is narrow science. The left region is broad science. The former stems from the exterior realms while the latter, from the interior realms (I, WE). Together they constitute good science

He has similar divisions for religion. He calls "deep religion" or "deep spirituality" that "which involves the direct investigation of the experimental evidence disclosed in the higher stages of development".[10] In the UL quadrant it is concerned with "soul" and "spirit" and in UR it has correlates in the brain mapping as mentioned earlier. He asserts that broad religion meets the same three criteria used for science – induction, experience and verification. This division results in the overlapping of religion and science. For example, Deep spirituality (UL) is investigated by broad science through its correlates (UR) .

According to Wilber "narrow religion" or "translative" religon offers meaning solace to self, myths, etc. It is what the common people understand by religon and involves belief in scriptures But even narrow religion can be mentioned scientifically in UR. The difference between these two subgroups is that unlike the followers of transformative religion, the adherents of narrow religion have no wish to drastically transform the subject of their beliefs.

31.8 The Pitfalls of Integrationsim

Those who follow a holistic or integral approach rightly believe that our life has many dimensions; and our concept of valid knowledge should not be based on the prejudices harbored by the rationalist. However, such approach creates a few hazards in epistemology as well as ontology or metaphysics. If we are not careful, our zeal for acquiring the "whole view" might lead us unsuspectingly to pitfalls. A brief survey of such possibilities is given below :

1. At the outset, it should be made clear that we can never have "a theory of everything" or "all-encompassing knowledge".

The words "all" and "everything" can lead to fallacies. For example, we cannot have "a set of all sets".[10a] Any approach such as all quadrant, systemic, etc. which tries to encompass *everything* suffers from the same reflexive fallacy. Any proposition about "all" can be adjoined to a part of it to obtain a new proposition or theory leading to an unending process.

2. The words such as "soul" and "spirit" do not seem to have any ontological significance, and are interpreted metaphorically only, on the basis of the individual's experience. "I am at peace", "I am in heaven", "I have a peak experience", etc. are believed to indicate spiritual experience. It is doubtful whether it can have an isomorphic correlation with the brain state (UR). Since personal experience is unique to the individual, it is doubtful whether we can ever read the mind from the brain mapping on the basis of some "science" though we may be able to have broad inferences. In some cases the pattern may be misguiding. From the EEG of an individual's brain we might conclude that he is in deep meditation, while in reality he is in a dreamless sleep.

Let us assume for the time being that the technological problem is overcome and we have reached a stage where we can establish isomorphic models between the mind and the brain. It will tell us that the mind and brain are only two facets of the same entity. Can UL tell us more than what we call psychology? When Wilber says that "science and religion are thus giving us some of the correlative facets – interior and exterior – of spiritual realities, and that is a key ingredient of their integration in a larger and more encompassing *Theory of Everything*", what does he mean?[11] Can we accept literally what the interior says if it has isomorphic pattern with the brain?

3. The region left of y axis relates to interpretation, hermeneutics and also such arts as painting and sculpture In what sense is it connected with science? For example, hermeneutics can only give us different views of what the author meant or the hybrid product of "the reader's participation with the writer's creation" Dilthy's "hermeneutic circle", Hirsch's "horizon" (author's outlook) and Gadamers "reader's horizon" can convert a text into thousands of interpretaion. I have made detailed comments elsewhere to show why hermeneutics cannot be called science. [12]

The following illustrations should explain epistemological and metaphysical problems that stem from the integral approach or rather its wrong interpretation :

E1

(a) Patañjali Yoga is an eight-step Indian system to attain "liberation" in which the last stage is called *samādhi.* Patañjali's famed *sūtra* enumerates some *siddhis* (powers) which a student acquires before reaching the goal of emncipation. Some of them are :

Knowledge of earlier births	(3-18)
Ability to fly	(3-42)
Clairvoyance	(3-25)
Ability to make oneself invisible	(3-21)

Let us suppose that different students of this system assert that they have acquired such abilities and their brains too show isomorphic patterns. How do we interpret the situation? All the above claims are testable and we know these statments can be disproved. Wilber is aware of such false claims and asserts that if narrow religion makes empirical claims, they must be tested.[13] In that case what knowledge have we gained from ULQ and URQ? At best it can be called knowledge relating to "psychological illusion" a practitioner of the yoga has experienced.

(b) X is a well-known swami who believes in non-dualism. About 30 students who have been tested for high intelligence, memory and aptitude for religious studies undergo rigorous training for 5 years under the swami. At the end of the training all of them are not only well-versed with various schools of Indian philosophy, but have experienced monism. Their belief in monism – everything is Brahman – is not theoretical. They feel they are Brahman just as the whole universe is Brahman. The students are also tested by well-known *sannyāsins* who are themselves *jīvanmuktas* (liberated in their own lifetime) All of them certify that these 30 students have realized Brahman.

What is our interpretation? Observe that all Wilbert's criteria for testing good science are met. Can we assert (1) monism is true (2) all the students have realized Brahman?

According to our criterion the subject belongs to nonscience since we cannot disprove the claim (Popper's test). Even if we find that the student's brain map has distinct characteristics, it only shows a correlation between a *belief* and the brain pattern.

(c) Kṛṣṇa is an important *avatāra* or incarnation of Viṣṇu, a god who sustains the Universe according to Hindus. In a certain town his worshippers have formed a society whose members believe in Kṛṣṇa's divinity. Every day they sing *bhajanas* (devotional songs), dance, and listen to the discourses of their *guru* (teacher) who tells them that after a sufficient number of sessions they will actually see Kṛṣṇa and will feel divine ecstasy. Most members after practicing their guru's injunctions do become ecstatic while dancing and praising the Lord and actually see Kṛṣṇa.

The society has empaneled a number of sages, who are themselves worshippers of Kṛṣṇa, to examine whether these members have attained the state of divine ecstasy. All of them testify that they have reached the stage where they can see Kṛṣṇa.

Here, too, Wilber's tests are satisfied. What is the inference? Can we conclude that Kṛṣṇa does visit the worshippers?

Our earlier analysis (chapter 21) should make you treat such experiences as pertaining to nonscience because Kṛṣṇa's visit cannot be disproved. The only conclusion we can draw is that after considerable training some people, especially those who are religious, begin to have experiences which common people do not have.

(d) In a certain tribal society a total solar eclipse is considered a sign of impending catastrophe. A team of scientists gathers the following data during one such eclipse – (1) Almost all members of the tribe undergo severe anxiety before and after the eclipse. (2) Brain mappings of those who were tested display similar pattern changes before and after the eclipse. These are interpreted as excessive pre-eclipse and post-eclipse dread. (3) Most tribal members mention the stories of the dreadful effects (earthquake, floods, disease, etc.) of the total eclipse in the past. However, most of these stories belong to the ancient period and have been handed down from one generation to another. (4) A few cases of fainting, severe trembling and facial contortions are observed by the scientists before and after the eclipse. One person is reported to have died as a result of cardiac arrest, immediately after the eclipse. The quadrant analysis would indicate that all quadrants provide knowledge consistent with the general attitude of the tribe towards the eclipse. However, the scientists need to verify whether any external calamities independent of the tribal belief have occurred after the eclipse in order to prove that the eclipse does lead to calamities. The abnormal behavior shown by the tribals and the death of a person in all probability arises from the collective dread the tribe experiences at the time of the eclipse.

In conclusion we may observe that a holistic approach widens our world view and provides new dimensions of reality which the conventional reductionist approach to the understanding of a phenomenon does not. This is epistemically significant and extremely useful in practice especially in such areas as integral medicine, ecology and social sciences.

It must, however, be realized that while psycho-spiritual dimension may motivate us to undertake a scientific enquiry, the findings can be called science only if they have characteristics mentioned in chapter 21. Isomorphism between the mind and brain (first and second quadrants) merely establishes a correlation, it does not per se verify any external event believed to be occurring solely on the basis of what the individual or collective mind feels.

Despite the pitfalls of integrationism, recent research based on Buddhist meditation and brain states have opened up a new dimension in the holistic view as we shall see in the next sections.

31.9 Body-mind and Mind-brain

In connection with an integral approach two controversies relating to the body mind connection and the mind brain connection have assumed considerable importance in recent years. While the mind and the body have been replaced by one single whole, viz. mind-body the question of the relationship between the mind and the brain is still unsettled though recent researches have convinced most scientists that the mind and the brain are inseparable.

On the one hand psychologists have tried to explore the new areas of research – visualization, meditation, phenomenology. On the other hand neuroscientists have tried to correlate mental states especially imagination with brain physiology. The new tools mentioned earlier in section 6 have provided greater insight into the mind brain complex. Scientists have been unabashedly trying to explore eastern methods of visualization without feeling guilty about mystical aura that surrounds oriental meditation. We can only briefly describe important results of the researches carried out recently, I have extensively borrowed from Varela and Depraz.[14] Imagination has been studied extensively vis-à-vis perception. Borrowing from Husserl and Sartre, the difference between imagination and perception appears much more than what earlier philosophers thought. According to Husserl imagination is a dynamic intentioanl act and not an abstract faculty. Its objects are mental images that lie within the mind. Perception is a positional act because the object is there to be perceived, while imagination is an act of consciousness that neutralizes every factual existence. Husserl uses the word "nonpositional" act for imagination.

Sartre goes even further and feels that imagination and perception are so widely separated that the gulf between them cannot be bridged. He regards imagination as totally free unlike perception which is conditioned.

However the studies on daydreaming and the analysis of narration by the daydreamer herself have shown that there is actually some "mixing" or transformation of the positional into nonpositional states and vice versa. This agrees with Buddhist view reflected in the practice of mindfulness and meditative quiescence (*śamatha*). As Varela and Depraz observe "... the very core of our temporality is an inseparable mixture of these two modes of apprehension".[15]

In certain respects memory like imagination appears different from perception because both are reproductions. But the first two can be differentiated in "inner consciousness". Agreeing with Bernet, Varela and Depraz conclude "In other words reproductive consciousness is the privileged place for the manifestation of unconscious, sedimentated habitus and desires".[16]

31.10 Brain Imaging

Brain imaging techniques mentioned above have proved extremely useful in correlating the mind and brain. A brief account of the findings is give below :

A 1. The inputs from the mental side are provided by meditative conditions especially through "tonglen". What we call imagination involves several capacities; memory, language and motor actions.

A 2. Physiologically, imagining stems from a network of many circuits and locations in the brain. These networks are highly active in high level vision in conscious activities. Apart from being a function of the task involved in imagining, they reflect the uniqueness of the individual.

A 3. There is a large-scale integration of what emerges from a plethora of mind body sites, the experienced moment is a synchronization of dynamic processing appearing as a fleeting emergence and an integrated whole. This is called "upward causality".

A 4.. Conversely, the large scale intergarion in a "moment of nowness" can in turn access any neural process. This two way process is dynamic, it also constitutes an autonomous couple in the sense, "no extra ontological ingredients are required for this reciprocal effective causation".[17] The fact that the globally emergent configuration is mirrored as constraints on physiological and even genetic process is called "downward causality".

From the other side, viz. phenomenological analysis, researches have gathered the following results :

B 1. Perception and imagination are different though closely related.

B 2. As mentioned earlier imagination may include mental events such as memory, daydreaming, fanstasy and dreaming.

B 3. Perception and imagination influence each other.

B 4. The gap between the experiential (what is felt by the meditator) and empirical (what is interpreted by the experimenter) cannot be bridged. This has far reaching consequences and will be discussed later.

B 5. Imagination also involves elements from the prereflexive or unconscious.

Buddhist views on meditation and visualization usually stress the pragmatic side viz. human transformation. The gist of their views is as follows :

C 1 "Tonglen" is a skill that effect changes in our spontaneous reaction to others or the world.

C 2 "Tonglen" uses selective visualization to effect changes in our association and response.

C 3 This transformation interlinks experience in visualization (global) and the brain states observed in imaging techniques.

C 4 The downward effect mentioned in (B3) has been observed not only by the traditional Buddhist methods of monitoring the meditator but is also attested by modern experiments involving studies of brain plasticity especially in sports and emotional development of children. Varela and Depraz conclude that "The three dimensions of the empirical the experiential description and transformation practices form a coherent whole, not contradictory views. They illuminate rather than exclude one another".[18]

31.11 Buddhism and Integral Approach

In section 31.8 pitfalls of the holistic approach were pointed out. Wilber's criteria for scientific investigation are less demanding than our tests mentioned in chapter 21. Using Wilber's criteria, one may say that such methods as "tonglen" afford a scientific basis for Buddhist epistemology. The major hurdle in our tests (chapter 21) was posed by meditation not being social knowledge. However, if we can establish a strong correlation between the prescribed results (e.g. emotional development), we may say that the technology is effective. A correlation between phenomenological interpretation of the results obtained from quadrant UL and the brain imagery pertaining to quadrant UR can help investigators to elevate this technology to the level of full-fledged science. Technology involves following a certain method to obtain a specific result without understanding the underlying scientific process. Many useful traditional remedies in medicine are based on pure experience.

However, when the underlying dynamics is understood in terms of a scientific model, there is a quantum jump. Scientific theories help the investigator to manipulate the input to obtain other possible results not contemplated by the initial technology. What we called generalization in science in chapter 21 can be facilitated only through such scientific theories.

There is a tremendous potential for the progress of psychology and neurosciences if furher research is undertaken. We have also to remember that one-one correspondence between a psychological state (quadrant UL) and brain imagery (quadrant UR) should make things much easier because this can be accepted as social knowledge, a necessary criterion for valid scientific viewpoint. If there is no such one-one relationship further research is needed for fine-tuning.

The researcher should also be aware of the limitations of such spiritual methods used in science :

1. The meditator's statements such as "I am in heaven", "I am liberated", etc. should be treated as metaphors.
2. The Buddhist view of re-birth is beyond the pale of science as it prevails today.
3. Any transendental interpretation such as those involved in *catuṣkoṭi*, is again beyond the scope of science.

It is necessary to see that Buddhist logic and the attendent spiritual methods use quadrants UL and UR prominently and even LL (for collective appraisal). Buddhist logic, therefore, appears to be well-integrated with Wilber's quadrant approach.

32

Conclusion

The foregoing discussion on Buddhism, science and RQ theories has covered almost all the aspects that are relevant for comparing (1) Buddhism with science (2) mystical elements in Buddhism with RQ theories. It is time for recapitulating and drawing appropriate conclusions. This is done under important heads, but there is bound to be some overlapping. I have also presented a table of comparison which briefly highlights similarities, pseudoparallels and dissimilarities.

1. Buddhism and Science

Buddhism has the right environment for science to grow. Generally it is rational, agnostic and liberal. We have commented in chapter 21, how it permits dissent. Though a religion, it is not a dogma. This liberal spirit is fortunately maintained even today. I have already mentioned the Dalai Lama's views earlier, but his most progressive attitude appears in his *Policy and Kindness*:

> Suppose that something is definitely proven through scientific investigation, that a certain hypothesis is verified or a certain fact emerges as a result of scientific investigation. And suppose furthermore, that the fact is incompatible with Buddhist theory. There is no doubt that we must accept the result of the scientific research.1

Buddhists do not recognize ego, soul, god and so on which most scientists consider as outside the purview of science.

Unfortunately, in practice the followers have not ventured to express views that would contradict the Buddha's pronouncements.

Even those, scholars who founded other "schools" were careful not to contradict the original doctrines of Gautama Buddha. Their deviation from tradition was facilitated by tactful reinterpretation of expressions and concepts. In Buddha's silence Buddhist logicians found enough space for manonverability.

There are two main reasons why Buddhists' contribution to hard science is not significant. First, their main goal was amelioration of human suffering and *nirvāṇa* for which Gautama's eight-fold path was adopted. The best Buddhist brains were engaged in exploring the inner space through meditation, rather than working in science laboratories. Second, Indian mathematics slowed down and almost stagnated after twelveth or thirteenth century. For advanced science especially physics, calculus is needed as a tool, which Indians as well as Buddhists outside India did not possess.

2. Is Buddhism Science?

As mentioned in Chapter 21 Buddhism can be called science only in a broad sense. It, however, cannot be treated as a hard science.

The Buddhist concept of verifying a theory is different from the criteria used by modern scientists. Buddhists emphasize individual experience. The modern idea of scientific verification involves objectivity. Any scientific theory which is verified empirically involves objective measurements independent of the investigator's personal likes and dislikes and feelings.

It has been already been pointed out that Buddhist experiments involving individuals and their "inner search" cannot be called social knowledge which we considered as an essential criterion for science.

Buddhism also contains principles or concepts which cannot be said to pertain to science. The cycle of birth and death raises a question as to what survives. Ostensibly it is "consciousness" that continues after death. This particular consciousness appears to contradict Buddhism's refusal to recognize an "identity".

Despite the Buddhist attitude of agnosticism in the generic sense, there are concepts such as the doctrine of *karma,* liberation (*nirvāṇa*), ultimate reality and so on which are not testable. You may try to use the Popper's falsification test in each case and you will find that the test fails. This aspect has already been discussed earlier. Fortunately there is one field, mind-brain connection, where Buddhist methods of meditation are used in conjunction with neurosciences and brain-imaging. This appears to hold a great potential for solving problems related to consciousness, memory and other features of what we call the mind-brain complex.

Buddhism may be considered a broad science in the same way as a systematic study of any religion.

We need to recall Wilber's criteria for science (chapter 31). His tests are less rigorous than the traditional criteria we mentioned in chapter 21 especially because he lays stress on acceptance by the community of peers who have already undergone through steps 1 and 2 mentioned in 31.7. This test makes objective measurement in social science less important. This places Buddhism higher than a "science of religion" and closer to hard sciences. It also reflects the modern trend to facilitate an integral approach to human needs.

3. Space, Time and Causation

It was pointed out in chapter 9 that for Buddhist logicians the world is dynamic and ever-changing. This is in consonance with modern scientific thought. The original source consists of the chains of insubstantial moments or point-instants which are efficient. There is no difference between space and time, and space and time cannot be separated from objects.

Unfortunately these momentary beings belong to the transcendent and thus are beyond the realm of science. However, Buddhist relate these things-in-themselves or noumena to the phenomenal world through a sort of isomorphic mapping. Thus the phenomenal world though unreal, too, is a series of momentary images constructed by the mind.

The doctrine of Dependent Origination when treated as a special theory concerns the cycle of birth and death which cannot be explained in terms of empirical world view. The doctrine of *karma* and the survival of consciousness remain two transcendental hurdles.

Mahāyāna thinkers adhere to the general theory which interprets the doctrine as interdependence. This in turn is construed as relativity and even unreality. The net effect of this doctrine was mentioned at the end of chapter 9. Briefly, it is the phenomenal world which is conditioned and secondly, its part cannot be seen in isolation, because the conditioned world and interdependence are two sides of the same coin.

As far as the quantum world is concerned it is as dynamic as the Buddhist world and its entities are ephemeral like point-instants. As in Buddhism, so also in quantum theory a cause cannot be isolated; we can only speak of functional dependence or rather interdependence. In Buddhism there is an excellent solution – there is ultimate reality which is not conditioned. RQ physicists cannot use this escape route because science demands positive evidence.

Nevertheless modern science has created pockets of mysticism such as the determinate evolution of wavefunction to which we have no access. (chapters 24, and 25)

4. Chance, Determinism and Free Will

It is difficult to discuss determinism and free will because there are hundreds of views in philosophy, religion and science.

In Buddhism despite the doctrine of dependent origination, there is room for free will. Gosāla Moskariputra a contemporary of the Buddha believed in extreme determinism. According to him "all things are inalterably fixed and nothing can be changed".[2] The Buddha called him the "bad man". He declared, "There is action, there is retribution, I maintain the doctrine of free actions" (*aham kriyāvādi*).[3] On the other hand Vasubandhu, the second Buddha denies free will. According to him : "Actions are either of the body or of speech, or of the mind. The two first classes those of the body and speech wholly depend upon the mind, and the mind wholly depends on inexorable causes and conditions".[4]

Buddhists, in fact faced a dilemma, Gautama believed in liberty but at the same time his doctrine *pratītyasamputpāda* required strict causal law. This is not a place to discuss how the dilemma was solved. Suffice it to say that the free will was interpreted as the "freedom inside the limits of Necessity... a freedom inside the prism (prison) of Dependent Origination".[5]

In quantum theory probability introduces similar antinomies, e.g. chance vs. determinism since probabilistic behaviour of quantum particles apparently counters determinism. However, according to William Band this anamoly is only an illusion. It arises from our misunderstanding of the cause-effect chain. According to our perception, A causes B IF B always follows A with a stress on IF. But in the absence of an alternative to A, the notion of cause is void. According to physicist Band, "There must be the possibility of giving meaning to the statement. IF A does not occur then B will not occur". From this angle, since there are no alternatives (~A is not allowed) determinism is negation of causality. According to Band, "Chance is essential to causality, because only by admitting chance is it possible to give any meaning to alternative situations yielding different results. We conclude therefore, that the uncertainty principle has strengthened the causal nature of physics rather than the reverse".[6]

5. Relativity Physics

In chapter 22 we mentioned that the word relativity was misinterpreted by common people. Einstein's theory deals with space, time and gravitation and those who interpret it to mean "everything is relative" show ignorance of what the theory means.

There is another group of intellectuals who are familiar with relativity concept in philosophy, sociology and so on. Relativity or relativism appears in philosophical sense in Buddhism especially in Nāgārjuna's philosophy (chapters 8, 14, 16, and 17) and also in Jainism (*Anekāntavāda* chapter 15) many commentators see a strong analogy between Einstein's relativity and philosophical relativity. It is therefore claimed that the relativity concept existed long before western science found it. Let me say emphatically that neither Buddhist logic nor Jaina philosophy anticipated Einstein's relativity. Some intellectuals have been led to a similar erroneous belief that the Vedas contain the theory of relativity. Even though *catuṣkoṭi* and *anekānta* have been interpreted in many ways (chapters 15, 16) by no stretch of imagination one can say that any of these doctrines have anything to do with relativity physics.

Not only lay intellectuals but even scientists seem to have been attracted to eastern mysticism and see in it exaggerated parallels with RQ theories. A few views of western scientists may be considered to evaluate the degree of parallelism. According to Capra, "Eastern philosophy unlike that of the Greeks has always maintained that space and time are constructs of pure mind."[7]

While many eastern schools contend that space and time are products of the mind, they divide reality into two parts empirical and transcendental. In Buddhism the empirical is conditioned while the transcendental is the ultimate reality. In Vedantic monism the former is an illusion while the latter is the real, the only Brahman. Most philosophies make it clear that the empirical and the real are not different; there is immanence of one in another. In western philosophy some schools like solipsism, do not recognize anything but one's own mind.

Again, quoting Aurobindo, Capra says that he speaks about a subtle change which makes the sight see in a sort of fourth dimension. Capra adds :

> The dimension of these states of consciousness may not be the same as the ones we are dealing in relativistic physics, but it is striking that they have led the mystics towards notions of space and time which are very similar to those implied by relativity theory.[8]

The fourth dimension Capra mentions above is the subjective and indescribable feelings of those who are engaged in such practices as meditation. Enough has been said in earlier chapters about such spiritual experiences and the difficulties in subsuming them in the category of science. Quoting Suzuki's comments on *Avatamsaka Sūtra,* Capra adds :

> The significance of *Avatamsaka* and its philosophy is unintelligible unless we once experience ... a state of complete dissolution where there is no more distinction between mind and body, subject and object ... we look and perceive that ... every object is related to every other object ... not only specially, but temporally ... As a fact of pure experience, there is no space without time, no time without space; they are interpenetrating.[9]

These views do contain some resemblance between the findings of quantum theory (interdependence, and entangled space time of relativity theory. However, different mystics have different views usually involving self-contradictions and ambiguities. We cannot selectively pick up only the positive paralles. We also explained in chapter 22 that despite the replacement of space and time by space-time, time retains its individuality and to call time the fourth "dimension" is to some extent metaphorical.

We may conclude that despite some resemblances between Einstein's relativity with Buddhist-Jaina views on philosophical relativity the analogies are of the type that does not warrant an assertion that relativity physics was anticipated by any Indian philosophical school or for that matter any other eastern thinkers.

Nevertheless, as pointed out in chapter 29, based on the general notion of relativism or relativity one may use the process of relativization to create a theory of universal Relativity to encompass various branches of knowledge which deal with the general notion of relativism. However, this exercise is beset with some problems, the most important being "when one false idol is reified another appears".

6. Quantum Logic

Perhaps the most mysterious features of quantum phenomena are the putative violation of the three laws of western logic which we discussed in chapters 20, and 27. Our analysis shows that there are different concepts of identity created for practical reasons. The purest form of identity A = A or A ≡ B where every proposition that is true of A is also true of B and vice versa, is nevertheless intact. Thus "identity crisis" in quantum physics is overcome when we define the identity of A at a given moment.

There is however, only one puzzle : the quantum world treats bosons as identical though they may be at different places. One hopes this conundrum will be demystified in due course when physics makes further progress.

We have explained at length in chapter 27 that neither the law of excluded middle nor that of contradiction is violated when we consider electromagnetic radiation as consisting of wavicles or partiwaves having both wave-like and particle-like properties.

7. Quanta and Buddhist Logic

Here the issue is not violation of Buddhist logic, but similarity between *catuṣkoṭi* and particle-wave duality. *Catuṣkoṭi* appears as four valued truth system :

A is B

A is not-B

A is both B and not-B

A is neither B nor not-B

We have fully analyzed *catuṣkoṭi* and *anekānta* (in Jainism) in chapter 15 and 16. There are many interpretations of both these doctrines; but we can safely say that in case of *catuṣkoṭi* the third and fourth options pertain to the transcendent or subliminal. Both these areas are irrelevant to physics. The last two options have no similarity with duality once quanta are recognized as partiwaves (wavicles).

Jaina philosophers' attitude is generally to avoid the transcendent. In case of an indescribable phenomena their interpretations are usually pragmatic where "simultaneity" is subservient to "succession". In any case, the introduction of partiwaves makes any similarity between duality and Jaina logic almost impossible, because the duality in physics itself is illusory.

8. Particle at two places

Those who are awed by dualism displayed by subatomic particles also contend that in the two-slit experiment a particle appears to be at two places simultaneously. I have pointed out at several places that we do not know subatomic particles in the same way as we know mountains, animals or trees. These quantum entities are beyond our perceptual macro world. We infer their existence only through their effects in the classical world.

It is possible that a photon splits into two parts, it is possible that the photon is like a rubber band but many times more flexible so that its two extensions through the slits behave like the original photon and can travel to a great distance without losing the bond with each other.

9. Quantum World in general

When physicists entered the quantum world, they were shocked and disoriented. It looked as if they had entered a strange world, a world that appeared to be a misshapen *avatāra* of their classical world. They were as dazed as Alice was when she entered the looking glass and the rabbit's hole.

The unfamiliar quantum world appears as mysterious as some of the Buddhist quasi-mysticism. Particles appear and disappear in a fraction of a second in the same way as Buddhist instant beings behave. These *kṣaṇikas* are non-material, unique, and project ephemeral (apparently) material objects. Quantum physicists meet similar inhabitants which appear, now as field and now as particles. The laws of identity, excluded middle and contradiction appear to vanish in the uncertain world. You simply cannot talk of "that thing", instead, you have to speak of interdependence of events just as Buddhist philosophers introduced mutual dependence or cooperation banishing traditional *svabhāva.*

In quantum phenomena, contraries appear to coexist (particle-wave duality) and it appears as if Buddhist catuskoti prevails allowing additional possibilities, viz.

x is A and non-A

x is neither A nor non-A

Entities and systems in quantum state become inaccessible for measurement and become measurable when they are magnified to the classical level.[10]

Can we identify quantum states with Buddhist ultimate reality which is not accessible to ordinary mortals? I doubt it. Or can we identify ultimate reality with the whole quantum world and assert that it has the following correspondence?

Quantum world – Ultimate reality, noumenal world

Classical world – phenomenal world

I doubt it, if there are similarities there are dissimilarities too. This would prevent us from establishing homeomorphic relationship between quantum phenomena and Buddhist logic.

10. *Śūnyatā* and RQ theories

It was pointed out in chapter 14 that *śūnyatā* is etymilogically connected with śūnya or void. This has led many scholars to link *śūnyatā* with quantum theory and cosmology. According to Capra, "Buddhists express the same idea when they call the ultimate reality *śūnyatā* – emptiness or the void – and affirm that it is a living void which gives birth to in the phenomenal world". The analogy of the philosophical "creative void" and the quantum field was considered earlier in chapter 28. Unfortunately, *śūnyatā* has been interpreted in so many ways that one can think of scores of parallels with *śūnyatā.*

Śūnyatā is non-substantiality, *śūnyatā* is nonultimacy (exactly opposite to the sense in the above quotation). *Śūnyatā* is conditionedness.

Again, *śūnyatā* is the indeterminate, unconditioned, undivided unutterable ultimate reality. *Śunyata* is *Samatā* (ultimate sameness of things), *Śūnyatā* is harmony, integration, non-exclusiveness.

Śūnyatā is *Nirvāṇa. Śāstra* also describes no less than eighteen kinds of *śūnyatā.* The crux of the matter is that a religious or metaphysical concept is usually interpreted in several ways indicating ambiguities and contradictions. It would be correct to say that *śūnyatā* is indescribable. This is only one example which shows hurdles in comparing Buddhist philosophy or any other eastern mysticism with theories in physics. Fortunately there are also apparent contradictions in the quantum world which mitigates adverse criticism on positive parallels. For example, in the EPR experiment when the state of a particle changes, that of its anti-particle changes instantaneously though (chapter 25) we know that any causal effect cannot travel faster than the velocity of light. Fortunately, no successful experiments have been performed to prove that the law of maximum velocity (c) is violated.

Table of Comparision

	Buddhism		*Science/RQ theories*
1.	Amelioration of suffering and nirvāṇa are the main goals.	1.	Science discovers Nature's laws and invents new products which may lead to improvement or deterioration (e.g. wars) of human conditon.
2.	Agnostic, no God, no soul.	2.	Metaphysics is beyond the scope of science.
3.	Belief in momentariness and everchanging world where identity loses meaning (chapter 9).	3.	Momentariness is admitted. For pragmatic reasons entities are considered. In RQ theories the everchanging world becomes patent; the concept of identity becomes dubious with extreme volatility. Mass and energy are *interconvertible.*
4.	Belief in (at least) two realities, empirical and ultimate (transcendental).	4.	Reality is one, but levels are many. There is also search for the ultimate "stuff" of which the world is created.
5.	Ultimate reality consists of insubstantial moments in different chains. These point-instants are unique and dimensionless. They are efficient. Existence equated with cause.	5.	Ultimate transcendental reality is irrelevent. But scientists may believe in the ultimate real stuff.
6.	The chain of moments is discontinuous, so is motion. Space and time are illusions belonging to em-	6.	Both continuity and discontinuity are admitted. Space and time are considered continuous. Post-

pirical world.	RQ physics replaces space and time by space-time, bringing them closer.
7. Phenomenal world is conditioned.	7. Phenomenal world is shaped by forces, substances, energy etc. based on some fundamental laws (gravity, magnetism, etc.).
8. Belief in survival of consciousness after death, and rebirth unless a person attains *nirvana.*	8. Survival after death considered improbable but science is open to experimentation.
9. Belief in the doctrine of *karma.*	9. This moral law, partly transcendental, is not relevant to science.
10. The concept of *svabhāva* replaced by *niḥsvabhāva* and interdependence (chapter 17). Nagarjuna's concept of functional dependence.	10. Post RQ physics treats universe as interconnected whole with subsystems.
11. Anyone is free to test the tenets through experience.	11. Science relies on empirical (not merely experiential) evidence with objective criteria. In such areas as neursciences experiential methods in conjuction with empirical approach are finding greater acceptance.
12. The world of momentary beings is field-like with potential for dynamic activities.	12. Field is a very useful concept in physics. In post RQ era there is a search for an all pervading quantum field.

13. Instead of "A causes B" Buddhists prefer to say B follows A or there is invariable concomitance.	13. Due to multiple causes, physics considers a system of entities subject to many laws.
14. Love and compassion are considered as important as intellectual understanding and insight. Sakharov's equation √Truth = Love is usually accepted.	14. Love and compassion are irrelevent to science.
15. In *catuṣkoṭi* logic there is apparent violation of the law of middle and contradiction. Nāgārjuna believes that the third and fourth alternatives are applicable only to the transcendental (chapter 9).	15. Apparent violation of these laws in particlewave duality, which disappears when *wavicles* are introduced.
16. There is philosophical relativism : *śūnyatā* is regarded synonymous with phiolosophical relativity.	16. Einstein's relativity pertains to physics and implies modification of Newton's laws. But universal relativity can be attempted through the process of reification and elimination of false idols (chapter 29).
17. The transcendental momentary beings are devoid of substance but are creators of phenomenal world.	17. Some physicists believe that even in empty space there is a putative quantum field which is creative (e.g. giving rise to particle-antiparticle). The void is a living void. Search for a unified theory GUT is only partly successful.

Now that we have analyzed in detail Buddhist logic, eastern mysticism, science and RQ theories what is our conclusion? What are our answers to the questions raised at the beginning? Is there parallelism between science and Buddhism? Are RQ theoreis analogous with eastern mysticism and Buddhist logic? From the conclusions drawn in this chapter you will appreciate that we have found a mixed bag.

The only answer I can think of is, with apologies to Jaina scholars, **Both, Yes and No.**

Chapter Notes

1. Introduction

2. The Riddle

1. See Tigunait (1983), p. 40. K. Venkata Ramanan (2002) p. 147 quotes from *Śāstra* to explain why the Buddha did not answer questions, fourteen in all, relating to *avyaktāni*.
2. In fact this principle is used in the electron microscope where electrons replace photons.

3. Identity

1. Forlov (1984), p. 187. This is perhaps the most useful form.
2. Russell (1995), p. 102.

4. Knowledge, Universals and Particulars

1. Forlov, p. 128.
2. Russell (1992), p. 4.
3. Russell (1998), pp.123-24.
4. Ibid., p. 124.
5. Russell (1992), ch. VIII.
6. Russell (1988), p. 124.

5. Perception and Concept Formation

1. There is no uniform terminology. Here the terms such as sensation, perception, etc. are borrowed from the objectivists. See Rand (1990).

2. Rand (1990), p. 7.
3. Ibid., p. 8.
4. Ibid., p. 10.
5. Forlov (1984), p. 136.
6. Rand (1990), p. 42.

6. Individuals and Classes

1. Russell (1992), p. 71.
2. Ibid., p. 75.
3. Russell (1992), pp. 99-100.
4. Ibid., pp. 99-100.

7. Śākyamuni's Teachings

1. Tigunait (1983), p. 44.

8. Development of Buddhist Philosophy

1. Stcherbatsky (I), p. 4.
2. Ibid, p. 6.
3. Ibid. (I), p. 9.
4. Stcherbatsky (I), p. 13.
5. K. Venkata Ramanan, pp. 37-38.
6. Stcherbatsky (I), p. 28.
7. Ichimura discusses at considerabe length some discrepancies relating to Nāgārjuna's biography in Article 2.
8. From *Kārikā,* K. Venkata Ramanan, p. 39.
9. Quoted from *Kārikā,* K. Venkata Ramanan, p. 40. *Śūnyatā-śūnyatā* implies that the conditionedness of the conditioned is not unconditioned.
10. Ibid., p. 42.
11 Ichimura, p. 120.

9. Momentary Beings and Causation

1. NBT, quoted in Stcherbatsky (I), p. 59.
2. NBT, Stcherbatsky (I), pp. 61-62.

3. Ibid., p. 63.
4. For a detailed discussion, see Stcherbatsky (I), p. 63.
5. Ibid., p. 79.
6. Ibid., p. 82.
7. Ibid., p. 83.
7a. The illusion of duration/extension can be attributed to imperceptible changes.
8. Ibid., p. 90.
9. Stcherbatsky (I), p. 91.
10. Ibid., p. 91.
11. Three categories of existence (*astitva*), viz. substance, quality, motion (b) four categories of "meaning" viz. universals, differentials, inherence and non-existence.
12. TSP, Stcherbatsky (I), p. 93.
12a. Stcherbatsky (I), p. 101.
13. NS, Stcherbatsky (I), p. 103.
14. Vasubandhu's account in *Abhidharmakośa* quoted in Stcherbatsky (I), p. 130.
15. Quoted in Stcherbatsky (I). The universal application of the doctrine is called the general theory.
16. Ibid., p. 137.
17. Ibid., p. 141.
18. From TSP, Stcherbatsky (I), p. 121.

10. Perception in Buddhism

1. NB, Wayman, p. 44.
2. NBT, Stcherbatsky (I), p. 149.
3. NB, Wayman, p. 44.
4. NBT, Stcherbatsky (I), p. 149.
4a. Quoted in Stcherbatsky (I), pp. 150-51.
5. Quoted in Stcherbatsky (I), p. 152.
6. Ibid., p. 153.

7. NBT, Wayman, p. 160.
   It appears that in case of common people 1, 2, 3 are the sequential stages. In case of yogins, truth is "contemplated" not perceived.
8. NBT, Stcherbatsky (I), p.160.
9. Quoted in Stcherbatsky (I), p.166.
10. Quoted in Stcherbatsky, p. 219.
11. Tatp, Stcherbatsky, p. 214.
12. Quoted in Stcherbatsky, p. 215.
13. Actually y is a complicated function since construction can take place after the projection of every x. There are bound to be slight differences in the construction by different observers on their personal dispositions. These nuances are ignored here. Similarly perception should also depend on the observer's location, etc. the object's location.
14 Two structures connected by $y = f(x)$ are isomorphic with respect to R, R' if and only if xRx' implies yRy'.
15. NVTT, quoted in Stcherbatsky (I), p. 223.

11. Inference

1. Stcherbatsky(I), p. 240.
2. NBT, Stcherbatsky(I), p. 250. The word identity should be understood in the right sense.
2a. Stcherbatsky (I), p. 251.
3. NB Wayman, p. 46.
4. Ibid., p. 54.
5. See, e.g. Ichimura, p. 132.
6. NB, Wayman, p. 50.
7. Ibid., p. 47.
8. Despite various interpretations of p.q the most favoured choice seems to be invariable concomitance in the temporal order p.q. Implication in western philosophy is different from p.q. For example, $p \Rightarrow q$ is always valid if p is false.

12. Syllogism

1. Quoted in Stcherbatsky (I), p. 275.
1a. The classes of similar instances / loci and dissimilar instances/loci are, of course, determined through observation or induction.
2. Use of western symbolic logic can lead to confusion. See S. 13.3 below.
3. See Ichimura, p.133 which is based on Vidyabhusana's *A History of Indian Logic* and Kitagawa's *A Study of Indian Classical Logic: Dignāga's system.*
4. Stcherbatsky (I), p. 277.
5. Stcherbatsky, p. 282.
6. Ibid., pp. 282-83, quoted from NB.
7. Burde(2004), pp. 65-68; some parts are reproduced almost *verbatim.*

13. Logical Fallacies

1. Adapted from Stcherbatsky (I), p. 323.
2. Adaptation from Dignāga. See Stcherbatsky, p. 326.
3. From NB and NBT. Stcherbatsky (I), p. 328.
3a. This was, of course, unknown in Dignāga's days.
4. NB and NBT, Stcherbatsky (I), p. 328.
5. Ibid., p. 331.
6. Ibid., (I), p. 331.
7. NB and NBT, Stcherbatsky (I), p. 337 (adapted).
8. NB, NBT, Stcherbatsky (II), p. 183.
9. NB, NBT, Stcherbatsky (II), p. 183.
10. Nyāya-mukha quoted in Stcherbatsky (I), p. 336.
11. NBT quoted in Stcherbatsky (I), p. 337.
12. Stcherbatsky (I), p. 340.

14. Śūnyatā, Logic and Dialectic

1. Burde (2009) discusses various interconnected concepts of *śūnya.*

2. Ichimura, p. xii.
3. Kuan-yin Bodhisattva embodies love and compassion. The cult which flourished in China after Dharmarakṣa's translation of *Lotus Sūtra* (ca 286 CE). Ichimura, pp. 20-32.
4. Ichimura, p. 27.
5. Ibid., pp. 28-29 for a detailed discussion.
6. Quoted in Stcherbatsky (I), pp. 478-79.
7. Stcherbatsky (I), p. 460.
8. TSP, quoted in Stcherbatsky(I), pp. 460-61.
9. Stcherbatsky (I), p. 476.

15 Anekāntavāda In Jainism

1. JTMF : "Introduction" by Nagin J. Shah, p. x.
2. Ibid. "Anekānta : both yes and no" by B.K. Matilal, pp. 3-4.
3. "A study of Syādvāda" in JTMF, p. 35.

3a. "Relativity and Absolutism", Ibid., pp 63-64.

4. *Many-Valued Logic*, quoted in JTMF, p. 78.
5. "The Logical Structure of Syādvāda", JTMF, p. 84.
6. JTMF, "The Logical Structure of Syādvāda", p. 80.
7. Ibid., p. 81.
8. JTMF in "Relativity and Absolutism" by V.M Kulkarni, pp. 64-65.
9. From Atsushi Uno's article "A study of *Syādvāda*", JTMF, chapter 3.

9a. Ibid., pp. 41-42. Quoting PNT and SBT Uno defines *saptabhaṅgī pramāṇa* as "statement of affirmation and negation, singly or jointly in seven different ways with the use of the term *syāt* without such inconsistency as arises from conflict (with perception) and in virtue of inquiry about each of the different attributes with regard to one and the same entity like soul(jiva)".

10. Ibid., p. 50.
11. Ibid., p. 46 .

11a. Ibid., p. 56.

16. Catuṣkoṭi in Buddhism

1 K. Venkata Ramanan has discussed the problem of extremes in chapter VI.
2. Ibid., p. 155.
3. *Śāstra*, quoted in K. Venkata Ramanan, p. 158.
4. K. Venkata Ramanan, p. 156.
5. Ibid., pp. 161.
6. Quoted in K. Venkata Ramanan, p. 161.
7. Ibid., pp. 161-62.
8. Ibid., p. 163.
8a. Quoted in Ichimura, p. 358.
9. Ibid., p. 359.
10. Ibid., pp. 359-60.
11. Quoted in Ichimura, p. 360n.
12. Quoted in Ibid., p. 372n.
13. Ibid., p. 377.
14. This is consistent with Dignāga's theory of *apoha.*
15. Ibid., pp. 70-71.
16. Ibid., p. 124.
17. For Bhagchandra Jain's detailed discussion see Ibid., pp. 124-25.
18. Ibid., p. 126.
19. Two fold naya refers to the usual bivalent system – *is* or *is not.*

17. Logical Impasse

1. For example, the doctrine of *Karma* cannot be fully explained on the basis of empirical reality.
2. Quoted in Ichimura, p. 151.
3. On account of contraposition of $p \Rightarrow q$.
4. If $q \Rightarrow p$ its contraposition gives $-p \Rightarrow -q$.
5. Ichipmura, pp. 157-58.
6. Ibid., pp. 162-63.
7. Ibid., p. 167.

8. Quoted in Ichimura, pp. 139-40.
9. Quoted in Ichimura, p. 139.
10. Ibid., p. 141.
11. Ibid., pp. 141-43,
11a. Ibid., pp. 143, 144. Quoted from *Vaidalyaprakaraṇa.*
12. See Ichimura, chapter II.
13. Ibid., p. 63.

18. Logic and Dialectic Outside India

1. Quoted in Ichimura, p. 209.
2. For further discussion on comparative contributions of these philosophers, see Ichimura, pp. 208-14.
3. Quoted in Ichimura, p. 213.
4. Ibid., p. 219.
5. Ichimura, p. 226.
6. Quoted in Ichimura, p. 227.
7. Quoted in Ichimura, p. 227.
8. Ibid., pp. 227-228.
9. Arbitrariness is a characteristic of a script.
10. Sêng-Chao quoted in Ichimura, p. 246.
11. Quoted in Ichimura, p. 253.
12. Quoted in Ichimura, p. 255.
13. Quoted in Ichimura, p. 246.
14. Smith, p. 129.
15. Ibid., p. 130.
16. Ibid., p.133.
17. Ibid., p. 132.
18. Wayman, p. 255.
19. Wayman, pp. 277-91.
20. Wayman, Ibid., pp. 280-81.
21. Stcherbatsky (I), p. 205.
22. Ibid., p. 58.

19. Knowledge, Wisdom and Love

1. K. Venkata Ramanan, p. 113.

2. Ibid., p. 115.
3. Ibid., p. 116.
4. Śāstra (254a), K. Venkata Ramanan, p. 134.
5. 59(b) quoted, Ibid., p. 137.
6. Ibid., pp. 139-40 from *Śāstra* (60a).
7. Ibid., p. 141 from *Śāstra* (61b).
8. Ibid., p. 143 from *Śāstra* (648 b).
9. Ibid., p. 147.
10. Ibid., p. 150 from Śāstra (75a).
11. Ibid., pp. 277-78.
12. Ibid., p. 280 quoting Śāstra (262 c).
13. Ibid., p. 294 from Śāstra (206 a).
14. Ibid., p. 294.
15. Ibid., p. 296.
16. Quoted in Ibid., p. 297.
17. Ibid., p. 308.
18. Wallace (ed.) "Imagining, Embodiment, phenomenology, and Transformation".
19. Ibid., p. 218.
20. Wallace (ed.), p. 221; quoted from the works of Altaiisa (982-1054 CE).
21. Ibid., p. 223.
22. One-page brief account of "tonglen" as methodology is given in Wallace, p. 222 by Varela and Depraz.

20. The Three Laws

1. Stcherbatsky (I), p. 401.
2. TSP quoted in Stcherbatsky, p. 403.
3. Stcherbatsky (I), p. 411.
4. Ibid., p. 414.
5. NB, Stcherbatsky (I), p. 419.
6. Quotation from NK, Stcherbatsky, p. 420.
7. Quoted in Stcherbatsky (I), p. 416, Ibid., pp. 423-24.

21. Buddhism and Science

1. These features are a modified version of those mentioned in Burde (2004) which in turn are based on Staal (1996).
2. Einstein (1979), p. 293 in his paper "Physics and Reality".

2a. However, in case of subatomic particles with high velocities, special relativity has to be used.

3. See, for example, Wilber (2000).
4. A hathayogi's claims and his subsequent failure are described in Kavoor (1990), p. 35.
5. Wallace, p. 96.
6. Ibid., p. 96.
7. Kirtisinghe (ed.), p. 147.
8. Forlov, p. 123.
9. Kirtisinghe (ed.), p. 147.
10. Ibid., p. 147.
11. Ibid., pp. 55-60.
12. Ibid., p. 55.
13. Ibid., p. 56.
14. Ibid., p. 56.
15. Ibid., p. 58.
16. Basham, p. 497.

22. Relativity : Interpretation and Misinterpretation

1. Einstein (1956), p. 54.
2. Ibid., p. 57.
3. Eddington, p. 10.
4. Ibid., p. 10.
5. In "Relevance of *Anekānta* in Modern Times", JTMF, p. 131.
6. "The complementarity Principle and *Syādavāda*", JTMF, p. 94.

6a. JTMF, p. 51. Etymologically *atom* means that which

cannot be split.

7. Tscherbatsky (I), p. 85.
8. Ibid., p. 79.

23. Subatomic Particles

1. From *Physics and Principles* quoted in Capra (1991), p. 61.
2. Capra (1991), p. 89.
3. Capra (1991), pp. 91–92.
4. Ibid., p. 92.
5. Words like flavor, color should not be interpreted literally. They are based on criteria not detailed here.
6. Capra(1991) chapter 15 gives seven examples with details.
7. Hawking (1989), p. 75.

24. Particle Wave Duality

1. Penrose, p. 235.
2. Ibid., p. 234.
3. Ibid., p. 236.
4. Ibid., p. 236.
5. The word wavicle has already been suggested by some commentators.
6. Penrose, p. 248.
7. Ibid., p. 248.
8. z (OP) can be similarly shifted or "non-localized" but we need not consider this case.
9. This is a simplified graph; three space dimensions are shown by a single dimension x; yz is the Argand plane in which ψ appears as a complex function.
10. Fourier transformation technique was developed by the French engineer – mathematician Joseph Fourier (1768-1830), and has many applications in physics.
11. w and z are called weightings or weights.

25. Quantum Systems : Intrusion and Disturbance

1. One light year is the distance travelled by light in one year. In one second it travels about 186,000 miles.
2. Penrose, p. 255.

2a. David Bohm developed the viewpoint that there could be "hidden" variables which were not accessible before measurements take place. See Penrose, p. 280.

3. Penrose, p. 250.
4. Probability of each alternative is square of the amplitude, i.e 1/2 the sum of the alternatives is 1/2 + 1/2 = 1, assuming the total probability is 1.
5. Penrose, pp. 292-93.
6. Ibid., p. 297.
7. Penrose, pp. 251-52.
8. Ibid., pp. 268-69.
9. Peterfreund, p. 255. The definition is due to logical positivists.
10. Penrose, p. 260.

10a. Penrose, p. 278.

11. Matthews, p. 18. The formula is complicated and is omitted here.
12. A commutator [A, B] = AB - BA.
13. Ibid., p. 19. A derivative is the instantaneous rate of change. For exmaple, velocity is the derivative of the distance with respect to time.
14. Ibid., p. 21.

26. Life, Cognition and Consciousness

1. Quoted in Capra (2003), p. 8.
2. Ibid., p. 8.
3. Ibid., p. 9.
4. Luici quoted in Capra (2003), p. 14. Alexander Oparin was a biochemist who wrote *Origin of Life* in 1929. He referred to prebiotic evolution as molecular evolution.

5. Capra (2003), p. 25.
6. Ibid., p. 32.
7. Ibid., p. 35.
8. Forlov (1984), p. 180.
9. Quoted in Guilford (1964), p. 70 from *Wolf Children and Feral Man* by J.A.L Singh and R.M Zingg.
10. See, for example, Capra (2003), pp. 47-50.
11. Ibid., p. 63.
12. Ibid., p. 64.
13. Penrose, chapters 9,10.
14. Penrose, p. 385, The subject is called "P.S." in medical literature.
15. Koestler, p. 173.
16. Quoted in Ibid., p. 173.
17. Ibid.
18. Ibid., p. 400.
19. Ibid., p. 404.

   An algorithm is a systematic procedure involving sequential operations which will give the solution to all the problems of a specific type. Euler's algorithm for finding the hightest common factor step by step is well-known. Algorithms are important in computer science. Any method not using an algorithm (say, a sudden insight leading to a quick solution) is non-algorithmic.

27. Violation of Logic

1. Penrose, p. 235.
2. Stcherbatsky (I), p. 424.

28. The Concept of a Field

1. Kirtisinghe in Bhikku Nana fiviko in "Aniccam – The Buddhist theory of imperpanence" p. 28.
2. Quotation., Ibid., p. 28.

2a. Quoted in Ibid., p. 28.

3. Burde (2004), chapter 15.
4. Penrose, p. 290.
5. Chopra (1993), p. 527.
6. Chopra (1990), p. 7.
7. Ibid., p. 159.
8. Ibid., p. 169.
9. To conform to monism, we may call this gap cosmic intelligence or cosmic consciousness.
10. Chopra(1990), p. 169.

29. Universal Relativity

1. Wallace (ed.) p. 367.
1a. Wallace, p. 374.
2. Ibid., p. 378
3. See chapter 21 for features of science.
4. K. Venkata Ramanan, p. 255.
5. Ibid., p. 256, commenting on the views in *Śāstra.*
6. Ibid., p. 256.
7. Ibid., p. 257.

30. Eastward Ho !

1. See Burde (2009).
2. Russell (1994), Chapter II.
3. Hawking (1989), p. 173.
4. Penrose (1991), p. 302.
5. Ibid., p. 304.
5a. See Burde (2004), and (2009).
6. See Burde (2004), Chapter 15 for a detailed discussion on this claim.
7. Quoted in Capra (1976), p. 246.
8. Quoted in Capra (1976), pp.163-64.
9. Capra (1976), p. 321.
10. Ibid., p., 339.
11. Ibid., p. 338.
12. Ibid., p. 339.

13. Burde (2004), chapters 6, 15.

31. Integration

1. Capra (1983), p. 27.
2. Wilber (2000), p. 40.
3. Ibid., p. 8.
4. Capra (2003), pp. 58-59.
5. Wilber (2000), p. 50.
6. Ibid., p. 50.
7. Ibid., p. 60.
8. Ibid., p. 61.
8a. Ibid., p. 62.
9. Ibid., p. 62.
10. Ibid., p. 77.
10a. This is a well-known antinomie called Russell's paradox.
11. Wilber (2000), chapter 4 , p. 282.
12. Burde (2004), pp. 98-104.
13. Wilber, p. 80.
14. "Imagining, Embodiment, Phenomenology and Transformation", in Wallace (ed.).
15. Ibid., p. 211.
16. Ibid., p. 212.
17. Ibid., p. 213.
18. Ibid., p. 225.

32. Conclusion

1. Quoted by Thupten Jinpa in Wallace (ed.), p. 77.
2. Stcherbatsky (I), p. 132.
3. Ibid., p. 132.
4. Ibid., p. 132.
5. Ibid., p. 134.
6. Band, p. 315.
7. Capra (1991), p. 179.

8. Ibid., (1991),p. 189.
9. Ibid., p. 189.
10. Penrose, p. 297.

Appendix

a) *Pañcāvayava* in symbolic logic (See Section 12.1)

1. *Pratijñā*	q(h)	h = hill
2. *Hetu* because	p(h)	
3. *Udāharaṇa*	(x) [p(x).q(x)]	
Anvaya	(α) [p(α).q(α)]	
Vyatireka	(β) [-q(β).-p(β)]	
4. *Upanaya*	p(h)	
5. *Nigamana*	q(h)	

b) Buddhist syllogism in symbolic logic. (See Section 12.2)

1. *Vyāpti*	(x) [p(x).q(x)]
Anvaya	p(α).q(α)
Vyatireka	-q(β).-p(β)
2. *Hetu* (implies *sādhya*)	p(h).q(h)

c) *Saptabhaṅgī* in symbolic logic. (See Section 15.5)

Let s(x) be a propositional function "there is a standpoint x"

p(x) a proposition true for x

~p≡ p is false

ip ≡ p is undeterminable

Then the seven alternatives can be written as :

1. (∃x) (s(x).p(x))
2. (∃x) (s(x).~p(x))
3. [(∃x) (s(x).p(x))].[(∃y) (s(y).~p(y))]
4. (∃x) (s(x).ip(x))
5. [(∃x) (s(x).p(x))].[(∃y) (s(y).ip(y))]

6. $[(\exists x)(s(x)].\sim p(x))].[(\exists y)(s(y).ip(y))]$
7. $[(\exists x)(s(x).p(x))].[(\exists y)(s(y).\sim p(y)].[(\exists z)(s(z).ip(z)]$

Note the following points :

(1) We can subsume all the interpretations of the third value (indeterminate, undeterminable, transcendent, etc.) under ip. The point (.) means conjunction *and.*

(2) In 3, 5-7 different variables are used. Using the same variable could lead us to the region of indeterminacy, uncertainty or transcendence, etc. which is accepted by a small minority of philosophers.

(3) It is necessary to remember that particular values of x, y, z are different, i.e. $x \neq y \neq z$ if indeterminacy stemming from simultaneity is to be avoided.

(4) When referring to the mundane reality symbolic logic is neither suitable nor necessary while discussing *catuṣkoṭi* or *saptabhaṅgī*, because the meaning of conjuction (.) when strictly adhered to (invariable concomitance) can lead to simultaneity of options.

At the empirical level the options may not be compatible.

However, these statements are metalinguistic in the sense they pertain to the statements about the statement p. Gokhale has suggested that a three term relations such as "y is z from x" should be used in place of the above model but has not pursued the idea further. The reason for such deadlock is that symbolic logic is not suitable beyond a certain point.

d) *Saptabhaṅgī* using relational calculus (See Section 15.5)

I think that using relational calculus we can express the sevenfold *saptabhaṅgī* in the following way. For convenience I shall use f to denote a relation Thus f(x, y) is the relational function expressing a binary relation, f(x, y, z) expresses a triadic relation and so on.

Let f(x, y, z) mean "there exists a standpoint (x) according to which the jar (y) has existence (z)".

Then *saptabhaṅgī* can be written as :

1) $f(x, y, z)$
2) $f(x, y, \sim z)$
3) $f(x, y, z) \wedge f(x, y, \sim z)$
4) $f(x, y, iz)$
5) $f(x, y, z) \wedge f(x, y, iz)$
6) $f(x, y, \sim z) \wedge f(x, y, iz)$
7) $f(x, y, z) \wedge f(x, y, \sim z) \wedge f(x, y, iz)$

There will be two broad cases

Case I - In any of statements 3-7 x's in different brackets have different values.

Case II - x's in different brackets in the same statement (3-7) need not be different.

Depending on the facts, case II will involve indeterminacy and contradictions while case I will be applicable to empirical reality without contradictions.

As remarked earlier most Jaina scholars would prefer case I. I am aware that this representation is hybrid. I have purposely retained $\wedge$ for "and", but it may be interpreted as invariable concomitance (.).

e) Modal Operator (See Section 15.5)

The truth value table Lukasiewicz appears as follows.

p	Mp	Lp
T	T	T
I	T	F
F	F	F

Instead of the original symbols we have used M and L after Gokhale. Gokhale has tried to adapt this three-value logic to *syādvāda*. Since, *syāt* can mean "possible", "perhaps", "maybe", etc. he expresses *saptabhaṅgī* in terms of this system. I have modified his model.

In what follows *ip* will subsume all kinds of uncerainties, logical as well as epistemic. Thus "ip" will mean the option indeterminable, undetermined, transcendental and so on. We have to remember that the three options are exhaustive. For convenience we shall use Jaina term *naya* for the category I leaving aside controversies of interpritation of *naya.* The seven fold logic now appears as :

1. Mp
2. M ~ p
3. Mp . M ~ p
4. M i p
5. Mp . M i p
6. M ~ p . M ip
7. Mp . M~p . M i p

We can interpret any one of these *bhaṅgas* with a little deliberation.

Suppose p is *naya* then so will be ~p and ip. Hence Mp, M~p, Mp.~p, M i p will all be true (T).

Ekāntavāda in Jaina logic means calling partial truth the whole truth or treating indeterminate view as necessarily true. For instance, if p is *naya* then Mp is true but Lp (condition of necessity) is false. This would be consistent with *ekāntavāda.* This is also called *nayābhāsa* or *durnaya,* i.e. a fallacy of *naya.*

BIBLIOGRAPHY

Acharya, S. S. (2001). *Rig Veda, Vols. I-IV.* Sanskriti Sansthan, Bareli.

———(1998). *Sama Veda.* Sanskriti Sansthan, Bareli.

———(2001). *Yajur Veda.* Sanskriti Sansthan, Bareli.

———(1998). *Atharva Veda, Vols. I-II.* Sanskriti Sansthan, Bareli.

Ahlfors, L.V. (1966). *Complex Analysis.* Kogakusha, Tokyo

Bag, A.K. (2003). *The Concept of Śūnya.* IGNCFTA, INSA, Aryan Book International, New Delhi.

Band, William (1964). *Introduction to Mathematical Physics.* Affiliated East-West, New Delhi.

Basham, A. L. (2001). *The Wonder That Was India.* Rupa & Co., New Delhi.

Berne, Eric (1968). *Games People Play.* Penguin, Middlesex.

Bose, A.C. (1970). *The Call of the Vedas.* Bharatiya Vidya Bhavan, Mumbai.

Burde, Jayant (2004). *Rituals, Mantras and Science: An Integral Perspective.* Motilal Banarsidass, Delhi.

———(2007). *Philosophy of Numbers.* Munshiram Manoharlal, New Delhi.

———(2009). *Śūnya and Nothingness.* Motilal Banarsidass, Delhi.

Burton, David (1989). *Elementary Number Theory.* UBS, New Delhi.

Capra, Fritjof (1983). *The Turning Point.* Flamingo, London.

———(1976, 1993). *The Tao of Physics.* Flamingo, London.

———(2003). *The Hidden Connections.* Flamingo, India.

Chidbhavananda, Swami (1965). *The Bhagvad Gita.* Sri Ramakrishna Tapovanan, Tirupparaitturai.

Chopra, Deepak (1990). *Quantum Healing.* Bantom N.Y.

———(1993). *Ageless Body, Timeless Mind.* Harmony Books, N.Y.

Clawson, Calvin C. (2004). *The Mathematical Traveller.* Viva, New Delhi.

Cohen, Leon W., Gertrude Ehrlich (1969). *The Structure of the Real Number System.* Affiliated East-West, New Delhi.

Deshpande,. Dhananjay (2001). *Vedanteel Vidnyan.* Popular Prakashan, Mumbai.

Durant, Will (1953). *The Story of Philosophy.* Pocket Books, New York.

Eddington, A.E. (1924). *The Mathematical Theory of Relativity.* Cambridge University Press, London.

Einstein, Albert (1979). *Ideas and Opinions.* Rupa & Co., Calcutta. (1956). *The Meaning of Relativity.* Oxford IBH, Calcutta.

Hawking, Stephen, W. (1989). *A Brief History of Time.* Bantam, N.Y.

Hawking, Stephen, Roger Penrose (1997). *The Nature of Space and Time.* OUP, New Delhi.

Ichimura, Shohei (2001). *Buddhist Critical Spirituality : Prajñā and Śūnyatā.* Motilal Banarasidass, Delhi.

Kirtishinghe, B.P. (ed. 1984). *Buddhism and Science.* Motilal Banarsidass, Delhi.

Krishnamurti, J., David Bohm (1985). *The Ending of Time.* Krishnamurti Foundation, Chennai.

Laanen, M.V. (2004). *Encounters with Infinity : A Metamathematical Dissertation.* New Age Books, New Delhi.

Matthews, P.T. (1968). *Introduction to Quantum Mechanics.* Tata McGrow-Hill, New Delhi.

Narayan, Shanti (1961). *A Text Book Of Modern Abstract Algebra.* S. Chand & Co., New Delhi.

O' Flaherty, Wendy Doniger (2000). *The Rig Veda.* Penguin, New Delhi.

Osho (2003). *The Fullness of Emptiness.* Sterling, New Delhi.

Page, Leigh, N.I. Adams (1955). *Principles of Electricity.* S. Chand & Co., Delhi.

Penrose, Roger (1991). *The Emperor's New Mind.* Penguin, N.Y.

Peterfreund, Sheldon P., Theodre C. Denise (1968). *Contemporary Philosophy and Its Origins.* East-West, New Delhi.

Rajam, J.B. (1960). *Atomic Physics.* S. Chand & Co., Delhi.

Rajaneesh, Bhagwan Shree (1979). *The Beginning of the Beginning.* Vikas, New Delhi.

Rajaraman (1999). *The Fundamentals of Computer.* Prentice-Hall, New Delhi.

Ramachandran, V.S., Sandra Blakeslee (1948). *Phantoms in the Brain.* Harper Collins, New Delhi.

Rand, Ayan (1984). *Philosophy. Who Needs It.* Signet (Penguin), N.Y.

———(1990). *Introduction to Objective Epistemology.* Meridian (Penguin), N.Y.

Russell, Bertrand (1988). *Logic and Knowledge.* Routledge, London. (N.Y.).

———(1948, 1992). *Human Knowledge.* Routledge , London.

———(1992). *The Principles of Mathematics.* Routledge, London.

———(1995). *An Inquiry into Meaning and Truth.* Routledge, London, (N.Y.).

———(1994). *Mysticism and Logic.* Routledge, London.

———(1995). *The Analysis of Mind.* Routledge, London.

———(1999). *History of Western Philosophy.* Routledge, N.Y.

Salmon, Weseley C. *Logic.* Prentice-Hall, N.J.

Sankaracarya (108), Sriyogesvaranandatirtha (1996). *Mantrasastra.* Keshav Bhikaji Dhavale, Mumbai.

Śaṅkarācārya, Bhāratī Kṛṣṇa Tīrthajī Mahārāja (1992). *Vedic Mathematics.* Motilal Banarsidass, Delhi.

Sartre, Jean-Paul (1966). *Being and Nothingness.* Pocket Books, N.Y.

Shah, N.J. (ed. 2000). *Jaina Theory of Multiple Facets of Reality and Truth (Anekāntavāda).* Motilal Banarsidass, Delhi.

Sharma, R.N. (2004). *Text Book of Symbolic Logic.* Surjeet, Delhi.

Simmons , G.F. (1963). *Introduction to Topology and Modern Analysis.* McGraw Hill, N.Y. (Kogakusha Tokyo).

Smith, Huston (1991). *The World's Religions.* Harper Collins, New Delhi.

Stcherbatsky, Th. (1963). *Buddhist Logic Vol. I-II.* Motilal Banarsidass, New Delhi.

Staal, Frits (1996). *Ritual and Mantras: Rules Without Meaning.* Motilal Banarasidass, Delhi.

Sterling, S.G. (1958). *Electricity and Magnetism.* ELBS and Longman, London.

Svanandasarasvati (—). *Patanjala Yogavidya.* Raghuvanshi Prakashan, Pune.

Swami Ashokananda (1995). *Avadhuta Gita of Dattatreya.* Sri Ramakrishna Math, Madras.

Tigunait, Pandit Rajmani (1983). *Seven Systems Of Indian Philosophy.* The Himalayan International Institute of Yoga science and philosophy of the U.S.A., Honesdale.

———(1996). *The power of Mantra & The Mystery of Initiation.* The Himalayan International Institute of Yoga science and philosophy of the U.S.A., Honesdale.

———(1999). *Tantra Unveiled.* The Himalayan International Institute of Yoga science and philosophy of the U.S.A., Honesdale.

Verma, K.D. (2008). *Vedic Physics: Towards Unification of Quantum Mechanics and General Relativity.* Motilal Banarsidass, Delhi.

Wallace, B.A. (ed. 2004). *Buddhism and Science.* Motilal Banarsidass, Delhi.

Wayman, Alex (1998). *A Millenium of Buddhist Logic.* Motilal Banarsidass, Delhi.

Woodroffe, John (1997). *The Serpent Power.* Ganesha & Co., Madras.

Index

Q

R

S